Tableau Desktop Certified Associate: Exam Guide

Develop your Tableau skills and prepare for Tableau certification with tips from industry experts

Dmitry Anoshin
JC Gillet
Fabian Peri
Radhika Biyani
Gleb Makarenko

BIRMINGHAM - MUMBAI

Tableau Desktop Certified Associate: Exam Guide

Copyright © 2019 Packt Publishing

Commissioning Editor: Ravit Jain
Acquisition Editor: Devika Battike
Content Development Editors: Athikho Sapuni Rishana and Roshan Kumar
Senior Editor: Sofi Rogers
Technical Editor: Dinesh Chaudhary
Copy Editor: Safis Editing
Project Coordinator: Aishwarya Mohan
Proofreader: Safis Editing
Indexer: Priyanka Dhadke
Production Designer: Nilesh Mohite

First published: December 2019

Production reference: 1231219

Published by Packt Publishing Ltd.
Livery Place
35 Livery Street
Birmingham
B3 2PB, UK.

ISBN 978-1-83898-413-7

www.packt.com

Subscribe to our online digital library for full access to over 7,000 books and videos, as well as industry leading tools to help you plan your personal development and advance your career. For more information, please visit our website.

Why subscribe?

- Spend less time learning and more time coding with practical eBooks and Videos from over 4,000 industry professionals

- Improve your learning with Skill Plans built especially for you

- Get a free eBook or video every month

- Fully searchable for easy access to vital information

- Copy and paste, print, and bookmark content

Did you know that Packt offers eBook versions of every book published, with PDF and ePub files available? You can upgrade to the eBook version at www.packt.com and as a print book customer, you are entitled to a discount on the eBook copy. Get in touch with us at customercare@packtpub.com for more details.

At www.packt.com, you can also read a collection of free technical articles, sign up for a range of free newsletters, and receive exclusive discounts and offers on Packt books and eBooks.

Contributors

About the authors

Dmitry Anoshin is an expert in analytics with 10 years of experience. He started using Tableau as a primary BI tool in 2011 as a BI consultant at Teradata. He is certified in both Tableau Desktop and Tableau Server. He leads probably the biggest Tableau user community, with more than 2,000 active users. This community has two to three Tableau talks every month led by top Tableau experts, Tableau Zen Masters, Viz Champions, and more. In addition, Dmitry has previously written three books with Packt and reviewed more than seven books. Finally, he is an active speaker at data conferences and helps people to adopt cloud analytics.

Jean-Charles (JC) Gillet is a seasoned business analyst with over 7 years of experience with SQL at both a large-scale multinational company in the United Kingdom and a smaller firm in the United States, and 5 years of Tableau experience. He has been holding Tableau and SQL office hours for multiple years to share his expertise with his colleagues, as well as delivering SQL training. A French national, JC holds a master's degree in executive engineering from Mines ParisTech and is a Tableau Desktop Certified Associate.

In his free time, he enjoys spending time with his wife and daughter (to whom he dedicates his work on this book), and playing team handball, having competed in national championships.

Fabian Peri's interest in decision analysis started after joining his first fantasy basketball league in 2006. His love for data analysis led him to pursue an MBA in information systems at the University of Tulsa, and then an MS in predictive analytics from Northwestern University. Since graduating, he has primarily worked in risk analysis and management for companies such as Amazon, GE Capital, and Wells Fargo. He is currently focused on using visualization to explore and interpret vast quantities of data.

Radhika Biyani is currently working as a recruitment insights analyst with Amazon. Before this, she worked as an analytics consultant with Version 1, where she consulted on several large-scale BI and analytics projects with clients across various industry verticals such as HR, finance, utility, supply chain, and more. She holds a master's degree in business analytics and has many certifications, including Tableau Qualified Associate. She enjoys attending meetups and is an active member of many meetup groups, including Tableau User Group Dublin.

Gleb Makarenko began using Tableau in 2018 and quickly fell in love with how intuitive and easy to use the software was. He was able to easily adapt to its interface and create powerful visualizations. That is when he decided to get certified on Tableau software in order to receive proper credentials that he could use on his resume, as well as learn about the intricacies of the software that he wasn't using at the time. With a bit of effort and research, Gleb was able to complete the examination. And he recommends the same to anyone who is serious about working with Tableau.

About the reviewers

Shweta Sankhe-Savale is the co-founder of Syvylyze Analytics. Being one of the leading experts on Tableau, Shweta has translated her expertise to successfully rendering analytics and data visualization services and training for numerous clients across a wide range of industry verticals.

Shweta is an empaneled trainer for Tableau Software APAC and conducts private and public Tableau training sessions across Singapore, Malaysia, Hong Kong, Australia, and India. She has successfully trained 2,000+ participants from 150+ companies, making her one of the foremost trainers on Tableau.

Shweta is also a published author with Packt Publishing, with a book titled *Tableau Cookbook: Recipes for Data Visualization*.

Marleen Meier has worked in the field of data science and BI since 2013. Her experience includes Tableau training, proof of concepts, implementations, project management, user interface designs, and quantitative risk management. In 2018, she was a speaker at the Tableau conference, where she showcased a machine learning project. Marleen uses Tableau, combined with other tools and software, to get the best business value for her stakeholders. She is also very active within the Tableau community and was one of the Dutch Tableau user group leaders before she moved to Chicago.

Marleen is also a published author with Packt Publishing, with a book titled *Mastering Tableau 2019.1*.

Packt is searching for authors like you

If you're interested in becoming an author for Packt, please visit authors.packtpub.com and apply today. We have worked with thousands of developers and tech professionals, just like you, to help them share their insight with the global tech community. You can make a general application, apply for a specific hot topic that we are recruiting an author for, or submit your own idea.

Table of Contents

Preface

There is no doubt that data is a key asset for organizations, and it is important to treat data right in order to get the most out of it. Tableau is a best-of-breed technology currently on the market that allows us to work with data, slice it, and do complex data analysis on the fly. However, it requires you to understand the key concepts of data analytics and how to *drive* Tableau in order to deliver value. Moreover, as we are working in a competitive environment, we should constantly improve our skills and learn new technologies, new features, and new data analysis methods to be on the cutting edge.

The goal of this book is to prepare you for the Tableau Desktop Certified Associated exam. This book is written by people who passed this exam and they will share their experience and resources so that you can also successfully pass the exam.

So, why is it important to obtain a Tableau certification? Well, the certification not only assesses our knowledge of Tableau, but it evaluates our ability to comfortably work with data and communicate with people using powerful visualization techniques. Moreover, it requires an understanding of overall **Business Intelligence** (**BI**) solutions and their role in an organization.

The idea behind Tableau is to democratize access to data. In other words, business users will use Tableau's functionalities to slice and dice data; connect various systems, databases, and files; visualize data; build dashboards; and explore data.

As a professional Tableau developer, you should know how to connect data, explore it, and slice and dice it. Often, you will have to build a dashboard or tell a story with data. It is good to know the best practices for data visualization in order to make your work effective. In some cases, you should calculate new metrics and leverage Tableau with table calculations or level of detail calculations. Sometimes, parameters can help you to filter data and add self-service functionality. Finally, you should have some knowledge of statistics and know how to use built-in functionalities for forecasting, trend lines, and clustering. You should know about Tableau Server and how to share and publish your work. This book will help you to cover all of these areas and not only prepare for the exam, but also help you to improve your overall skills in analytics.

This book will help you to prepare for the Desktop Specialist and Desktop Certified Associate certifications. In addition, it will provide you with the foundational knowledge for Desktop Professional. Based on my experience, Desktop Specialist isn't anywhere near as valuable as Desktop Associate.

Before diving into the Tableau lessons, let's review the success stories of the authors and learn more about their Tableau journeys in their own words.

Dmitry Anoshin, Tableau Desktop and Server Qualified Certified:

"I have worked with Tableau since 2011. Most of the time, I was working on data warehouse projects and used Tableau as a primary BI tool. I didn't spend much time on great visualizations and complex calculations. Also, I was responsible for Tableau Server deployment and support. My employer never asked me to complete a Tableau certification. Just recently, I was involved in Tableau communities and user groups and decided to pass the exam and fill the gaps in my knowledge. After some preparation, I was able to pass the Tableau Desktop Qualified Certification and Tableau Server Qualified Certification. It wasn't easy and it took a lot of extra effort. But it is totally worth it. Now, I feel more confident in my skills and can demonstrate my knowledge to my colleagues and employer."

Gleb Makarenko, Tableau Desktop Qualified Associate Certified:

"I began using Tableau in 2018 and quickly fell in love with the intuitiveness and ease of use of the software. I was able to easily adapt to its interface and create powerful visualizations. I decided to get certified on Tableau software to receive proper credentials that I could use on my resume, as well as learn intricacies that I wasn't using at the time. With a bit of effort and research, I was able to complete the examination and would recommend doing the same to anyone who is serious about working with Tableau."

JC Gillet, Tableau Desktop Qualified Associate Certified:

"I have worked with Tableau since 2014. For the first few years of my career, I was using Tableau mostly for its map feature, as I found this was a very efficient way to convey insights. I started to use it almost exclusively in 2018 as it was my new team's BI tool. Once you get past its few quirks, it is a really powerful and easy-to-use platform. It seemed like a natural step for me to take the certification exam once I found myself being the local expert on Tableau. Now, I hold a widely recognized qualification that I can use to promote myself to my current and future employers. I even learned a few things while taking the exam!"

Fabian Peri, Tableau Desktop Qualified Associate Certified:

"I was first introduced to Tableau in 2015 as a graduate student. It was recommended to me by my professor for a data visualization assignment. After a few days of use, I understood how it could help the stakeholders at my company gain insights from vast quantities of data. Since then, Tableau has been my preferred visualization tool. Although I have been working with Tableau for years, I was hesitant to take the Tableau certification exam because I did not know if it would be of any use. During my last job search, I realized that a Tableau certification would set me apart from other candidates. After reading numerous resources I passed the certification exam – the entire process was a great learning experience. In addition, it gave me confidence in my skills as a Tableau developer."

Radhika Biyani, Tableau Desktop Qualified Associate Certified:

"I was first introduced to Tableau in 2016 as a master's student while working on a data visualization assignment. I fell in love with it and, since then, it has been my preferred visualization tool. When I started using it on a day-to-day basis for my clients in an analytics consultant capacity, I knew that being Tableau Certified would help me gain the trust of any new or potential clients easily. I got certified in 2017 and studying for the certification helped me learn certain nuances of the tool that I wasn't familiar with, despite using Tableau on a day-to-day basis. These made my work faster, more efficient, and better and I still use those skills in my job to date. I would totally recommend the Tableau exam to anyone who wants to take their skills to the next level!"

Now that we have covered what the certification is in general and have learned why it is important to prepare for and pass the Tableau exam, it's time to learn about the key topics of Tableau that will help you to successfully prepare for the Tableau Desktop Certified Associate exam and pass it with a score of more than 75 percent in less than 2 hours. Good luck!

Who this book is for

This book is for business analysts, BI professionals, and data analysts who want to get certified as a Tableau Desktop Associate and solve a range of data science and BI problems using this example-rich guide. Each chapter is packed with self-assessment questions so that you can become well versed with Tableau Desktop's offerings. Some prior experience of Tableau Desktop is expected.

What this book covers

Chapter 1, *Building Your Data Model,* will help to understand how to connect to your data and use Tableau's data modeling capabilities.

Chapter 2, *Working with Worksheets,* will show you how to use the data that you have prepared to begin building your visualizations in order to share insights. This chapter will demonstrate how to use Tableau's worksheets to conduct your analysis.

Chapter 3, *Analyzing Data Using Charts,* teaches you about the various chart types that are available in Tableau. The chapter will also discuss how formatting can help create more effective visualizations.

Chapter 4, *Visualizing Geographic Data,* dives deeper into map visuals and will enable you to understand more about the mapping capabilities in Tableau. This chapter will explain how to create, navigate, and customize maps.

Chapter 5, *Understanding Simple Calculations in Tableau,* helps you to create simple calculations that can be leveraged across the various visuals that we have read about in the previous chapters.

Chapter 6, *Tableau Table Calculations,* looks at more advanced table calculations, where the results of the calculations observed in this chapter will be used for building further calculations.

Chapter 7, *Level of Detail Expressions,* covers the three types of level of detail expressions available in Tableau and explains how they can be used to aggregate data at a level that is either more granular or less granular than the specified dimensions.

Chapter 8, *Leveraging Analytics Capabilities,* covers some of Tableau's analytics tools, enabling you to create reference lines or bands, cluster data in similar buckets, identify trends, and forecast what your data will look like in the future.

Chapter 9, *Building Your Dashboards,* will walk you through features and best practices that will help you to build actionable and informative dashboards.

To get the most out of this book

Readers without any prior knowledge of Tableau can get the most out of this book.

Download the example code files

You can download the example code files for this book from your account at www.packt.com. If you purchased this book elsewhere, you can visit www.packtpub.com/support and register to have the files emailed directly to you.

You can download the code files by following these steps:

1. Log in or register at www.packt.com.
2. Select the **Support** tab.
3. Click on **Code Downloads**.
4. Enter the name of the book in the **Search** box and follow the onscreen instructions.

Once the file is downloaded, please make sure that you unzip or extract the folder using the latest version of:

- WinRAR/7-Zip for Windows
- Zipeg/iZip/UnRarX for Mac
- 7-Zip/PeaZip for Linux

The code bundle for the book is also hosted on GitHub at https://github.com/PacktPublishing/Tableau-Desktop-Certified-Associate-Exam-Guide. In case there's an update to the code, it will be updated on the existing GitHub repository.

We also have other code bundles from our rich catalog of books and videos available at https://github.com/PacktPublishing/. Check them out!

Download the color images

We also provide a PDF file that has color images of the screenshots/diagrams used in this book. You can download it here: http://www.packtpub.com/sites/default/files/downloads/9781838984137_ColorImages.pdf.

Conventions used

There are a number of text conventions used throughout this book.

`CodeInText`: Indicates code words in text, database table names, folder names, filenames, file extensions, pathnames, dummy URLs, user input, and Twitter handles. Here is an example: "Mount the downloaded `WebStorm-10*.dmg` disk image file as another disk in your system."

Bold: Indicates a new term, an important word, or words that you see on screen. For example, words in menus or dialog boxes appear in the text like this. Here is an example: "Select **System info** from the **Administration** panel."

Warnings or important notes appear like this.

Tips and tricks appear like this.

Get in touch

Feedback from our readers is always welcome.

General feedback: If you have questions about any aspect of this book, mention the book title in the subject of your message and email us at `customercare@packtpub.com`.

Errata: Although we have taken every care to ensure the accuracy of our content, mistakes do happen. If you have found a mistake in this book, we would be grateful if you would report this to us. Please visit `www.packtpub.com/support/errata`, selecting your book, clicking on the Errata Submission Form link, and entering the details.

Piracy: If you come across any illegal copies of our works in any form on the internet, we would be grateful if you would provide us with the location address or website name. Please contact us at `copyright@packt.com` with a link to the material.

If you are interested in becoming an author: If there is a topic that you have expertise in and you are interested in either writing or contributing to a book, please visit `authors.packtpub.com`.

Reviews

Please leave a review. Once you have read and used this book, why not leave a review on the site that you purchased it from? Potential readers can then see and use your unbiased opinion to make purchase decisions, we at Packt can understand what you think about our products, and our authors can see your feedback on their book. Thank you!

For more information about Packt, please visit `packt.com`.

Section 1: Getting Started with Tableau

1

In this section, you will learn about the concepts of Tableau and how to install Tableau Desktop.

This section comprises the following chapter:

- Chapter 1, *Building Your Data Model*

1
Building Your Data Model

Data analysis and visualization go hand in hand. Tableau allows users to perform in-depth data analysis and share results via interactive visualizations. Tableau includes numerous data modeling capabilities that allow users to make sense of data and to obtain meaningful insights, without having to deal with advanced database concepts. Data modeling is an important concept, and the more data you are working with, the more important it is.

As the amount of information we work with grows, we need to be able to efficiently perform analysis. Data modeling allows us to not only prepare for our analysis but to also make it as efficient as possible. At the end of the day, we use data to help us make better decisions. Spending time learning how we can model the data will help us identify what questions we can answer, and how to answer them. Regardless of the size of the data you are working with, Tableau will help you glean insights with ease.

This chapter will explain how to connect to your data and use Tableau's data modeling capabilities to begin your analysis.

The following topics will be covered in this chapter:

- Initial preparation
- Connecting to your data
- Building your data model
- Preparing your data

Technical requirements

This chapter uses the Global Superstore dataset, which can be found at `https://www.tableau.com/sites/default/files/getting_started_data_sets.zip`.

Once extracted, you will see two files:

- `Global Superstore Orders 2016`
- `Global Superstore Returns 2016`

 We believe that following along is the best way to learn and become comfortable with any application. Follow along using the examples provided in this chapter, or find a dataset that you are interested in.

Initial preparation

Before connecting to your data, you need to do a few things. First, you must look for data that will answer your questions. Once you have validated that it exists, where it is stored and how to acquire access/permissions (if necessary). In most cases, you will be connecting directly to a database using a username and password. However, you can also connect to files such as Excel workbooks on your local machine. You can even use a combination of both if needs be.

The Global Superstore dataset

The Global Superstore dataset is data from a fictional global retail chain that sells office supplies. In the real world, you will most likely be connecting to databases; however, working with Excel files is similar – sheets in Excel are treated similarly to tables in a database. The data in these workbooks is similar to what you would see in a database.

The Global Superstore dataset consists of one Excel workbook and one Excel CSV file:

- Global Superstore Orders 2016 (.xlsx)
  Sheet 1: Orders
  Sheet 2: People
- Global Superstore Returns 2016 (.csv)
  Sheet 1: Global Superstore Returns 2016

The Orders sheet contains sales data where each record (Row ID) represents a single transaction:

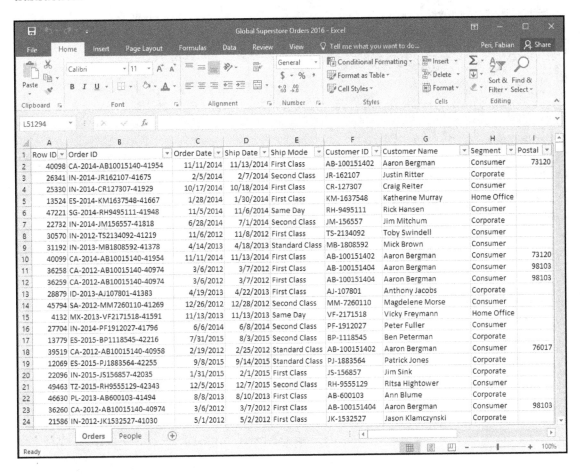

The `People` sheet contains a mapping of persons to region:

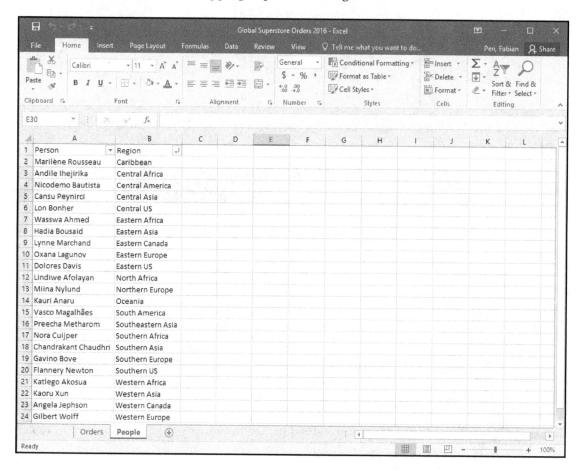

The `Global Superstore Returns 2016` sheet contains order IDs for returned orders by region:

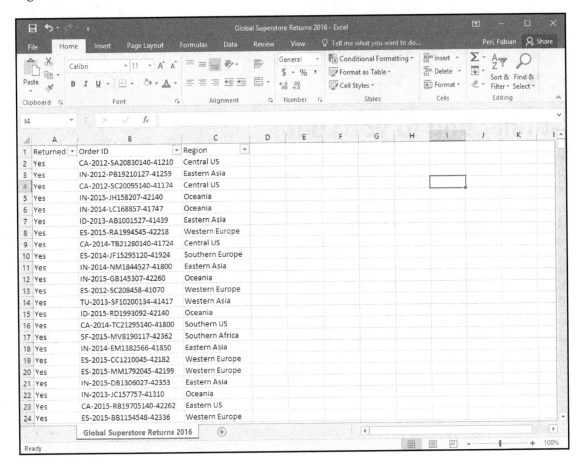

We have found the data we need for our analysis, we know where it's located, and have access to use it. Now we will move on to connecting to the data source with Tableau.

 It is always a good idea to get an idea of the data you are working with by viewing a few records. If you are working with an Excel file, open it in Excel to get a feel for the dataset.

Connecting to your data

Before diving into your data, you have to connect to it. Tableau allows you to connect to numerous data sources. You can connect to files on your local machine, to databases on servers, or other database sources. Tableau allows users to connect to numerous data sources – for a full list, visit Tableau's website to view a comprehensive and up-to-date list. The types of data sources you can connect with are listed in the **Connect** pane of the start page. Files that you have recently connected to will appear on this page as well.

Depending on which version of Tableau Desktop you are using, you will have access to different built-in connectors. Search for your required connection type to connect to your data. If you are connecting to a commonly used connector then it is almost certain to be available. If the file or database that you need to connect to is not available in the **Connect** pane section, you can create a custom connection using **Other Databases (ODBC)** or a **Web Data Connector**. You can see a list of all of the native data connection types Tableau allows in the **Connect** pane by clicking on the **More...** button (under the **To a File** or **To a Server** sections):

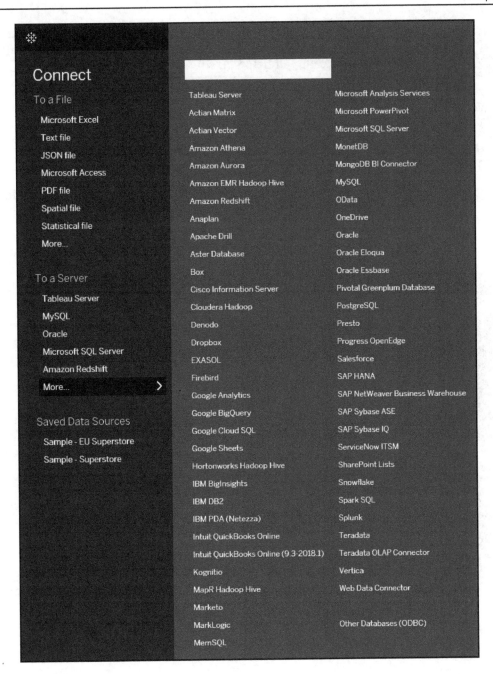

If the data source you want to connect to is not available in the **Connect** pane, do a little research online. There are often helpful suggestions made by the community that will help you solve questions or issues that you will run into.

Now we will move on to connecting to the Global Superstore Orders dataset.

Connecting to the Global Superstore dataset

Click on the **Microsoft Excel** button in the **Connect** pane. It will be under the **To a File** section. Your file browser window will open. Navigate to and open the `Global Superstore Orders 2016` Excel file:

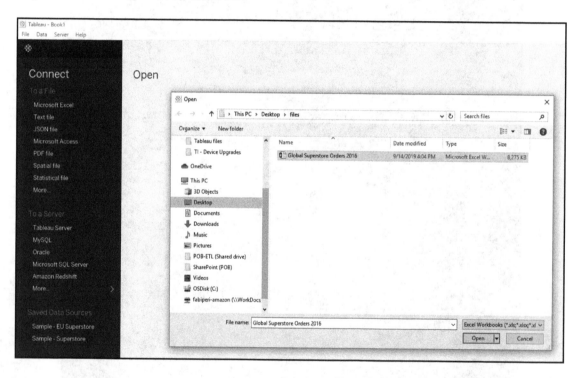

After connecting to the data source, you will be taken to the **Data Source** screen. From this screen, we can select which tables (in this case, sheets) that we want to use in our analysis:

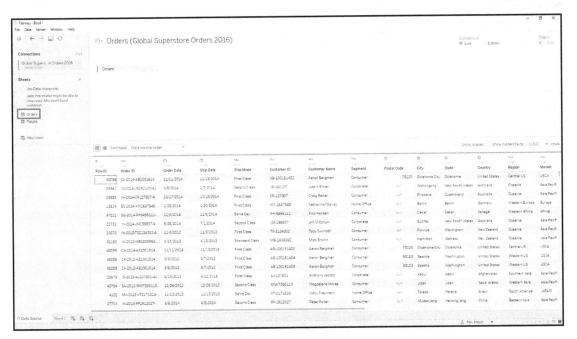

Double click the **Orders** table icon in the **Connections** pane (under the **Sheets** section) or drag the **Orders** table icon to the canvas. You will then see orders in the canvas (rectangle name icon with a blue border to the left). You will also see a sample of 1,000 rows in the data grid. We previously mentioned how important it is to view your data before you start working with it. The data grid is an easy way to do this.

The **Data Source** page allows you to prepare the data for analysis. Once connected to a data source, you can make changes to how Tableau imports and interprets tables. Take a look at the preceding screenshot, which shows the **Data Source** page after connecting to and importing the orders sheet from the *Global Superstore Orders 2016* dataset.

There are four main sections of the **Data Source** page. These sections are highlighted in the following screenshot. Next, we will look at these sections in detail, starting with the left pane:

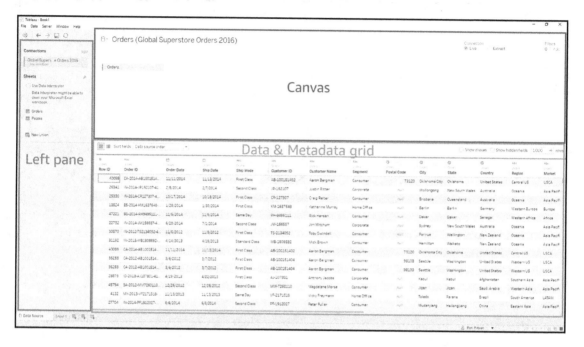

The left pane

The left pane shows connection details for the data sources you have connected to. This section allows you to add additional data source connections using the **Add** button.

When connected to flat files (for example, Excel), the **Connections** section will show the Excel workbook you are connected to with the sheets listed here. In the preceding screenshot, Global Superstore Orders 2016 is the Excel workbook and the sheets are Orders and People.

When connected to databases, the left pane will display the server name, the database, schema, and tables listed in the following screenshot:

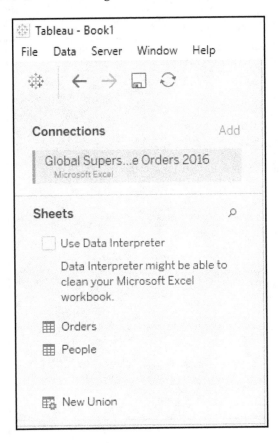

If you hover over the right of the connection name, a down caret will appear. This allows us to make extra changes to the connection, such as renaming it.

You can view records in any table that you are connected to by hovering to the right of the table name, then clicking the **View data** icon. This is shown in the following screenshot:

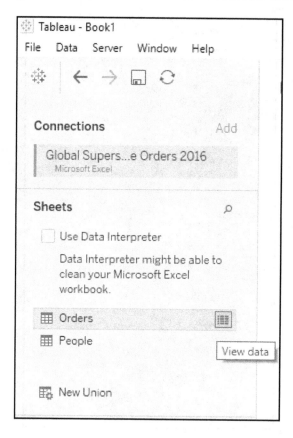

This results in the following popup:

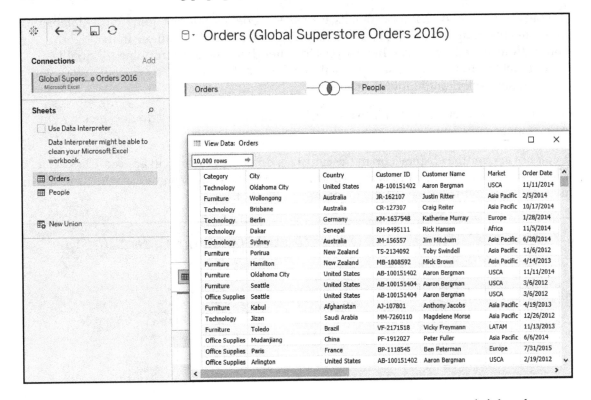

If you need to go back to the start page, click the Tableau logo in the upper left-hand corner of the screen (under **File**).

The canvas

The canvas displays data import details as well as modeling options (joins, cross-database joins, data blending, custom SQL, and data prep). The tables that you see in the **Connections** pane is what you have access to. After dragging and dropping (or double-clicking) tables from the left pane, you will see them in the canvas. You can only work with data that has been brought into the canvas.

Once a table has been imported into the canvas, it can be renamed by double-clicking on the rectangle name icon.

If you hover over the **Orders** icon in the canvas, a down caret icon will appear. Click on it to view additional modifications that you can make to the table. You can see the drop-down menu along with the options in the following screenshot:

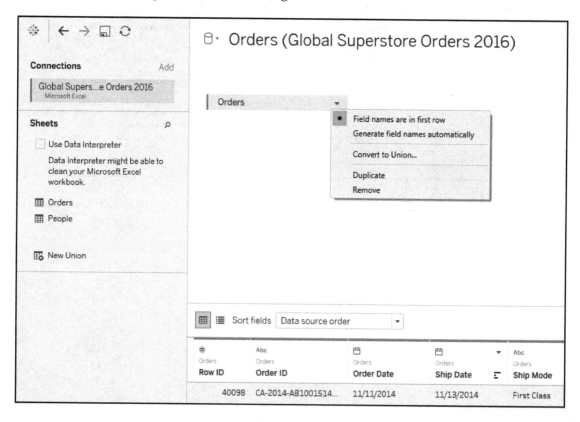

The data grid

The data grid is a tabular view of the imported data (the default display is a view of the first 1,000 records). The data grid is displayed in the following screenshot along with a sample of the records:

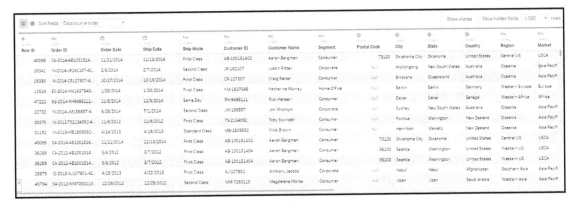

You can rename columns by double-clicking on their names as shown in the following screenshot:

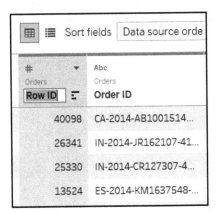

After connecting to a data source, Tableau automatically identifies the data types of columns. Occasionally, columns will be incorrectly classified. For example, Tableau might interpret a field that contains dates as an integer data type, rather than a date data type. You can change the datatypes of columns by clicking on the data type icon and selecting the new data type, as shown in the following screenshot:

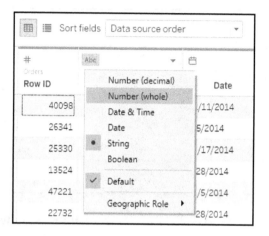

If you hover over the top-right of the column name, a down caret will appear. This allows us to make extra attribute changes to the column. You can see the drop-down menu along with the options in the following screenshot:

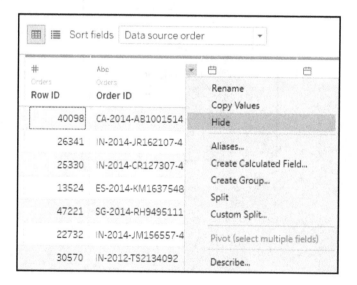

> In Tableau, there are usually multiple ways to accomplish the same task. Figure out what works best for your workflow and go with that.

The metadata grid

The metadata grid allows you to get a glance of the fields you have imported, the source tables, and the remote field name (the name of the field as it is in the data source). Click on the **Manage metadata** icon (to the left of **Sort fields**) to get an overview of the data source structure.

You can perform all the same operations on columns that you could in the data grid view (for example, rename columns, change the datatypes of columns, and so on). The following screenshot shows how field name, table, and remote field name are presented in the **Manage metadata** view:

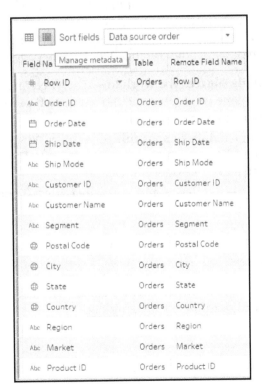

Once you have imported a table into the canvas, you can quickly explore field names and data types by clicking on the **Manage metadata** icon. This is an excellent view to validate what you are importing.

In the next section, we will talk about what must be done before you build visualizations.

Building your data model

Building your data model consists of how you combine your data before you analyze it. There are numerous factors to take into account when determining a data model structure – the amount of data, type of data, granularity of the data, number of data sources, and so on. The **Data Source** page is where we will set up how Tableau interprets the data from the data source. The settings we modify on this page tell Tableau where to find the data (for example, network location, server name, and more) and what data is available, and it allows us to customize the data that is brought in (for example, change field names, create new columns based on calculations, and more).

Tableau allows you to easily combine data from different sources. Here are the various ways in which we can join data together on the **Data Source** page.

- **Data from a single source**: The workflow when needing only one table is simple – drag the table name (or double-click) from the left pane onto the canvas. You will only need to make one data connection.

- **Data from a single database but multiple tables**: When using multiple tables in the same database, the canvas gives you the ability to join and union tables. You will only need to make one data connection.

- **Data from multiple databases and multiple tables**: If you are connecting to multiple databases and need to use data from many tables then you can use cross-database joins.

- **Data blending**: This shows data from two different sources that are at a different grain. You will need to make multiple data connections.

Now that we have a general overview of what we can do on the **Data Source** page, let's move on to how we can further refine our data model.

Preparing your data

Once the data sources have been defined, you can apply various actions to help tidy your data before analysis. We will begin by discussing data types and how to work with them.

Working with data types

If you have worked in data analysis before, you know how important it is to work with the right data types. Tableau allows users to make all the common data type conversions in a few different places. We will discuss data types in much more detail in the coming chapters but just remember that you can change the type of data in the metadata panel. The available data types in Tableau are presented in the following table:

Icon	Data type
Abc	Text (string) values
🗓	Date values
🗓	Date and time values
#	Numerical values
T|F	Boolean values (relational only)
⊕	Geographic values (used with maps)
⬓≈	Cluster group (https://help.tableau.com/current/pro/desktop/en-us/clustering.htm)

After you have connected to your data, click the **Manage metadata** icon in the center of the page (left of the **Sort fields** drop-down menu). The metadata grid view will appear:

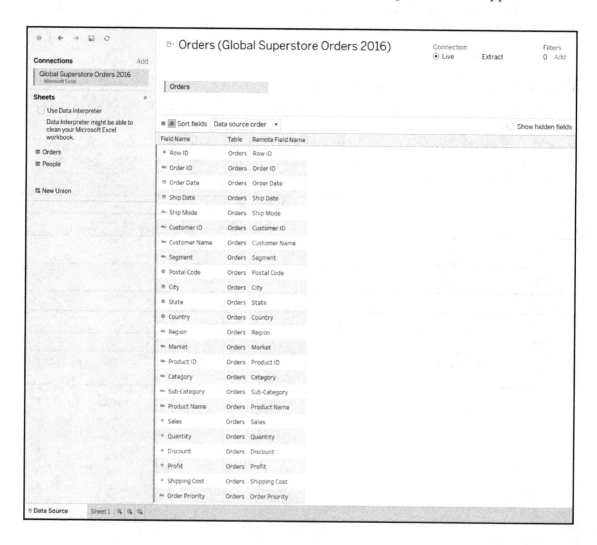

To change the data type of a field, click on the data type icon to the left of the field name. Here, you can convert between types of data. Various geographic data types are also available in the pane:

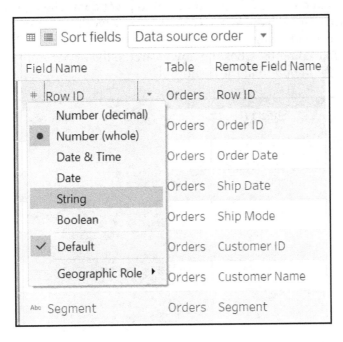

One example of when you may want to change data types is when you import dates as a string instead of a date. You can click the icon and convert it to a date field without having to make any changes to the source data.

Pivoting data

If you've worked with Microsoft Excel or data in a tabular format before, you have probably pivoted data. Generally, you want to pivot data when it is in a cross-tab format to work with it in Tableau. While wide data may work well for reporting, data should be long when conducting the analysis. After you have connected to your data source, select multiple columns. Click the down caret to the upper-right of the column name and click the **Pivot** option in the menu:

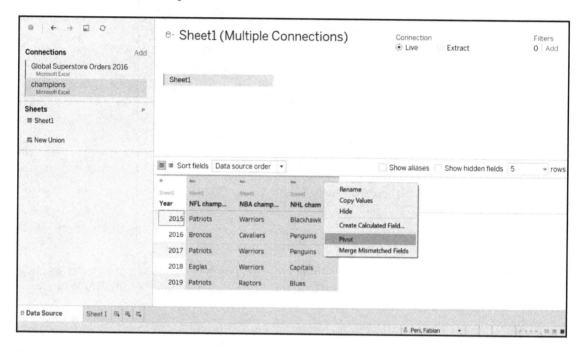

The columns that you have previously selected will be pivoted. Always validate your data after you make any transformation; this will give you confidence in the results of the analysis. You can add or remove additional columns to the pivot in a similar manner – click the down caret of the field that you are interested in and follow the instructions:

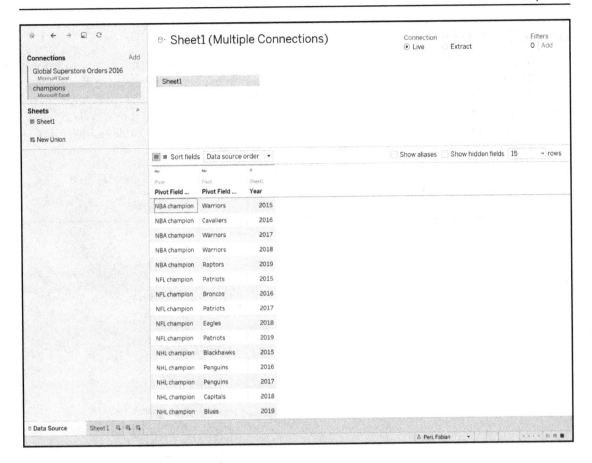

 You can use custom SQL to pivot data in tables from databases. Note that the pivot data option in Tableau Desktop is only available for selected data sources such as text files, Google sheets, Microsoft Excel, and PDF files. If you are working with SQL then you must use custom SQL to pivot your data.

Splitting fields

If one of your fields is a string and you need to split it up, you can use Tableau's split into multiple fields options. When you are on the **Data Source** page in the data grid, click the down caret icon next to a column, then click the **Split** option. The split will be automatic, but you can get more control of the split if you click the **Custom Split...** option. When using the automatic split option, the field is split on a common separator that Tableau identifies. In the following example, it is a space between the first and last name.

An example of when you would want to use this option is if you had full names in a column and needed the first name and last name in different columns:

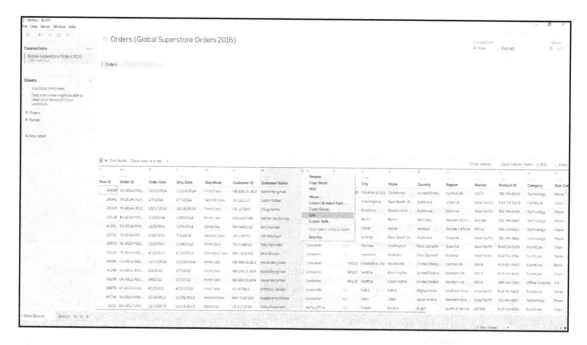

After splitting the column, you can see that there are two new columns – one containing the first name and one containing the last. You can rename the column by double-clicking on the column name:

Orders	Calculation	Calculation
Customer Name	**Customer ...**	**Customer ...**
Aaron Bergman	Aaron	Bergman
Justin Ritter	Justin	Ritter
Craig Reiter	Craig	Reiter
Katherine Murray	Katherine	Murray
Rick Hansen	Rick	Hansen
Jim Mitchum	Jim	Mitchum
Toby Swindell	Toby	Swindell
Mick Brown	Mick	Brown
Aaron Bergman	Aaron	Bergman
Aaron Bergman	Aaron	Bergman
Aaron Bergman	Aaron	Bergman
Anthony Jacobs	Anthony	Jacobs
Magdelene Morse	Magdelene	Morse

Filtering data

Tableau is built to work with big data, but your performance takes a hit as the size of your data increases. One of the best ways to manage the performance of your analysis is to limit the amount of data that Tableau needs to read. On the **Data Source** page, you can include a data source filter.

To add a data source filter, click the **Add** button in the **Filters** section of the canvas. An **Edit Data Source Filters** menu will appear. Click **Add** and select the filter you would like applied. You can add more filters or remove added filters using the same method:

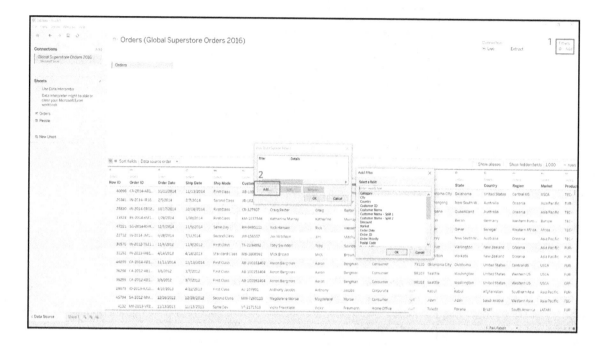

Combining data

When performing data analysis, you will often work with data in multiple tables. Tableau allows you to combine data sources using multiple methods. The four primary methods are as follows:

- Joins
- Cross-database joins
- Unions
- Blends

The following sections will explain each of these methods in detail.

Joins

Joining the data allows you to combine tables using common fields in order to perform analysis. You can think of joining tables as extending a table by adding columns from a source table to a target table. You can combine tables using a common field (a column present in both tables) in Tableau. Based on the related field, we can combine rows from multiple tables. If the tables you are using are from the same source (database, workbook, and so on) then the procedure involves a single connection. Working with tables from the same data source is computationally more efficient; however, it is not a requirement.

The `Orders` table should already be in the canvas.

Double-click or drag the `People` table to the canvas (an inner-join icon will appear between the rectangular icons for each table name that is in the canvas).

Select/change the join type (when a new table is brought into the canvas section, Tableau will look for a column to join on – in the case of our example, it has joined on `Region`, which is a column in both sheets).

You can click the blue inner-join icon to make changes to how the tables are being joined. You may want to edit the join type (for example, inner-join to left) or perhaps even edit the clause itself by adding more conditions to it. The following screenshot shows the results of the join between the `Orders` and `People` sheets:

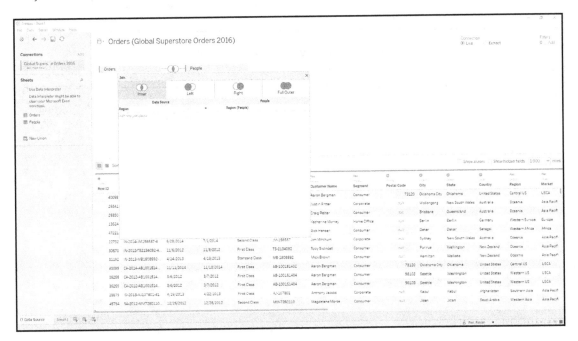

You can view the data in the data grid after joins to visually inspect for errors.

The join types

The four basic SQL join types are all supported by Tableau: **inner**, **left**, **right**, and **full outer**. Prior to joining data, you must verify that the data types from the common field used in the join are the same:

Type of join	Description	Venn diagram of join
Inner join	The result set includes all records that have a matching value in both tables. For the Global Superstore Orders 2016 example, this will return all records from the Orders table for which there is a matching person in the People table.	Inner
Left join	The result set includes all records from the left table (Orders) and matching records from the People table. For records where there is no match, NULL values will appear.	Left
Right join	The result set includes all records from the right table (People) and matching records from the Orders table. For records where there is no match, NULL values will appear.	Right
Full outer join	The result set includes all records from both tables regardless of whether there is a match or not.	Full Outer

The maximum number of tables that can be joined in Tableau is 32. Tables also have a limit of 255 columns.

Some instructions for joins are as follows:

1. Click and drag (or double-click) the second table from the left pane onto the canvas.
2. Tableau will automatically attempt to detect a common field from both data sources in order to join both tables.
3. Click the **Join** icon to change the join type or to change the join operation by adding/removing additional clauses. When finished, close the **Join** dialog box.
4. Validate the join so that the data pane will reflect how you want the data to be ingested by Tableau in the data grid. To remove a join, click the **x** button icon by the join condition.

Next, we will move on to a similar type of join – the cross-database join.

Cross-database joins

A cross-database join is an inner, left, right, or full outer join between two or more tables that are in different databases. You will often encounter multiple databases systems that house different information. Order information may be in an Amazon Redshift database while information about store locations may be in an SQL Server database. To join information from different sources, you will need to use a cross-database join.

There may be multiple reasons why data resides in different databases but that is beyond the scope of this chapter.

The four types of joins mentioned previously are available with cross-database joins. Cross-database joins require a multi-connection data source setup. This means that you need to create a new connection to each database for each of the tables that you want to join. We have already connected to the `Global Super Orders 2016` Excel workbook and brought in the `Orders` table. We want to join orders with the `Returns` table but it is in a different file (`Global Superstore Returns 2016.csv`).

 Although we are working with data in flat files, the process is similar when working with databases. Each connection will be to a database instead of a flat file.

In the following screenshot, we see that we are connected to a data source (`Global Superstore Orders 2016`). The `Orders` sheet has already been imported onto the canvas:

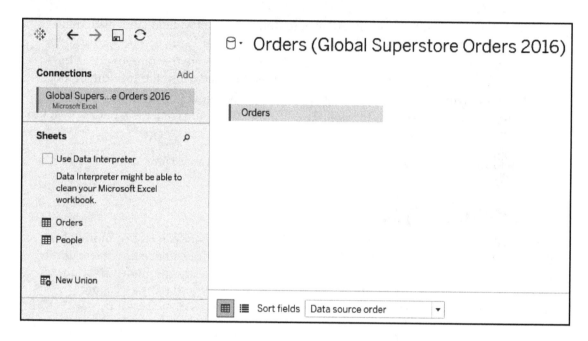

To join the `Returns` table to the `Orders` table, connect to `Global Superstore Returns 2016` by clicking on the **Add link** option in the **Connections** pane. From here, navigate to the file and double-click it:

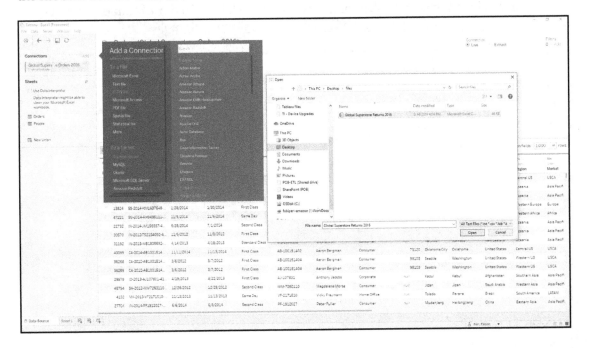

Once the second connection is added, you will see the connection name under the pre-existing connection as well as all the tables under the **Files** section of the **Connections** pane. Double-click the `Global Superstore Returns 2016` table name (or drag it onto the canvas) and Tableau will try to automatically join these tables. In our example, the join is done on the `Order ID` column, which is a common field in both tables:

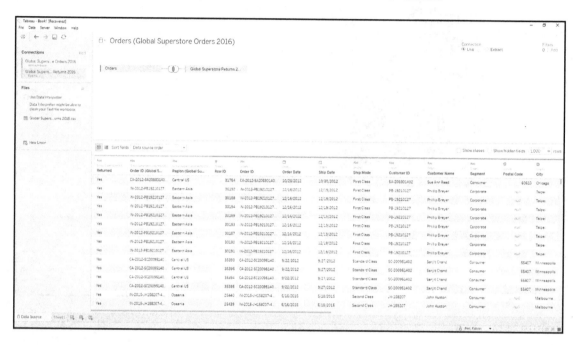

When you cross-join tables, Tableau will color-code them according to their source. Note that the `Orders` table in the canvas has a blue left border indicating that it is from the `Global Superstore Orders 2016` workbook. Similarly, the table from the `Global Superstore Returns 2016` flat file has an orange left border in the canvas. The borders of the rectangular table button in the canvas corresponds to the color of its connection. When viewing the data grid after a cross-database join, the top borders of columns will be color-coded to the connection name as well.

Some instructions for cross-database joins are as follows:

1. Click the **Add** button in the **Connections** pane to add a new connection. A connection to another data source must be made prior to joining a table that is stored in that source.

2. Select a second table under the new connection then click and drag (or double-click) the second table from the left pane onto the canvas. Tableau will automatically try to join the tables using a common field.

3. Click the **Join** icon to change the join type or to change the join operation by adding/removing additional clauses. When finished, close the **Join** dialog box.

4. Validate that the join was done properly. The data grid will display the results of the data after the join and should help you to easily identify whether there are issues with your join.

 Cross-database joins are extremely powerful as they are often the easiest way to join tables from different databases.

Next, we will describe how Tableau can union data.

Unions

A union is another way to combine your data. When you union two tables, you append the rows from one table to another. Since you are effectively stacking tables on top of each other, there is one important condition that must be satisfied – the data types of the columns that will be stacked need to be compatible. You should not stack a date column on top of a text column.

The following table includes a description of a union along with a Venn diagram visual to help you visualize how a union operates:

Union	Description	Venn diagram of Union
Union	The result set of a union is all records from the first table appended to all records from the second table.	Union

To illustrate unions, we will append the `Orders` table to itself; this will yield a result set where every record is duplicated. Make sure the `Global Superstore Orders 2016` connection is highlighted then click and drag the `Orders` table to the canvas on top of the `Orders` table rectangular button already in the canvas. Drop it on top:

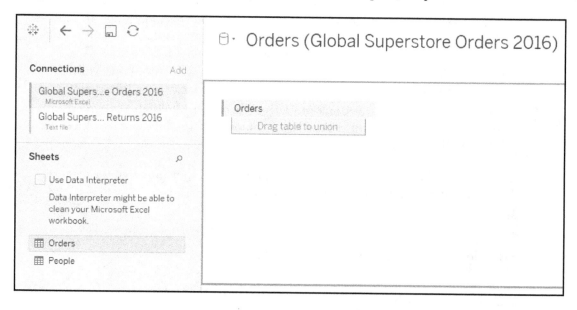

You will see a plus symbol to the right of the `Orders` table icon and table icons peeking out underneath. This indicates that the union was successful:

If you right-click the `Orders` table icon, a submenu will appear. Click on **Edit Union...**:

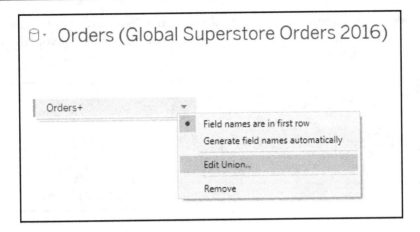

The **Specific (manual)** menu allows you to see how many tables are in your union. You can also union tables by dragging tables on the canvas of the **Specific (manual)** menu:

A second option is for Tableau to automatically include tables in your join based on wildcard criteria that you set up. This is useful when you would like to append numerous tables that may have different date suffixes:

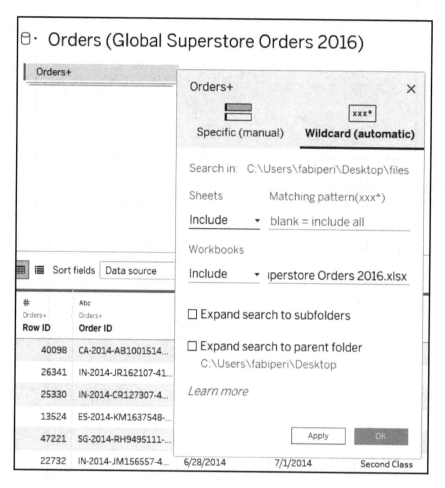

In Tableau, you cannot union tables from different databases (cross-database unions), but this may be changed in future updates. While you cannot union tables from different databases, you can union tables (sheets) from different Excel workbooks. Tableau has released a tool called **Tableau Prep Builder** that allows you to union data across multiple connections but that is beyond the scope of this chapter. For more information on Tableau Prep, visit the product page at `https://www.tableau.com/products/prep`.

Next, we move onto blends and how they differ from joins.

Blends

Like joins and unions, data blending allows you to work with data from different sources. Blends allow you to show data from two or more sources in the same view. The difference between a blend and a join is that when you blend, you are not combining data at the row level. A blend is a relationship. It allows data from different sources to be displayed in the same sheet. A data blend is primarily used when you need to show data from two different sources that are at a different grain.

When you connect to a database, Tableau automatically displays a blue checkmark next to the connection icon (see the following screenshot). The blue checkmark indicates that it is the primary, or first connected to, data source. After adding a second connection, an additional icon will appear, this time with an orange checkmark. Instructions for blends are as follows:

1. Make sure that the workbook contains at least two sources of data. You can do this by clicking **Data > New data source** in the menu.
2. The primary data source is the database icon with the blue checkmark; the database icon with the orange check mark is the secondary source. Click on the secondary database icon in the **Data** pane to use fields from this source.
3. The orange link icon indicates the field on which the data sources are blended using. If the link icon is gray, click it to activate the blend.
4. Use fields from the secondary data source as you would in the primary data source.

The following screenshot displays the **Data** pane once a successful blend has been made:

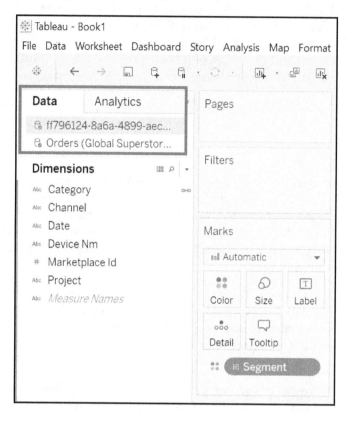

We have learned a tremendous amount of how to connect to, prepare, and join our data before analysis. In the next section, we will summarize what we have learned in this chapter.

Summary

We have gone through some ways to model data in Tableau. At this stage, you know how to connect to a data source. You should also have seen how important the **Data Source** page is when it comes to modeling your data. You can make your life so much easier if you use many of the features that are available in this section.

The main takeaway for data modeling in Tableau is that it helps you prepare your workspace to answer questions using data. Taking the time to understand your business or project requirements will help you perform a better analysis. Tableau allows you to quickly connect to and build visualizations but the **Data Source** page should not be ignored. Tableau also adds extra features with new releases. In the next chapter, you will learn how to use the data that you have prepared to begin building your visualizations in order to share insights.

Questions

Answer the following questions to test your knowledge of the information in this chapter.

1. To connect to multiple tables in multiple data sources, what must be specified?

a. A blend
b. A cross-database join
c. A join

A: b. A cross-database join

2. What types of joins are supported by Tableau?

A: Inner join, Left join, Right join and Full outer join

3. You can change the data types of fields in Tableau's **Data Source** page.
a. True
b. False

A: a. True

4. Tableau has a row limit.
a. True
b. False

A: b. False

Further reading

You can check out the following link for more information about the topics that were covered in this chapter:

- Full list of supported connectors (data sources Tableau can connect to): `https://help.tableau.com/current/pro/desktop/en-gb/exampleconnections_overview.htm`.

Section 2: Answering Questions with Data

In this section, you will use the knowledge you acquired from the previous chapters and practice answering questions using the Tableau functionality and connecting different data sources.

This section comprises the following chapters:

2
Working with Worksheets

Now that we have connected to our data sources, we can begin to glean insights. You will discover these insights using the worksheet tab. A worksheet is where you will build charts and tables using the data you have connected to. If you have used Microsoft Excel in the past, Tableau's sheet structure should be familiar. The workbook is the Tableau file you have open. Within the workbook, you will work with sheets. There are three different types of sheets:

Sheet Icon	Sheet description
	Worksheet – This is the primary workspace in which you will be working with your data.
	Dashboard – This is a collection of worksheets on one page with filters to personalize the view.
	Story – This is a collection of worksheets and/or dashboards sequenced in a presentation format.

This chapter will explain how to use Tableau's worksheet to conduct your analysis. The following topics will be covered in this chapter:

- Introduction to worksheets
- Exploring the data and analytics panes
- Shelves and cards

Introduction to worksheets

After connecting to a data source, you will see a worksheet tab entitled **Sheet1** in the lower menu ribbon. Click on it:

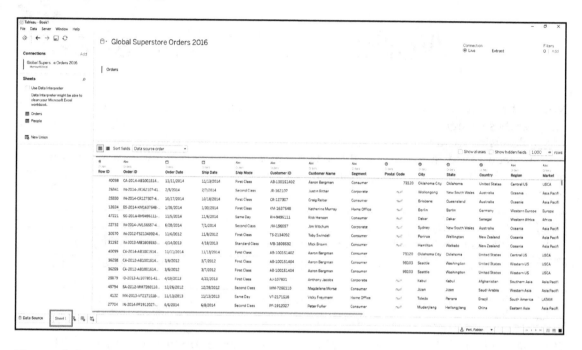

The worksheet page contains many items (menus, toolbars, panes, cards, shelves, and so on). You can think of the worksheet as the canvas on which you will paint your story or the view of the data you wish to present:

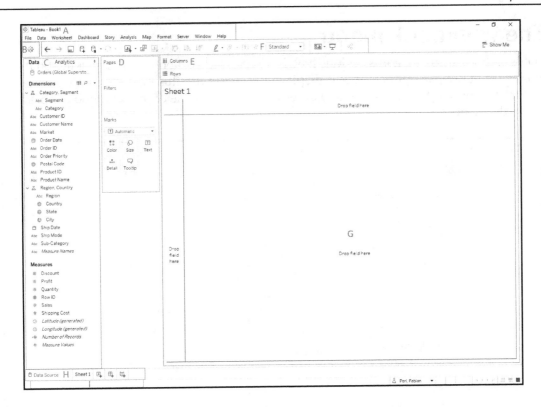

We will walk through the individual components of the worksheet here:

Section	Description
A	**Workbook menu**: This contains the workbook name, main menu, and options for the tableau workbook.
B	**Data Source page**: Click this icon to go to the Data Source page.
C	**Data and Analytics pane**: This contains the fields from data sources and options for manipulation and organization.
D	**Cards**: Drag fields from the data pane onto cards to edit and format the visualization.
E	**Shelves**: Drag fields from the data pane onto shelves to add data to your view.
F	**Toolbar**: This provides menu and analysis options for the worksheet.
G	**View**: This is the canvas where you create visualizations.
H	**Sheets**: These are tabs to create additional worksheets, dashboards, and stories.
I	**Status bar**: This displays a summary of the fields in the view.

Now that you are familiar with the main items of the worksheet, we will dive deeper into each individual component. We will begin by looking at the workbook menu.

The workbook menu

The workbook menu contains options that pertain to the workbook. After clicking on the worksheet button, an options pane is displayed. You can use this menu to create a new worksheet, format the worksheet, and other options. The name of the workbook appears above the menu ('Book2'):

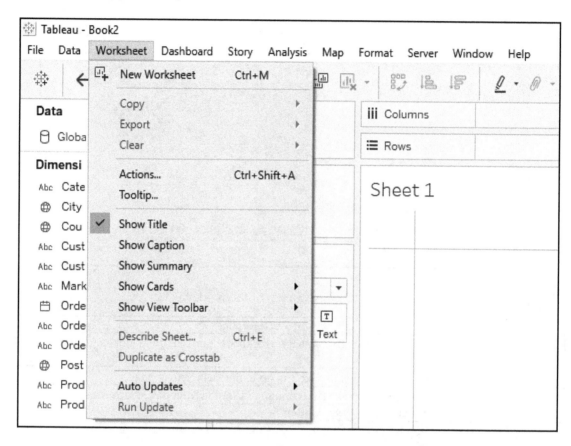

Options that are grayed out are unavailable. As you work with data in the worksheet, options will become enabled as conditions are met. For example, the **Clear** button is grayed out because the worksheet is empty. Once data is in the view, the **Clear** option will become available.

Toolbar

While working with data on the worksheet, you can perform commonly used actions. We will walk through the individual components of the worksheet toolbar located below the workbook menu. You can show or hide the toolbar by clicking **Window** > **Show Toolbar**:

Button	Description
	Tableau icon: Click this icon to go to the Data Source page.
	Undo: This undoes the last action performed. You can undo unlimited actions within the same session. Actions are not saved between sessions.
	Redo: This redoes the last action performed. You can redo unlimited actions within the same session. Actions are not saved between sessions.
	Save: This saves the workbook (using the .twb extension by default).
	New data source: Click this icon to go to the Connect pane page.
	Pause Auto Updates: When you make data changes to a worksheet, the current view may change. How fast the worksheet refreshes depends on many factors, one of them being the size of the data connected to it. When working with larger datasets, it is often beneficial to pause the view until all changes have been made. This can improve performance as you will not have to wait for the view to refresh after every action. Click the down-caret to the right of the **Pause Auto Updates** icon to customize how the view is refreshed.
	Run update: If you have enabled **Pause Auto Updates**, you can use the **Run Update** button to manually refresh the view.
	New worksheet: This creates a new worksheet. Click the down-caret to select between creating a new worksheet, dashboard, or story.
	Duplicate worksheet: Creates a copy of the current worksheet.
	Clear worksheet: Clears the current worksheet. Click the down-caret to the right of the clear worksheet icon to customize how the view is cleared.
	Swap rows and columns: This swaps fields in the columns and rows shelves.
	Sort fields ascending: This sorts the data in ascending order for a chosen field.
	Sort fields descending: This sorts the data in descending order for a chosen field.
	Highlight action: This enables/disables highlighting for the current sheet. When you enable highlighting, you select a field that you want to use as a highlighter. The down-caret will display a list of available fields to use for the highlight action. When a field is used as a highlighter, it tells the visualization which marks to highlight.
	Group members: Use this to quickly group members of a field. You must select multiple field headers for this option to become available.

[T]	**Show mark labels**: This enables/disables mark labels in the visualization.
🖈	**Fix axes**: When a continuous field from the data pane is added to a shelf, an axis is generated in the visualization. Use this button to select between a locked or dynamic axis.
Standard ▾	**Fix size**: Choose how the view is resized. Select from the following: • **Standard**: The view is automatically resized based on the size of the window. • **Fit Width**: The width of the view encompasses the entire width of the window. • **Fit Height**: The height of the view encompasses the entire height of the window. • **Entire View**: The view is set to the entire size of the window.
📊 ▾	**Show/Hide cards**: Choose which cards are displayed on the worksheet. Click the down-caret to the right of the **Show/Hide** icon to customize card options.
🖥	**Presentation mode**: This activates the full-screen view.
⚂	**Share workbook with others**: Click to publish the current workbook to your Tableau Server.
⊫ Show Me	**Show me**: This is where you select what type of visualization you will create.

There are usually a few ways to perform the same action in Tableau, taking advantage of the toolbar to save time. Understanding these commonly performed actions is an important part of developing visuals. Take the time to play with the buttons in the toolbar. Remember, you can always use the **Undo** button to reverse changes.

Exploring the Data and Analytics panes

The **Data** and **Analytics** panes are two distinct panes. The **Data** pane is where you will work with fields from your data sources. The **Analytics** pane is where you will apply various analytical tools and techniques to the data in your view. Options in the **Analytics** pane will not be available (grayed out) until you have worked with data in the **Data** pane.

The Data pane

The **Data** pane displays all of the fields that are available in your data source. After connecting to a data source, fields are categorized as one of two roles—dimension or measure. Dimensions are represented as blue pills when set in shelves, while measures are green. The color of the icon in the **Data** pane corresponds to the role as well.

The field manipulation options from the data source page (data grid) are also available after right-clicking a field. The following screenshot shows the **Data** pane and its available fields:

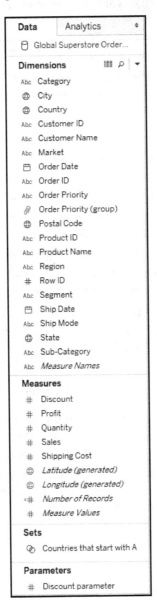

You can use options in the data pane to create additional field types, which we will describe in the following sections.

Data pane fields

After setting up the data source page, Tableau classifies the imported data into types. There are six data types:

Data icon	Data type	Description
T|F	Boolean	The value is one of either two values (for example, true or false)
🗓	Date	Date values (for example, 2009-01-20)
🗓🕐	Date & Time	Date and time values (for example, 2009-01-20 12:00:00)
⊕	Geographic	Geographic values such as countries or zip codes (for example, USA or 74104)
#	Number	Numeric values (for example, 4)
Abc	Text	String values (for example, Washington)

You can always change the data types of fields. Tableau assigns a data type during the import phase. Use the data source page or the **Data** pane to manually edit data types.

These six data types fall under one of the two data roles:

- **Dimensions (blue fields)**: These are fields that are of the Boolean, date, date and time, geographic, and text value data types (that is, qualitative data). Dimensions are the level of detail displayed in your analysis.
- **Measures (green fields)**: These are fields that are of the numeric data type (that is, quantitative data). Measures are numbers. They can also be summarized and aggregated based on conditions you define. By default, Tableau aggregates measures.

An example of a visualization using one dimension (country) and one measure (profit) is shown in the following example. Notice how the dimension field is blue in the **Columns** shelf while the measure field is green in the **Rows** shelf. Blue pills are discrete, while green pills are continuous:

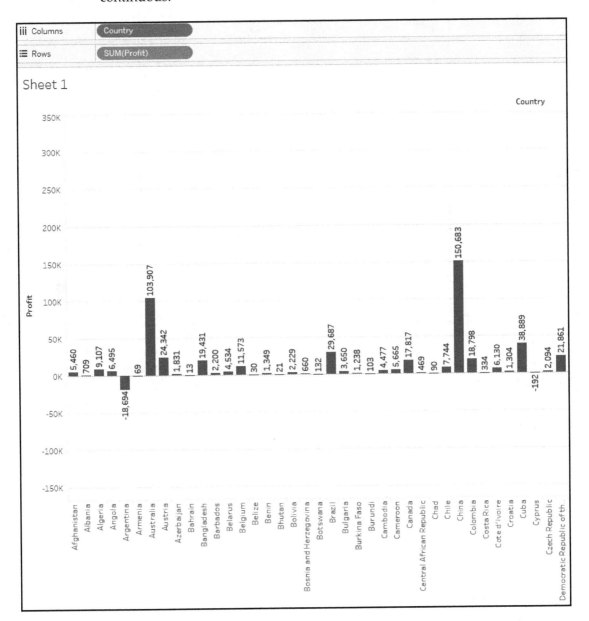

Dimensions and measures can also be of the continuous or discrete type. Once again, use the color of the fields to help you identify these two categories. You can change the type of field by right-clicking the field and selecting either **Discrete** or **Continuous** in the menu:

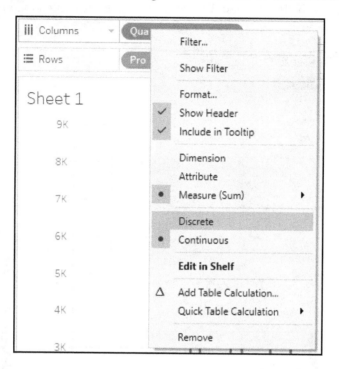

Knowing the difference between continuous and discrete fields is an important skill. You should spend some time researching the differences. A summary is provided in the following sections.

Continuous data

Continuous data can be any number within a range (the range can be infinite). There are infinite possibilities of what the number could be. For example, height is continuous. The shortest human verified by Guinness World Records was 21 ½ inches tall. The tallest was 99 inches tall (8'3"). Think of 21 ½ inches as the beginning of a number line and 99 inches as the end of the number line. A normal person's height could take on any value along this line:

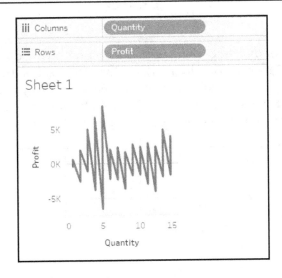

Discrete data

Discrete data is countable and distinct—it can only be certain values. For example, the number of parents you have is discrete —you cannot have half of a parent. In the following example, the quantities are defined (1, 2, 3,..., 14):

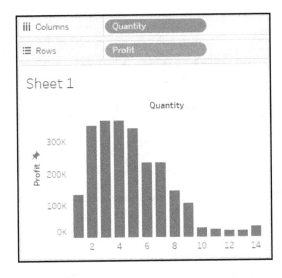

In the previous section, we went over the different data types and roles once data is available in the data pane. In the following section, we will discuss how to group data based on field values by creating sets.

Sets

Sets can either be static or dynamic (changes based on underlying data). Sets are defined using the fields in the **Data** pane or with marks in the visualization (not dynamic). You can think of sets as groupings or filtered results of your data. One way to create a set is to right-click the field in the **Data** pane and then select the **Create - Set** option. In the following screenshot, we will create a set based on values in the **Country** field:

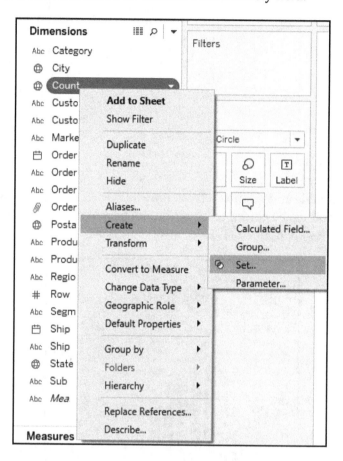

The **Edit Set** menu will appear. Select all of the field values for your desired set by clicking the checkbox next to each value. In the following example, all countries with a name starting with the letter *A* are selected. The name of this set is `Countries that start with A`. Created sets are shown in the data pane below the measures section:

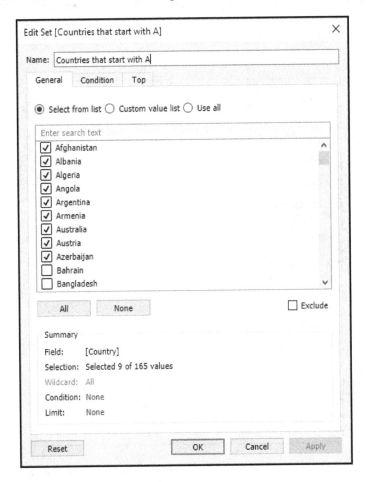

The next section explains how to give users the ability to edit values used in filters and calculations.

Parameters

Parameters are dynamic values that a user can change. These values are used in calculations so that the results are dependent upon the user's input. Parameters are an extremely powerful tool that allows values in calculations to be set dynamically. To create a parameter, either click the down-caret in the **Data** pane or right-click anywhere in the **Data** pane and select **Create Parameter** from the menu. The following screenshot illustrates this process:

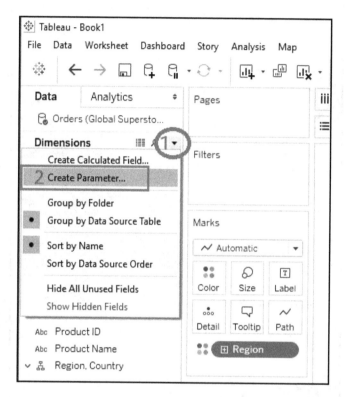

The **Edit Parameter** menu requires a few pieces of information. For this example, we are naming the parameter `Multiplier`. The data type is **Integer**, meaning that it will accept only integers as inputs from the user. The current value is the default one (set to 1), and the display format is how the value is formatted. The Allowable values section states whether a user can select any value (**All**) from a list of predefined values (**List**), or within a predefined range of values (**Range**). The following screenshot shows the **Edit Parameter** menu:

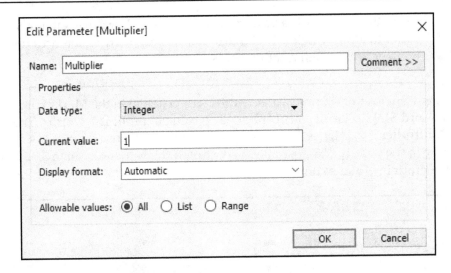

In the following screenshot, a calculated field was created using the `Multiplier` parameter. The calculated field is named `p. Profit * Multiplier`. The `p.` prefix will be a visual cue to us that this field uses a parameter. The result of this calculation will be the `Profit` multiplied by the `Multiplier` parameter (an integer that the user chooses):

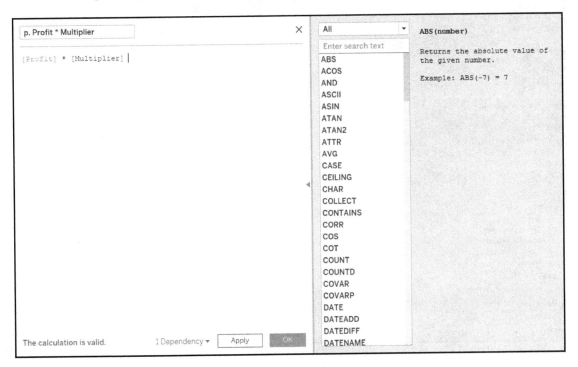

Using the `p.` prefix is a best practice that the author prefers to make it easier to identify fields. Feel free to follow your own preferences for nomenclature when creating fields.

The following visualization shows two measures (green fields) in the **Marks** card: **SUM(Profit) and SUM(p.Profit * Multiplier)**. The value of profit is 1,426,457. The value for **p.Profit * Multiplier** is 2,934,915. This is the profit doubled because `Multiplier` is set to 2 (see the value in the `Multiplier` parameter control). If the value was set to 3, it would multiply the profit by 3 and so on:

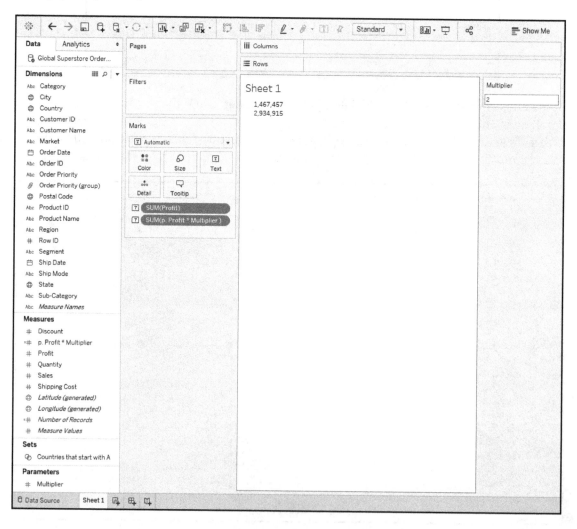

We will explain the calculated fields in more detail in the following section.

Calculated fields

In the preceding example, we created a calculated field—a field that was not in our original data source. To create a calculated field, either click the down-caret in the **Data** pane or right-click anywhere in the **Data** pane and select **Create a calculated field** from the menu. If we want to compute the profit margin, we can do so with a calculated field. The profit margin is the sum of profits divided by the sum of sales refer to the following screenshot for the calculation:

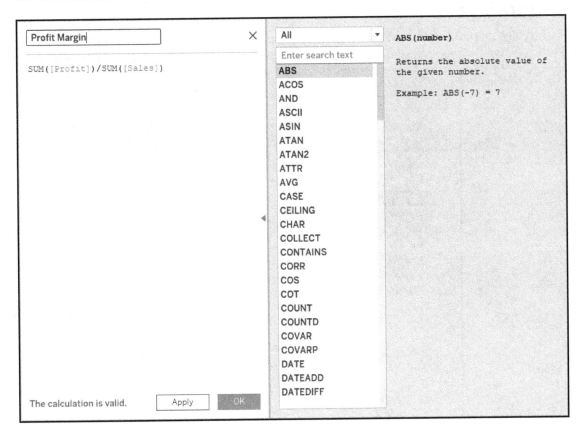

 Tableau provides a handy reference guide for calculated fields with examples (to the right of the calculation editor).

Calculated fields are treated like any other field. They are categorized as a dimension or a measure based on whether the result of the calculated field is quantitative or qualitative. The ability to create fields to use for your analysis is powerful and one that you will use repeatedly. There are many uses for calculated fields. They are easy to use and will help to solve many questions when you begin analyzing your data. We will learn more about calculated fields in later chapters (see `Chapter 5`, *Understanding Simple Calculations in Tableau*, and `Chapter 6`, *Tableau Table Calculations*).

In the next couple of sections, we will describe how to keep your data pane organized.

Hierarchies

Hierarchies help to organize data in the **Data** pane. They also make it easier for users when drilling down in visualizations. In the following example, we are creating a geographical hierarchy. First, right-click the **Country** field and select **Hierarchy**:

Once **Country** is under the **Geography Hierarchy** folder, three additional fields were dragged under the **Geography Hierarchy** folder—**State**, **City**, and **Postal Code**. The following screenshot shows that when **Country** is placed in the **Rows** shelf, a +/expand icon appears. When a user clicks on this, the next item in the hierarchy will populate (**State**) and so on. Hierarchies should make sense intuitively:

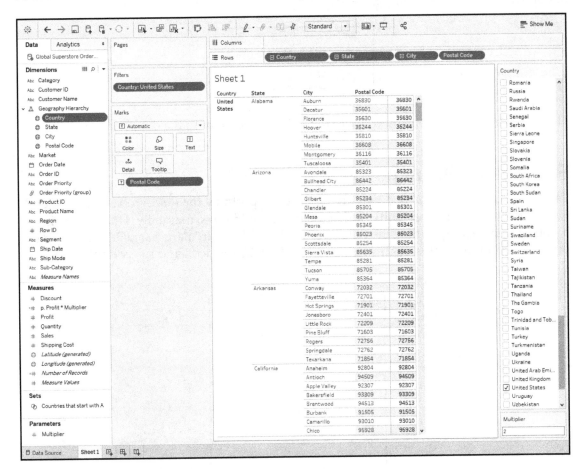

 Only dimensions can be added to hierarchies. To add a measure to a hierarchy, it must first be converted into a dimension.

You should use hierarchies for a more organized and efficient visualization. In the following section, we will discuss another way to organize data in the **Data** pane.

Grouping data fields

When working with fields in the **Data** pane, there are a few ways to stay organized. One of them is to place similar fields in folders. To create a folder, right-click on a data field and select the create folder button. Once a folder is created, drag and drop fields under the folder, similar to how we did for hierarchies:

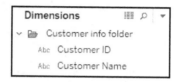

The default organization method is where fields are grouped by the data source table.

Replace References

Earlier, we created a calculated field that multiplied profit by the `Multiplier` parameter. If we wanted to replace profit with another field, we could do so manually. However, this becomes cumbersome if the same field needs to be replaced in many calculations. Tableau provides a solution to this. Right-click on the field to be replaced and select **Replace References**:

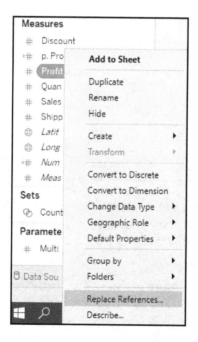

A menu will appear that gives you the option of selecting what field to replace the old field with. In the following example, we want all references of **Profit** to be replaced by **Discount**:

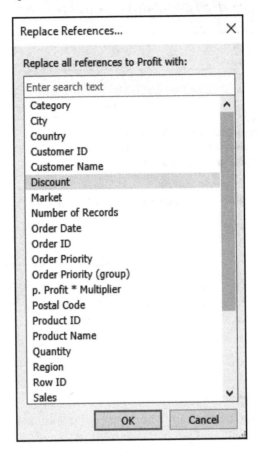

After clicking **OK**, the calculated field is updated with the replaced reference.

If you ever want to know additional details for a particular field, then right-click the field in the **Data** pane and select the **Describe Field** button. A window similar to the following will appear:

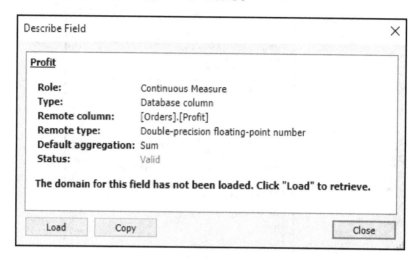

We have discussed many of the features and options available in the **Data** pane. In the next section, we will highlight some of the tools and features available in Tableau's **Analytics** pane.

The Analytics pane

To access the **Analytics** pane, click the tab at the top of the left sidebar. The **Analytics** pane allows users to summarize and apply various analytical techniques to the view. Analytic objects can be added by dragging and dropping from the **Analytics** pane onto the view. If an object is grayed out in the **Analytics** pane, this means that it is not available based on the type of data in the current view. In the following example, the **Average Line** object (under the **Summarize** section) is brought into the view:

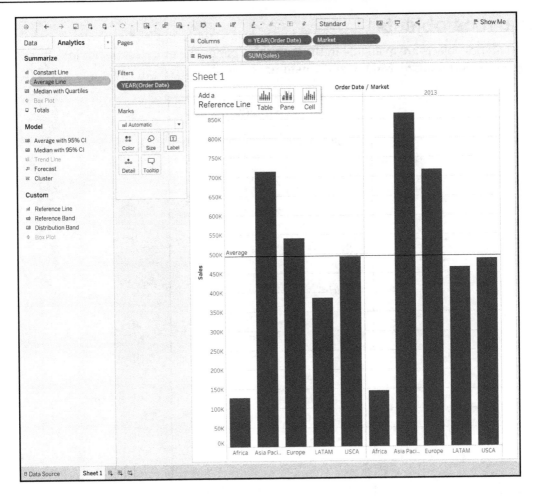

Depending on the analytics object you wish to use, there are various options available. For the average line object, there are choices to set the scope of the average—table level, pane level, and cell level. The analytics object assist menu (for example, **Add a Reference Line**) should help you make the right choice for your needs. You can add multiple analytic objects to a view. To delete an object, right-click the item in the view and select **Remove**.

Analytics objects

The analytics objects are available in the **Analytics** pane. The objects are split into three categories—**Summarize**, **Model**, and **Custom**:

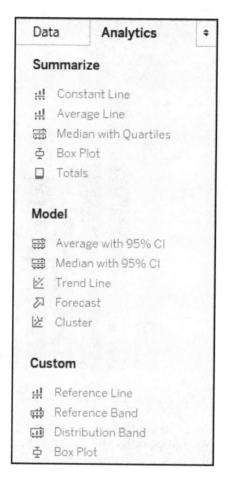

A short description of each is provided in the following sections.

Summarize

The **Summarize** section allows you to apply calculations to the data in the visualization. The following summary calculations are available:

- **Constant Line**: A line whose value is set by the user.
- **Average Line**: A line whose value is the average of a specified measure or measures.
- **Median with Quartiles**: A line whose value is the median of a specified measure or measures with distribution bands.
- **Box Plot**: Adds a box plot to the view.
- **Totals**: Adds the totals (subtotals, column grand totals, or row grand totals) for values in the field.

Model

The **Model** section allows you to apply statistical models to the data in the visualization. The following models are available:

- **Average with 95% CI**: This is the line whose value average of a specified measure or measures with distribution bands. The bands are set to a 95% confidence interval.
- **Median with 95% CI**: This is the line whose value is the median of a specified measure or measures with distribution bands. The bands are set to a 95% confidence interval.
- **Trend Line**: This is the line whose value is configured using the type of trend selected (linear, logarithmic, exponential, and polynomial).
- **Forecast**: This is the forecast whose value is configured using the type of forecast model selected (automatic, automatic with seasonality, or custom). Tableau forecasts are based on the exponential smoothing technique. Exponential smoothing is a technique that places more weight on recent observations.
- **Cluster:** This applies cluster analysis based on the number of clusters selected by the user.

Custom

In addition to the **Summarize** and **Model** objects provided in the preceding sections, Tableau offers **Custom** objects:

- **Reference Line**: This is the line whose value is a constant or calculated value of a specified field.
- **Reference Band**: This is a shaded band whose value is the distance between two constants or calculated values of a specified field.
- **Distribution Band**: This is a shaded band whose value is a distribution of values of a specified field.
- **Box Plot**: This adds a box plot to the view.

There are no limits to the number of analytic objects you can use in a visualization. In the next section, we will discuss shelves and cards. Shelves are where you will place fields to build your visualization. Cards allow you to add detail and customize the visualization.

Shelves and cards

Where fields are placed will affect the layout of the visualization. As you work more with the tool, you will gain a better understanding of how to best approach building visualizations. You should always take the time to try multiple approaches.

You can add fields to shelves and cards by dragging and dropping. You can also double-click fields in the **Data** pane and Tableau will attempt to display the data using best practices; however, this does not always yield the desired results.

Shelves – Columns and Rows

Placing fields in either the **Columns** or **Rows** shelves creates headers in the view. It is important to remember that visualizations are built using marks, which are just records in your data source. You can add multiple fields to both the **Columns** and **Rows** shelves. In the following example, **Market** and **Regions** are the rows by which sales are displayed (bar chart):

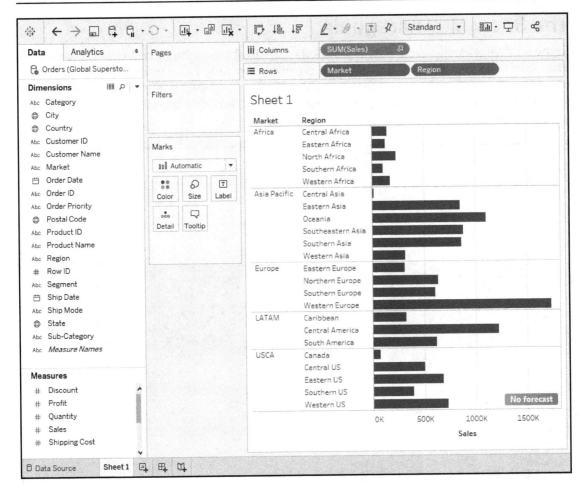

TIP

Right-click on the pills in the **Rows** and **Columns** shelves to see additional field options.

As fields are places on the shelves, Tableau will attempt to select the best chart type. In the preceding example, a bar chart was chosen to display sales by market and region. To change chart types, utilize the **Show Me** chart guide in the upper right-hand corner of the application.

The Show Me chart guide

In the following example, two fields (**Market** and **Sales**) are highlighted in the **Data** pane. The **Show Me** chart guide indicates that there are 10 possible types of charts you can create using these fields (see the charts that are colored). The horizontal bar chart type is shown with an orange border, indicating that this is Tableau's recommended chart type based on best practices:

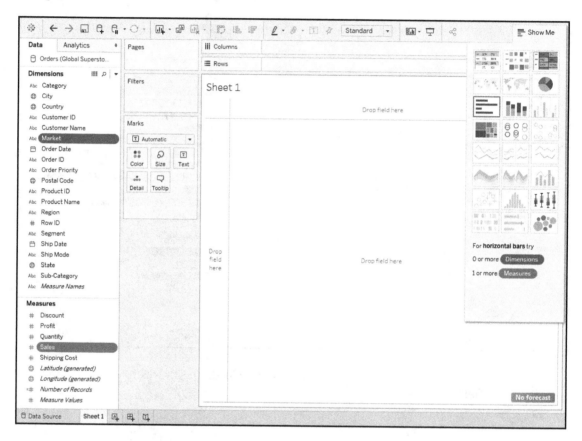

 Tableau's recommended chart type works by analyzing specific fields. It then generates a recommendation for the most effective visualization type based on the properties of the data.

Knowing what type of chart type to use is one of the most important decisions you will make when creating a visualization. For more information on this topic, we suggest searching for guides on how to select the best chart type for your data.

The Marks card

The **Marks** card is where you will refine your visualization with details. In the following example, the **Market** field has been added to the **Color** mark and the sum of sales was added to the **Label** mark. Adding these two fields to the **Marks** card colors the bars by market and displays the sum of sales as a label to the right of the bar:

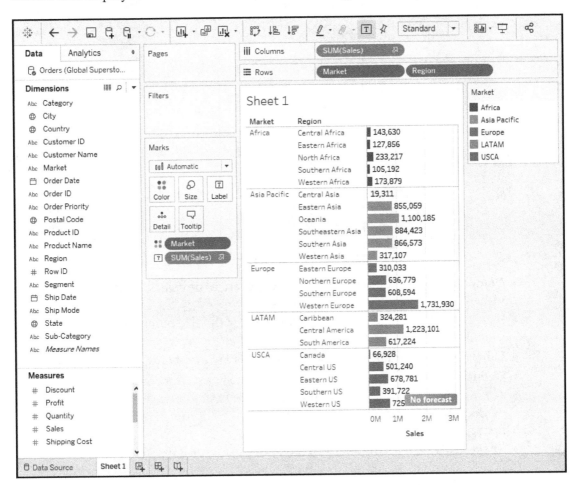

There are seven components of the **Marks** card:

- **Shape**: The **Marks** drop-down menu changes the visualization in the view:

- **Color**: Drag a field onto the color mark to change the colors of marks in the visualization.
- **Size**: Drag a field onto the size mark to change the size of marks in the visualization.
- **Label**: Drag a field onto the label mark to display a text label in the visualization.
- **Detail**: Select the level of granularity for data shown in the visualization.
- **Tooltip**: Tooltips are an information menu that appears when you hover over marks. They are extremely useful for conveying additional information about the mark.
- **Shape**: This changes the shape of the marks in the visualization.

While these components may seem trivial, they are extremely important to the overall look and feel of the visualization. Good design should be intuitive. Learning how to use these components will help your users to digest information efficiently. Similar to knowing what chart type to use for your data, selecting marks is also a science.

Knowing how to properly use color, size, and shape will elevate the quality of your visualizations. Proper mark usage makes it easier for users to understand and use dashboards. We suggest you read more about dashboard design principles to take full advantage of Tableau's **Marks** options. If you are looking for a book suggestion, we highly suggest Stephen Few's *Information Dashboard Design: Displaying Data for at-a-Glance Monitoring*. It is an excellent guide to learn how to build meaningful dashboards.

In the following section, we will discuss how to add interactivity to visualizations using filters.

The Filters shelf

Dragging and dropping fields onto the **Filter** shelf will allow you to filter the view. It also allows you to give users the ability to filter data in the worksheet. In the following example, we want to allow users to be able to filter the view based on **Market**. After dragging the **Market** field to the **Filters** shelf, a **Filter** menu appears:

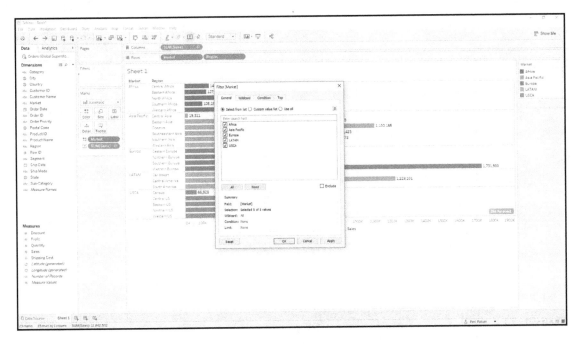

After clicking **OK**, right-click on the **Market** field in the **Filters** shelf, and click **Show Filter**.

You can now see the **Market** filter on the right-hand side of the screen. Add or remove the checkmarks next to the field values to filter the view, as shown in the following screenshot:

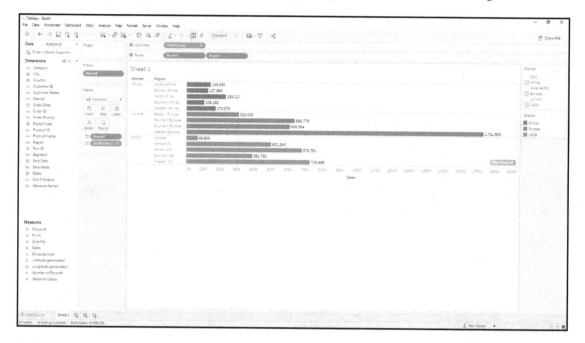

You can edit the filter settings by clicking on the down-caret in the **Market** filter:

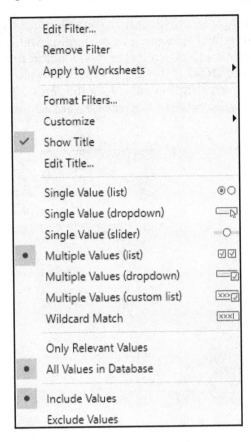

There are numerous ways to customize filters on the worksheet. Play around with different settings to discover what works best for your analysis.

The Pages shelf

The **Pages** shelf allows you to create distinct views based on specific values of a field. The most commonly used field in the **Pages** card is a date field. After placing a date field in the **Pages** card, you can use the menu to see how the data looks at different snapshots in time. In the following example, the **Order Date** field was added to the pages shelf. The **Order Date** pages menu is shown on the right-hand side of the screen. You can move forward or backward to see the sum of sales by year. You can also create animated visualizations using fields in the **Pages** shelf:

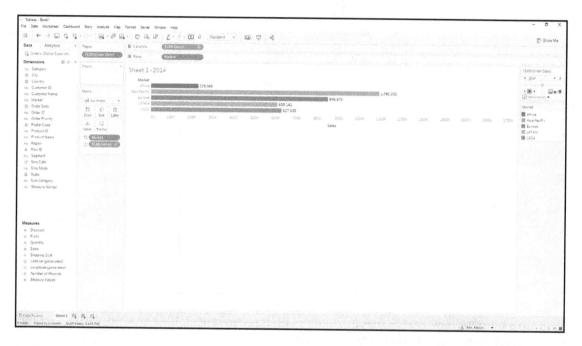

In the preceding section, we learned how to build and refine visualizations. Building a good visualization depends on many factors. Knowing the features on the worksheet page will help you build effective visualizations that are easy to use and understand for the end user.

Summary

In this chapter, we have learned about the components and features of the worksheet page. You should feel comfortable navigating the worksheet page, working with fields in the **Data** pane, applying analytic functions, and creating visualizations. As stated at the beginning of this chapter, the worksheet is the canvas on which you will paint your story. Familiarizing yourself with the worksheet will allow you to tell the best story.

In the next chapter, we will learn about the various chart types available in Tableau. We will also discuss how to use filters, sets, and groups and perform quicker analysis. Finally, we will talk about how formatting can help to create more effective visualizations.

3
Analyzing Data Using Charts

Now that you can connect to data and understand the various elements of the worksheet, it is time to start analyzing data. Data analysis and visualization go hand in hand in Tableau. Data visualization enables us to quickly understand and interpret the various trends in data. Tableau provides extensive options to slice and dice the data, and view it in different formats using visualizations, sets, filters, hierarchies, and so on. This chapter will detail each of these formats.

The following topics will be covered in this chapter:

- Key charts in Tableau
- Sorting your data
- Creating filters, sets, groups, and hierarchies
- Formatting your visuals

Technical requirements

This chapter uses the Global Superstore dataset, which can be found at `http://www.tableau.com/sites/default/files/training/global_superstore.zip`.

Key charts in Tableau

Tableau provides a variety of charts that are super quick and easy to create. All charts in Tableau are created based on marks, where marks are the rows in your dataset for any given combination of dimensions and measures. To create a chart, you have two broad options:

- Select the dimensions and measures you want to plot and click on the **Show me** window. The **Show Me** window is a special window where all of the default charts in Tableau and their details can be found. For example, select **Category** from **Dimensions** and **Sales** from **Measures**. Use the *Ctrl* key (the *Command* key on macOS) to select multiple elements.

The **Show Me** window can be seen in the following screenshot:

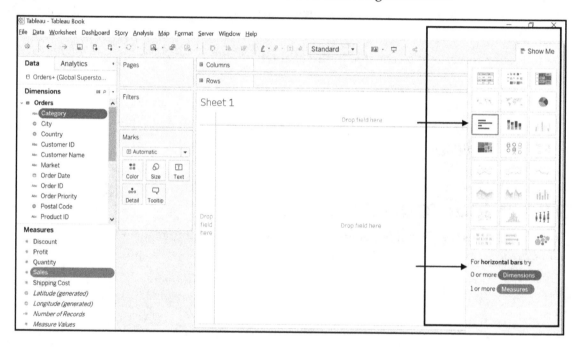

As you can see, the **Show Me** window currently contains 24 graphs. However, only one is highlighted with an red square around it, seven others are activated, and the rest are grayed out. The highlighted graph is the graph recommended by Tableau based on your data. The graphs that are grayed out are those that can't be created with a combination of the chosen fields. To discover what is needed to generate a graph, you simply hover over it. For instance, in this case of the bar graph, we can see that, for **horizontal bars**, we need **0 or more Dimensions** and **1 or more Measures**. Similarly, if you hover over other charts, it will list their requirements. Once your data meets the requirements, you can select the chart type and it will be displayed on the screen.

- Drag and drop the dimensions and measures directly onto the sheet's **Rows**, **Columns**, and **Marks** shelves.

The following screenshot displays a combination of items, using which you can create charts directly without using the **Show Me** Window:

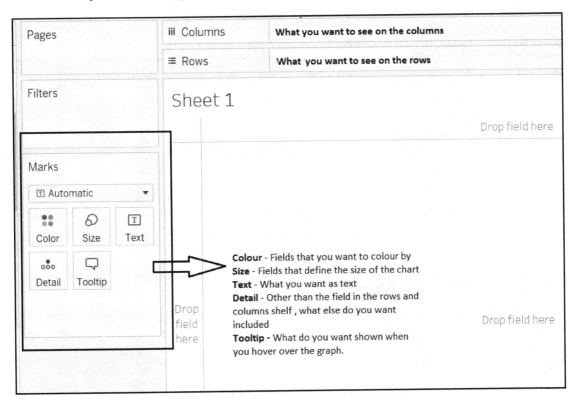

These options are also going to be useful when enhancing the standard chart types on the **Show Me** window to create more advanced charts.

Using `Category` and `Sales`, if you want to see the categories and their sum of sales listed as a value, you can drag `Category` to the **Rows** and then `Sales` to the **Text Label** on the **Marks** shelf. This will create **Fig(a)**, as shown in the following screenshot. Similarly, if you remove `SUM(Sales)` from the text shelf and drag it to the **Columns** shelf, you get the horizontal bar graph shown in **Fig(b)**:

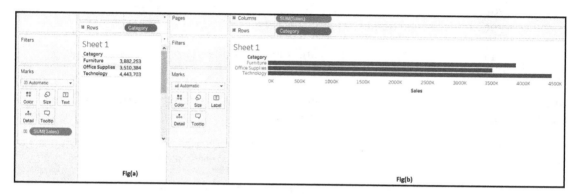

It is important to note that whenever you pick up a measure to bring into a worksheet, it will always aggregate automatically, based on the best aggregation type for that data. The most common aggregate types are **Sum** and **Average**. You have the option to change the aggregate type of a measure. If you do not want to see the measure as an aggregate, you can also deselect **Aggregate measures** and view it as raw data with no aggregation.

Now that you know how charts can be created, we will move on to the next section where we will discuss important chart types and when to use them.

Text tables (cross-tabs)

Text tables are similar to Excel grids, that is, they contain rows, columns, and values in a grid. These tables are very useful when there is limited data, and you want to see the exact number quickly, or if you need to find the intersection points between categories (equivalent to a cell in Excel).

For example, what was the total **Shipping Cost** for **Office Supplies** in the **Consumer Segment**?

To create this table, follow these steps:

1. Select `Segment`, `Category`, and `Shipping Cost` and select the text tables icon (the first graph) from the **Show Me** window.
2. Alternatively, put `Segment` and `Category` on **Columns** and **Rows**, respectively, and then place `SUM(Shipping Cost)` on the **Marks** text shelf, as shown in the following screenshot:

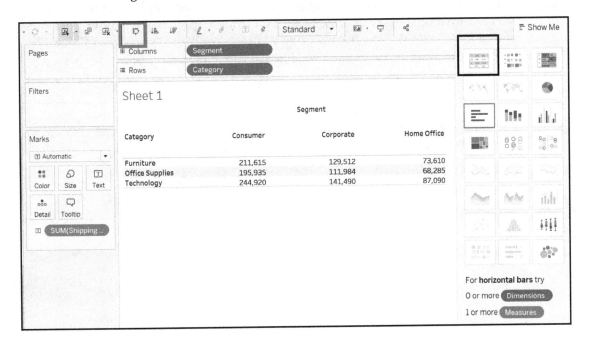

We can quickly see that the **Shipping Cost** for **Office Supplies** in the **Consumer Segment** is **195,935**. In this example, I have used **Segment** in **Columns** and **Category** in **Rows**, but you can reverse these as necessary.

To quickly swap **Rows** and **Columns** for any graph, you can click on the **Swap** button, highlighted in red in the picture, or just use the *Ctrl + W* shortcut.

Highlight tables

Highlight tables are an extension of text tables (or cross-tabs), discussed in the previous section. A highlight table is obtained by adding a field to the **Marks Color** shelf. They are useful for quickly seeing trends in data. For example, what if you were asked which **Category** and **Segment** of the product has more sales than **Office Supplies** in **Consumer**, but less profit? One way to solve this would be to look at all of the segments that have more sales than **Office Supply** in **Consumer**, and then look at the profits for each of those and see whether they are more or less than the profit for **Office Supply** in **Consumer**. An alternative way to look at this is to quickly bring SUM(Profit) on to the **Marks Color** shelf, and change the **Marks** type to **Square**. This will create the graph shown in this screenshot:

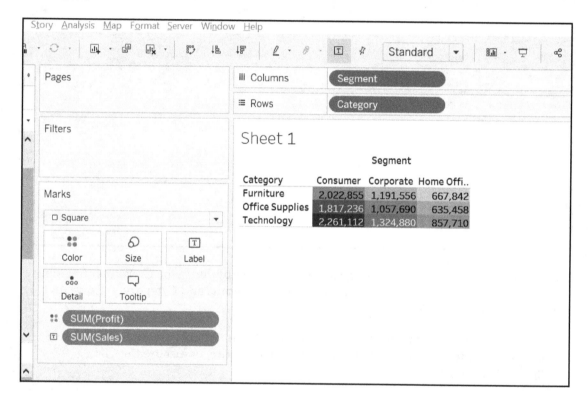

You can quickly see that, based on sales only, **Furniture** and **Technology** within the **Consumer Segment** have more sales than **Office Supply** in the **Consumer Segment**. Now, looking at the color for **Profits**, you quickly know that as **Furniture** is colored lighter than **Consumer**, it has fewer profits than the consumer.

 By default, the automatic gradient of colors in Tableau for measures goes from lowest to highest. Also, by default, any value below 0 is orange, and **greater** than 0 is blue.

Maps (symbol and filled)

Maps are one of the most important visuals present in Tableau that quickly and effectively help to visualize any kind of geographic data. To identify a geographical field, look for the globe icon next to the field. Based on the geographical field, Tableau generates two fields, **Latitude** and **Longitude**. These are used to pinpoint the exact locations on the map. It is not necessary to use the auto-generated **Latitude** and **Longitude** fields; you can also upload your own geocoding, which we will cover in more detail in Chapter 4, *Visualizing Geographic Data*.

For now, our focus will be on the two map types available in the **Show Me** menu: the symbol map and the filled map. Symbol maps can show up to two measures, whereas filled maps can show only one. Symbol maps are useful to show very granular data or if you need to represent multiple measures on the graph. Filled maps, on the other hand, are very effective for showing a single measure. They also are useful for low-level data, such as that at the city or postcode level.

For example, to view the distribution of `Sales` by `Segment` in each country, you would use a symbol chart, as shown in the following screenshot:

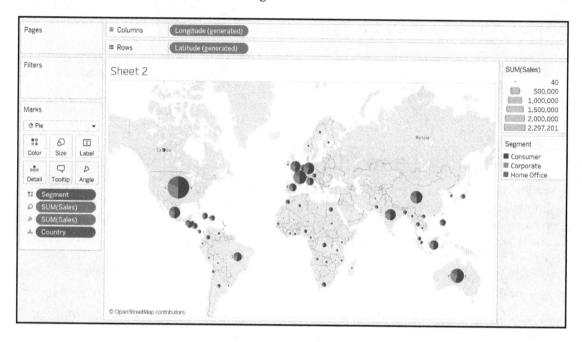

On the other hand, to view which state on the west coast of the USA had the highest sales, you can use a filled map, as shown in the following screenshot:

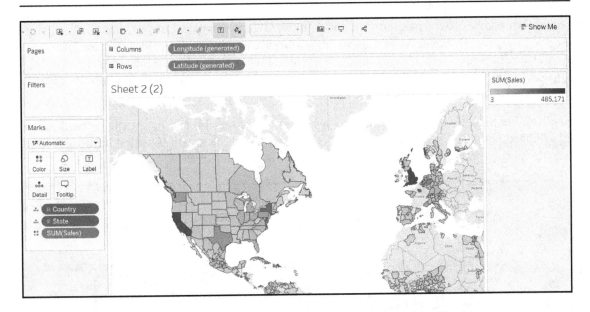

One quick glance at the map and we can tell that California has the highest sales on the West Coast.

Bar charts

Bar charts are one of the easiest tools for making quick comparisons across categorical data. Bar charts compare data on a linear scale and quickly make it easy to compare data points across dimensions. Tableau has three types of bar chart variants available in the **Show Me** menu:

- Horizontal bar charts
- Stacked bar charts
- Side-by-side bar charts

Simple bar charts are the best kind of charts to use whenever questions are asked about the largest or smallest values, what dimension values are in the top or bottom five, and so on. As these values are all displayed on a linear scale, they are also useful for quick approximations of data. For example, which product's sales are approximately half of the product with the second-highest number of sales?

Reading the preceding question, it looks a bit convoluted, but it can be quickly solved using a bar chart using `Product Name` and `SUM(Sales)`. Once the graph is sorted according to the descending values of sales, we get the following bar chart:

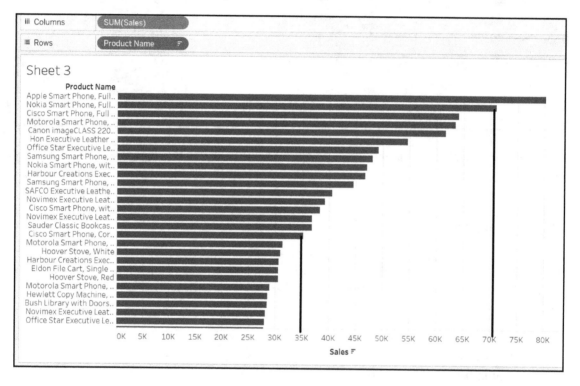

A quick glance at the graph shows the second-highest product to be a Nokia smartphone with sales worth approximately **70k**. Half of this is **35k** and, again, a quick glance at the graph shows us that the product in question is **Cisco Smart Phone**. As the value of sales used is not exact in this example, it saves us time in calculations, allowing us to quickly reach our results.

The higher the complexity of the dimensions that you want to compare against, the more you can nest your bar graph to easily get results. The following example compares values across **Category**, **Segment**, and **Market**:

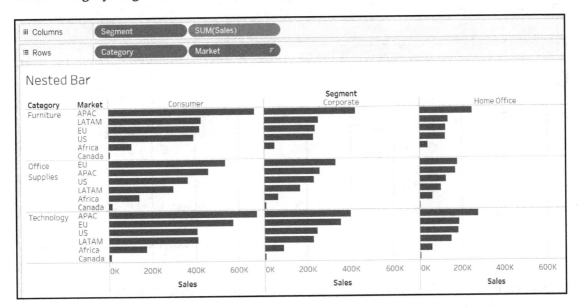

A pattern quickly emerges, with the **Consumer Segment** having the highest sales across regions and categories as compared to **Corporate** and **Home Office**. We can also quickly see that while **APAC** leads the **Technology** category in the **Home Office Segment**, **Europe** is the leader for the **Office Supplies** category in the **Home Office Segment**. Canada has the least sales across all segments and categories.

Bar charts are the best tool for comparison of the same value against multiple dimensions.

Now, let's move on from simple bar charts to stacked bar charts. The latter is useful for understanding proportions. An example that uses stacked bar charts to see the proportion of quantity shipped using different shipping modes and segments can be seen in the following screenshot:

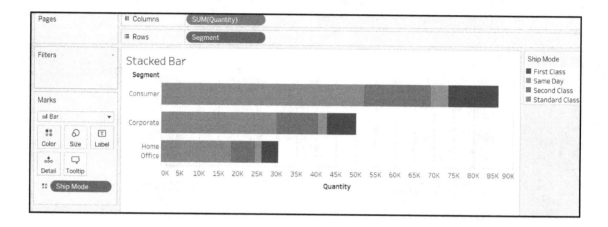

Consumer had the highest proportion of its quantity shipped under **Standard Class Ship Mode**.

Do not use stacked bar charts if there are too many dimensions to compare as it can become very confusing. Instead, use side-by-side bars or nested bars.

Side by side bar graphs provide another way to compare measures. The main difference from a stacked bar is that the axis remains the same in a side-by-side bar chart. For instance, if we change the preceding stacked bar graph to a side by side bar, we obtain the following:

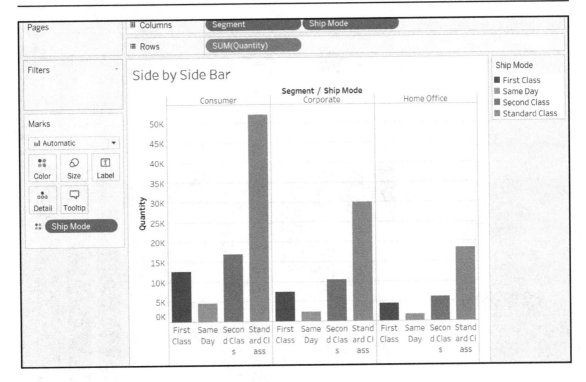

It is the same information presented in a different format. If you want to compare and need absolute value comparisons, side by side graphs are the ones to use. However, if you are more interested in the proportions when comparing and how they change, stacked graphs are the way to go.

Stacked bars are also generally used to represent the percentage of the total population.

For example, to view the percentage of sales distributed by shipping mode across regions, you will do the following:

1. Create a simple stacked chart using `Region`, `SUM(Sales)`, and `Ship Mode`.
2. Right-click `Sum(Sales)`. Select **Quick Table Calculation | Percent of Total**.
3. You will notice there is no change in the graph yet. This is because the table calculation isn't being calculated as Table across. To change this, once again right-click `Sum(Sales)`. Select **Compute Using | Table Down**.

This should give you the graph as follows:

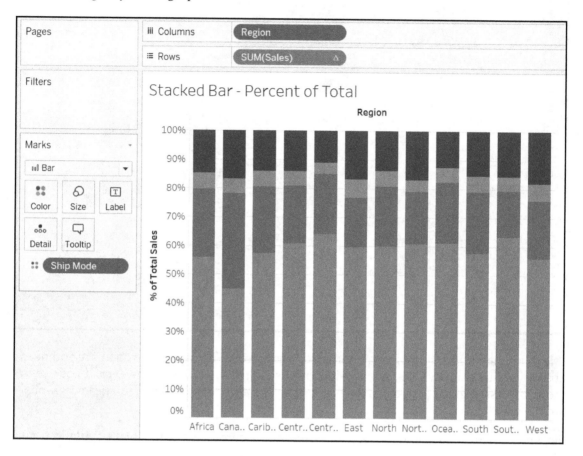

Heat maps and treemaps

Heat maps and treemaps are useful for when looking for patterns in highly granular and detailed data. Heat maps use a combination of size and color to show trends. For example, which subcategory has the lowest profit in the region that has the highest quantity sold? To answer this question, we create a heat map similar to the following screenshot:

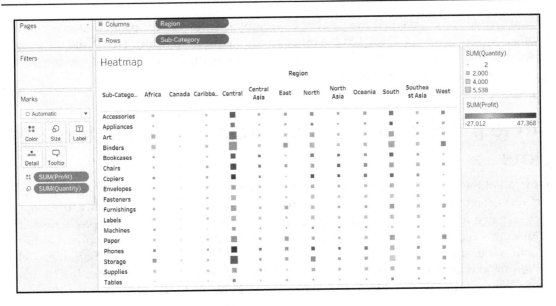

Using the heat map, we can quickly see based on the sizes of the squares that the **Central** region has the highest quantity sold and the **Tables** sub-category within it has the least profit.

Treemaps are another type of graph that is useful for looking at broad trends. They allow you to show up to four measures. For example, in the example shown in the following screenshot, we can look at SUM(Profit) (color), SUM(Quantity) (size), and SUM(Discount) (text value) across regions and markets:

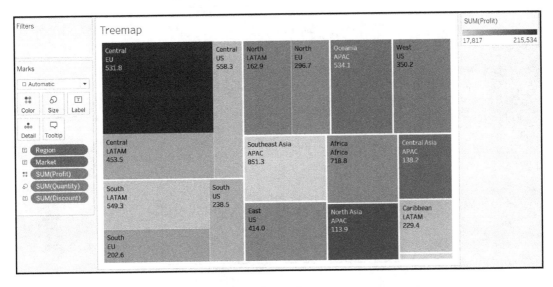

We can, in one glance, see that the **Central EU** region has the highest profit and sales, having a total discount of **531.8**. On the other hand, the profit of **South East Asia** in the **APAC** region is quite low, despite the sales being quite high. The market also has the highest discount value for all markets at **851.3**.

Circle plots, side by side circles, and scatter plots

So far, all of the graphs we have discussed have been used to analyze aggregate measures. The next category of graphs benefits more from analyzing measures in their raw or unaggregated form, though, it is not a prerequisite for their usage. These graphs are useful for detecting outliers in the data or seeing the relationship between two measures. Outlier detection is useful in understanding how much outliers influence statistical measures such as the sum and average. Outlier detection also becomes very powerful in detecting fraud or errors. For example, which three customers were responsible for the highest individual sales?

To view this, we create a **Circle Plot** for **Sales** and **Customer Names**. Once we have the circle plot created, you'll realize that the **Columns** shelf still shows SUM(Sales) in the measures. To remove this, you must go to the **Analysis Menu** and unselect **Aggregate Measures**.

Once this is done, you'll see a graph like the following:

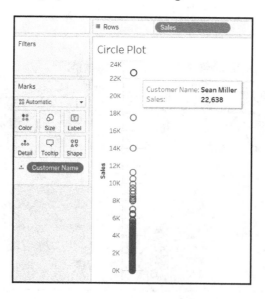

Hovering over the top three candidates' circles, we find that Sean Miller, Tamara Chand, and Raymond Buch have the highest individual sales values. Considering how much of an outlier Sean Miller's sales value is, it could also be a potential error in the data.

Side by side circle views are similar to side by side bar graphs and more useful when looking at unaggregated data, though they can be used for aggregated data as well. For example, to find how the priority of an item varies in terms of price across regions, we can use a side by side circle graph like the one shown in the following screenshot:

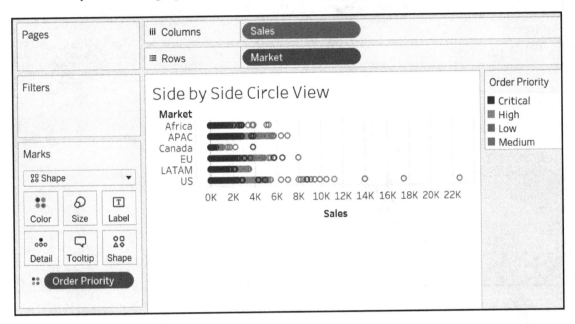

In the preceding screenshot, we can see that lower-values sales have higher-order priority than higher-value sales in general across all markets.

Scatter plots are useful for understanding relationships between the measures themselves. For example, what is the relationship between shipping cost and sales across various categories of products? Looking at the following screenshot, it is easy to see that there is less variance in the shipping cost and sales value of furniture than there is for technology. Some of the highest and lowest shipping costs are seen for the **Technology** category for similar values of **Sales**:

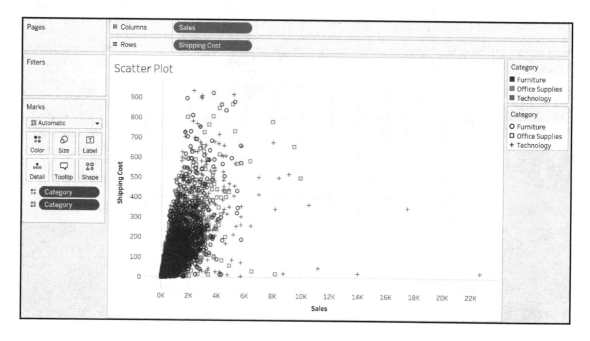

Line charts

Line charts are the best way to show data related to time. They connect distinct data points presenting them continuously and can show time either as discrete or continuous entities. Discrete time series are useful for comparison of one-time dimensions across another, for example, to find out which two quarters had the least difference in sales across all four years. One quick glance at the **Discrete Line Chart** graph tells us the answer is Q2 and Q3. Continuous line charts, on the other hand, are useful for understanding the overall trends across time. For example, in the following graph, we can quickly see that sales have increased overall across the 4 years irrespective of the seasonal variations:

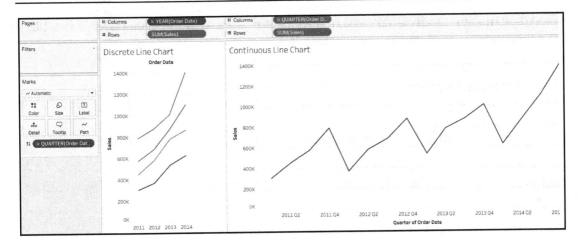

If you right-click on the date, you can change the level of detail the **Date** is displayed at. The date menu divides the dates into two date sections. The first group provides by default discrete date parts and the second continuous date values, as shown in the following screenshot:

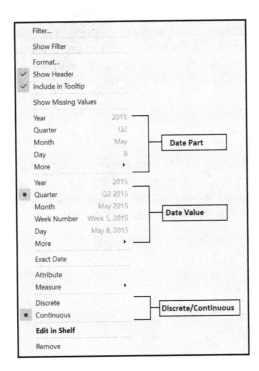

The **Date Part** values individual parts of the date, for example, if the date is December 10, 2018, then the various date parts would be as follows:

- Day: 10
- Month: December
- Year: 2018

The discrete line chart in the preceding example uses the **Year** and **Quarter** date parts.

Date values, on the other hand, are dates truncated to the level you have selected. For example, if you had the date December 10, 2018, the date value at different levels would be as follows:

- Day: 10 December 2018
- Month: December 2018
- Year: 2018

The preceding continuous line chart uses the **Quarter** date value, which will truncate the dates to the level of quarters.

 Though, by default, date parts are discrete and date values are continuous, we can use the discrete and continuous options to change this. The key difference is that discrete values will show headers while continuous values will show axes when displaying the visualization.

Histograms

Histograms are useful for viewing the distribution of continuous data into ranges or bins. They are used to determine whether a measure is left-skewed, right-skewed, or normally distributed and are widely used when describing demographic statistics such as the age distribution of the population or the distribution of wealth among a certain population.

The way histograms work is that they divide the entire dataset into bins (ranges of data). For example, if we want to understand how **Quantity** is distributed, we get the following:

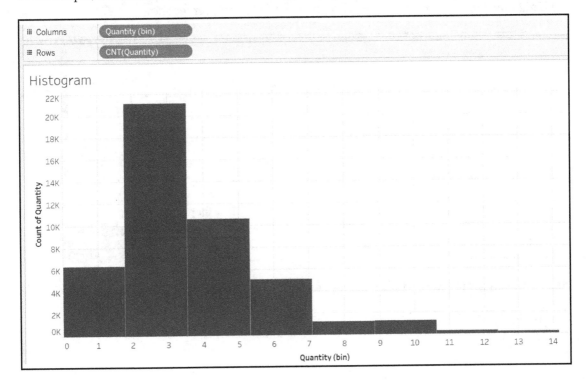

A count of 2 or 3 seems to be the most common quantities sold, whereas larger numbers such as 12 and 13 are rare. You can also notice in the distribution that the mean of the data (3.66) is on the right of the median (3.18). Such a distribution is called a right-skewed distribution. The reverse of this is a left-skewed distribution. If both the left and right sides are balanced, it is termed a normal distribution.

Whenever you create a histogram, you will notice that, in the **Dimensions** shelf, a new **Dimension** called `Quantity (Bin)` appears. You can edit this bin by right-clicking on it in the **Data** pane and selecting **Edit**, as shown in the following screenshot:

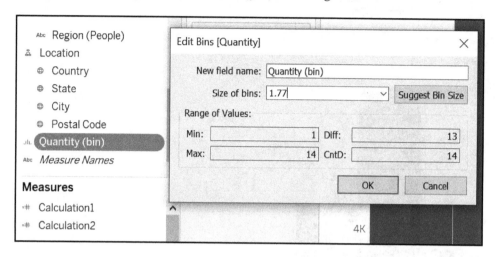

Here, you can set the **Size of bins**, **Range of Values** to include, the name, and so on.

If any question asks about the skew of the data or the left-/right-tailed distribution, then you need to use a histogram.

Box and whisker plots (box plots)

While circle charts are useful for detecting outliers for continuous measures, box and whisker plots (simply referred to as box plots) are useful for understanding the statistical distribution of a continuous measure in terms of the median and interquartile ranges. The box and whisker plots consist of five key components: the median, the upper hinge, the lower hinge, the upper whisker, and the lower whisker. The median is the midway point or the 50th percentile of the data. The upper and lower hinges show the first and the third quartiles, respectively. The whiskers extend up to 1.5 times the **Interquartile Range** (**IQR**) from the hinges, where IQR is the difference between the upper and lower quartiles. We can change the whisker limits to extend up to the minimum and maximum values in the chart too.

For example, what is the interquartile range for **Quantity** in **APAC**?

To answer, we use **Market** and **Quantity** to create a box and whiskers plot. Like with circle and scatter plots, you need to go to **Analysis** and unselect **Aggregate Measures**. We get the following graph:

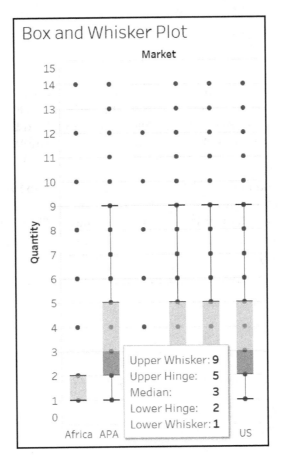

For **APAC**, we can see the **Lower Hinge** is **2** and the **Upper Hinge** is **5**, so *IQR = 5-2 = 3*.

The upper whisker can extend 1.5 times the IQR from the upper hinge, so *5+ (1.5*3) = 9.5*. The closest data point lower than this in the dataset is 9, hence the upper whisker gets the value 9. Similarly, the lower whisker can extend 1.5 times the lower hinge, so *2-1.5*3 = -2.5*. The lowest data point in the dataset closest to this value is 1. Hence, the lower whisker is at 1.

Remember, the *Interquartile Range (IQR) = Upper Hinge - Lower Hinge.*

The lower and upper whiskers extend to 1.5 times the IQR.

Gantt chart

Gantt charts are a popular project management tool used for tracking the time between activities. The chart consists of tasks or events on the vertical axis and time intervals on the horizontal axis. One popular use of a Gantt chart is to understand the project management schedules and the dependencies between the various events. Another common use is to understand the time difference between events.

For example, a popular method is to look at the average **Order to Ship Time** across the different shipping modes and any other dimension/s such as Order Category/Sub-category/Market. We will look at this example for **Market**. To create the Gantt chart, we will need a calculation for Order to Ship Time. We can create one as follows (**Analysis | Create Calculated Field**):

Now, to create a Gantt chart, we set up the chart as follows:

- **Columns:** Day(Order Date)
- **Rows:** Market and Ship Mode
- **Marks Color:** Ship Mode (Optional)
- **Size:** Avg(Order to Ship Time)

We have converted this to be the average since it makes more sense to understand the average **Order to Ship Time**:

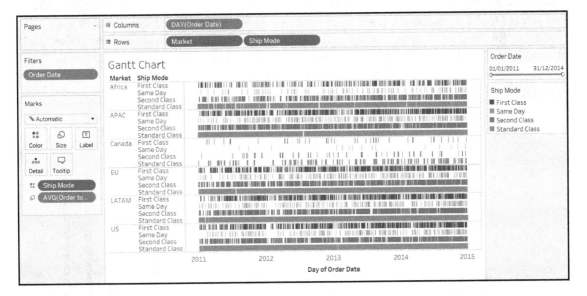

We can quickly see the time across the different shipping modes. If we filter for smaller ranges, the Gantt chart becomes more effective.

Combination charts

Combination charts allow us to view a combination of values in the same visual, for example, a line chart to show the sum of sales and a bar chart to show the profits. An example of a famous combination chart is a Pareto chart.

Combination charts allow us to compare data either on the same axes or use two separate distinct axes to work with the data. A minimum of two measures is needed to create a combination chart. To create a combination chart, select `Profit`, `Sales`, and `Order Date` and select **Dual Combination** from the **Show Me** menu. By default, the chart will get created at the level of `Year(Order Date)`. Right-click on it, and change it to be at the level of a quarter. You will obtain the following graph, where you will see `SUM(Profit)` is shown as a bar chart and `SUM(Sales)` as a line chart:

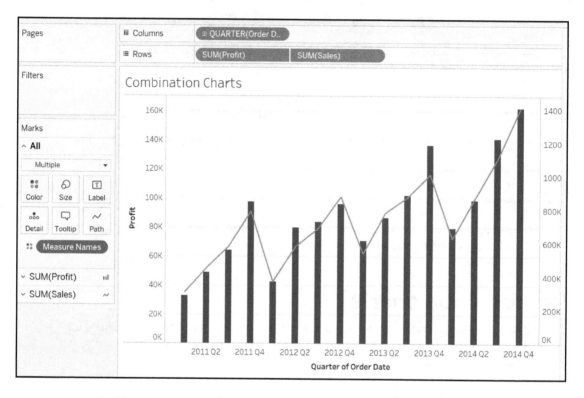

From the graph, if you don't pay close attention to the axes, it appears that the scales of `SUM(Profit)` and `SUM(Sales)` are the same. However, we can see from the axes that **20K** in profits corresponds to **200K** in sales value.

To synchronize the axes, right-click on one of the axes and select **Synchronize Axis.** This changes the graph, as shown in the following screenshot:

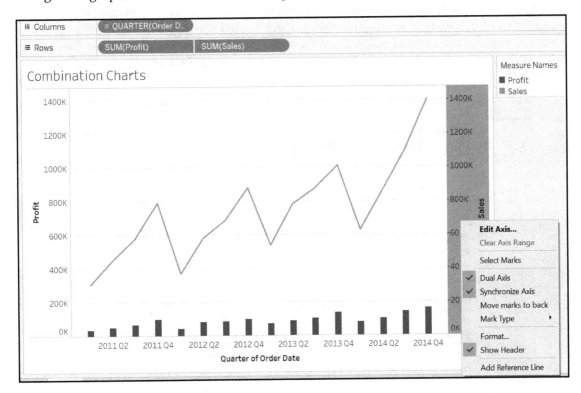

Now that we have learned about the various types of charts available in the **Show Me** menu, how to create them, and when they are most useful, let's look at some of the key properties that be can be used to enhance these visuals.

Sorting your data

Sorting data allows for patterns to be quickly visible. Tableau allows us to have simple ascending and descending sorting, manual sorting, nested sorting, and sorting based on some calculation. We can sort not only on the fields displayed on the graphs but also in any other field. To sort data, we can use any of the quick sort icons shown in the following screenshot:

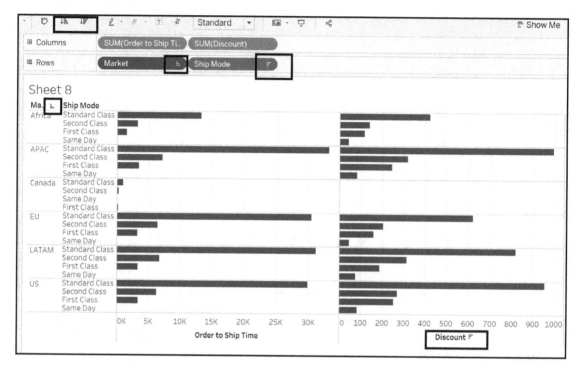

To view the sorting for each dimension, right-click on each of the dimension pills. Once you click on it, you will see options to **Sort By** multiple categories; here, you select from **Data Source Order**, **Alphabetical Order**, **Manual Sorting**, **Field**, or **Nested**. For example, in the preceding, `Market` was sorted using **Data Source Order: Ascending** and `Ship Mode` was sorted using **Nested** based on the `SUM(Discount)` field. You can select any field and aggregation here, and they don't need to be necessarily used in the graphs. Another way to sort is to drag the fields in the graph manually.

For stacked graphs, sorting stacks can be done by moving the legends. In the following example, as **US** was at the bottom of the **Color** legend, it appeared as the bottom category in the graph. Shifting **US** to the top in the **Color** legend also changes its position in the graph:

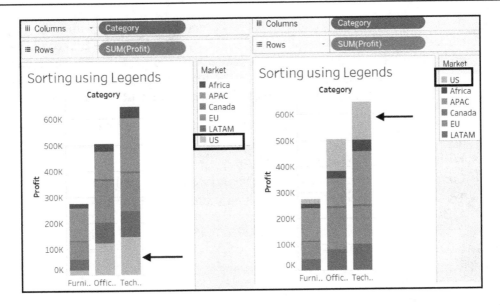

Now that you can create the various charts and know how to sort data, let's look at what other features can be used to enhance your data and visuals.

Creating filters, sets, groups, and hierarchies

Beyond sorting the data, Tableau provides many other ways to enhance visuals. Filters, sets, groups and hierarchies are some important ones. We will look at each in detail in this section, starting with filters.

Filters

Filtering is a major part of data analysis. Tableau allows us to filter using dimensions or measures. Filtering in Tableau follows this order of operations:

1. Extract filters
2. Data source filters
3. Context filters
4. Filters on dimensions
5. Filters on measures

To apply filters to any visual, drag the field to the **Filters** shelf, or select within the graph what to include/exclude. For example, to find `Profit` by `Market` for the **Standard Class** shipping mode, drag `Ship Mode` to the **Filters** shelf. Once you drag it to the shelf, you will be asked how you want the data filtered. This mode differs for dimensions and measures. For dimensions, there are the options of **General**, **Wildcard**, **Condition**, and **Top**:

- **General**: Allows us to include/exclude from a list, use a custom list, or use all of the values
- **Wildcard**: Useful for pattern matching
- **Condition**: Filtering based on other fields or custom calculations
- **Top**: Creates a subset of top/bottom fields and filters using those

The filters get evaluated from the left to right tab, so general tab filters get evaluated first and the top tabs last.

The **General** filter tab is the most used, and for this example, we will simply select **Standard Class** from the **General** tab, as can be seen in the following screenshot, and click **OK**:

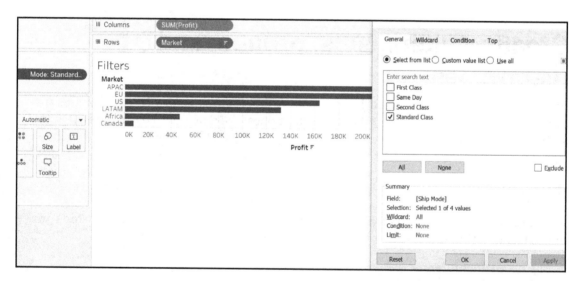

Once you click **OK**, the filter gets displayed on the screen and becomes a quick filter for easy access. If it doesn't get displayed on the screen by default, then right-click on the **Dimension** and choose the **Show Filter** option.

Quick filters have many options that can be accessed by clicking on the options button on the top right of the filter, as shown in the following screenshot. Explore the various options to use as per your requirement:

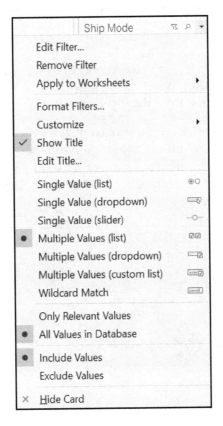

Another way to filter data for any visual is to select the data you want to see in the visual and, in the option box that appears, select **Keep Only** or **Exclude**, as can be seen in the following screenshot:

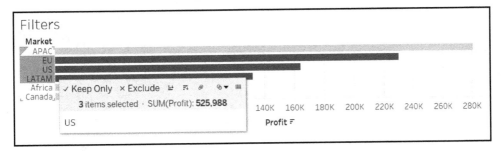

Sets

Sets are custom fields that are used to define a subset of data. The defined subset can be dynamic or static and can be used to create different visuals. We can also combine multiple sets. Sets have the advantage of being reusable across all worksheets, and they get added to the dataset's metadata too.

Dynamic sets: These are sets based on certain conditions that can lead to different results as the data changes. **Top n** or **Bottom n** sets are common use cases of this. For example, what percentage of the total sales came from the top 10 countries?

To solve this, we will create a set for the top 10 countries by sales first. Right-click `Country`, select **Create** and then **Set**. Then, under **Create | Set**, rename the set `Top 10`, and go to the **Top** tab. In the **Top** tab, we will define the condition for the set. Select **By field**, and change the field to **Sales**. The aggregation automatically changes to **Sum**. Click **OK**. Refer to the following screenshot for the steps:

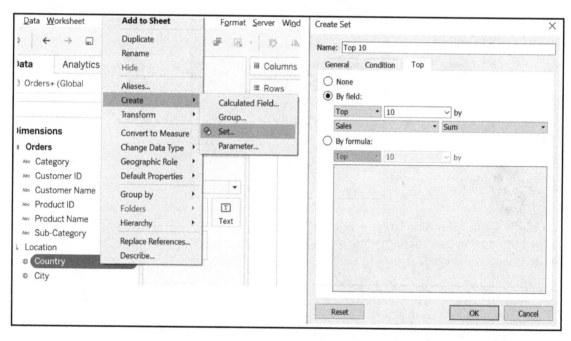

You will notice that, under the **Sets** category, a new set has been created:

Once you bring this to the shelf, it will show two values: **In/Out**—**In** includes values for all members within the set, and **Out** is for all numbers not in the set. To view the percentage of sales by the top 10 countries, we will now add SUM(Sales) to the graph and create a quick table calculation by right-clicking SUM(Sales) | **Create Table Calculation** | **Percentage of Total**. You should get the results shown here:

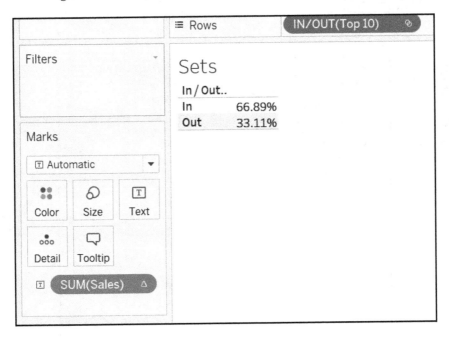

This gives us the result showing 66.89% of the total sales come from just the top 10 countries. Instead of seeing the values in terms of **In/Out**, to see the actual set members, right-click on the set and select **Show Members in Set**.

Static Sets: These sets have fixed members. For example, in the preceding example, if instead of having the top 10 countries set using a condition, we would have selected the United States and the United Kingdom in the **General** tab, and it would have become a static set:

Another way to create such a set is from the visual directly. Select the values you want to group and select **Create | Set**. Once you select this, it gives you additional options to exclude such values or to add them to the **Filter** shelf and more. An example of where this is useful is to identify outliers in data and then, using the set, exclude them from other visuals as well:

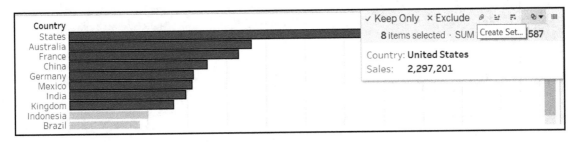

Groups

Groups are useful for categorizing data under common labels. Groups simply add another layer of labels/headers over existing data and can only be used with dimensions. Examples of grouping would be to correctly categorize data, for example, NY and New York all under a common header of New York, or to create regional groups per manager depending on their territories.

Creating groups is similar to creating sets. You can create a group directly from the visual by selecting the chart and then clicking on the paper clip icon for grouping:

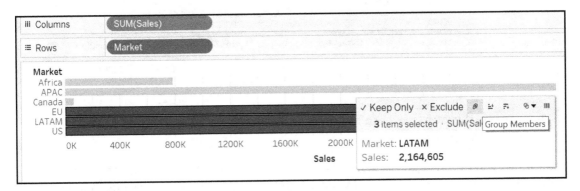

Once you group the items, you will see `Market (group)` appear in the **Dimensions** shelf. Right-click and select **Edit Group**. You will see the menu as follows:

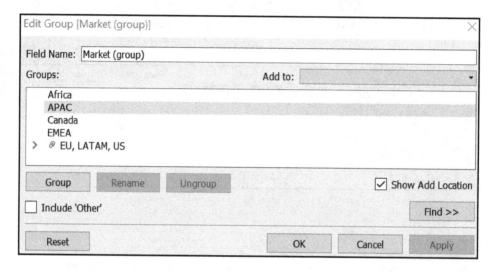

Here, you can group other members together, ungroup current members, and rename the groups as well as choose to include an **Other** group. As an example, let's combine **Africa** and **EMEA** by selecting both, clicking on **Group**, and then naming it `EMEA++`. Also, check the **Include 'Other'** button and click **OK**. Now, bring `Market` on the **Rows** shelf after `Market(group)`. You will see the graph shown here:

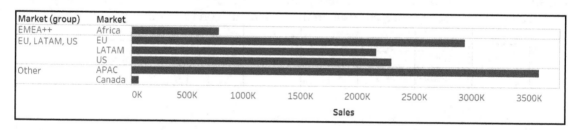

As you can see, the various `Market` types have been grouped together under the labels we chose in `Market(group)`.

Another way to perform grouping is to select the **Dimension** the elements of which we want to group, right-click and select **Create** | **Group**. This will open the same menu as you saw when clicking on **Edit Group** before.

Hierarchies

Hierarchies provide a good way to visualize data at a high level and then drill down to deeper details if needed. Common examples of hierarchies are date hierarchies (Year, Quarter, Month, and Day), location hierarchies (Country, State, and City), or a Product Category and Product Subcategory hierarchy. To create a hierarchy, click on the dimensions you want to add to the hierarchy, for example, Category and Sub-Category, then right-click **Hierarchy** and select **Create Hierarchy**. To add to a pre-existing **Hierarchy**, select **Add to Hierarchy**:

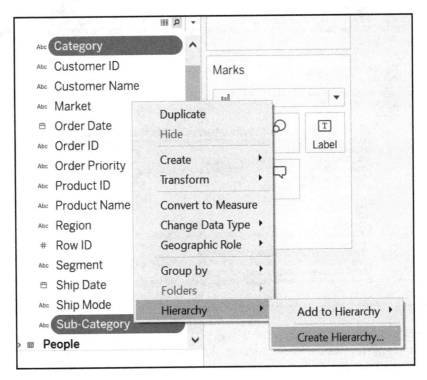

Once the hierarchy is created, it can be used in the graphs easily. By using hierarchies, we eliminate the need to use multiple visuals to represent the same data. Instead of having separate graphs to show data for sales at the `Category` and then `Sub-Category` level, a hierarchy allows us to toggle between both views on the same sheet. The **+** icon is used to expand the hierarchy while **–** is used to contract it. The following example shows how the created hierarchy expanded:

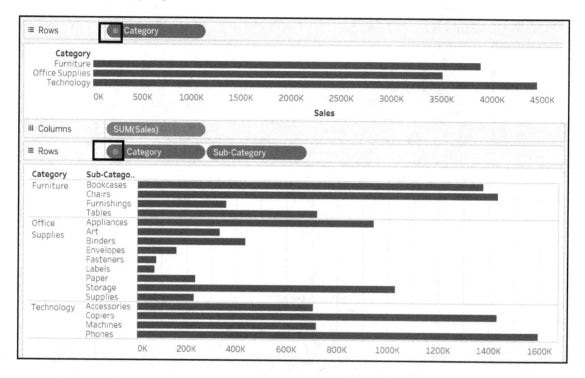

Now that we are familiar with the various ways in which we can enhance visuals using capabilities of grouping, sets, and hierarchies, let's shift our focus on to the more visual formats that we quickly apply to enhance our visuals.

Formatting your visuals

There are various formatting options available for the visual in Tableau at both the worksheet level as well as the individual graph level.

At the worksheet level, three important cards can be displayed:

- **Title**: To show the title of the sheet.
- **Caption**: A description of what the sheet is displaying, with all of the details of the filters applied.
- **Summary**: Provides a quick summary of descriptive statistics for the visual, such as the sum, average, and median.

You can choose to display any of these, by selecting **Worksheet** from the **Menu** bar and then **Show Title/Caption/Summary**.

At the visual level, you can display/edit the following:

- **Labels**: Values in the text for the visual points displayed.
- **Annotations**: Annotations with data highlighting points, marks, or labels—these can contain what you want to display.
- **Axes**: The axes label names, range of values displayed, normal or logarithmic axes—to view the options for the axes, select and right-click the axes and then select edit axes.

The following screenshot shows the labels and axes:

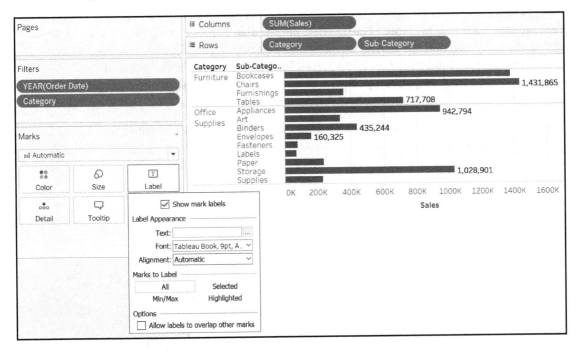

And the following screenshot shows annotations (point and area):

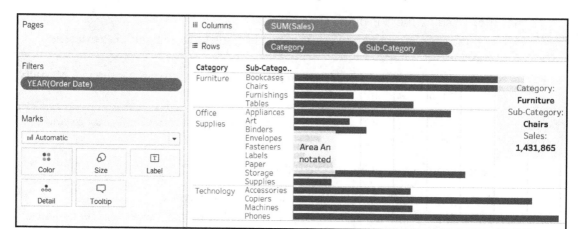

To add any of these, we can simply right-click on the visual and see the options available.

Summary

In this chapter, we learned about the most common types of charts that can be created in Tableau and when to use which chart. This chapter also detailed how filters, sets, groups, and more can be used to enhance the visuals and perform quicker analysis. As mentioned at the start of this chapter, Tableau is a visual tool and these basic elements of understanding will go a long way in way in saving time and performing quicker analysis for the exam, as well as for creating an effective and meaningful analysis for the future.

In the next chapter, we shall dive deeper into map visuals and understand more about mapping capabilities in Tableau.

4
Visualizing Geographic Data

For centuries, maps have been used to convey meaningful data. We are used to seeing maps representing data commonly around us, be it with Google Maps calculating distances, Uber tracking the cost and distance of locations, or weather forecasts looking at each region, and so on. In the last chapter, we learned a bit about the two standard map charts available in the **Show Me** menu, and how we can use these to visualize geographic data. In this chapter, we will dive deeper into the various mapping capabilities of Tableau and cover the following topics:

- Mapping basics
- Map navigation – geographic search, pan and zoom, mark selection, and scaling
- Map features – layering and custom territories
- Modifying locations
- Importing and managing custom geocoding
- Connecting to spatial data
- Using the background screenshot map
- Creating density maps

Technical requirements

This chapter uses the following datasets:

- Global Superstore dataset, which can be found at `http://www.tableau.com/sites/default/files/training/global_superstore.zip`.

- The London Wards dataset, which can be found at `https://data.london.gov.uk/download/statistical-gis-boundary-files-london/08d31995-dd27-423c-a987-57fe8e952990/London-wards-2018.zip`.

- The 311 calls dataset, which can be found at `https://data.nola.gov/City-Administration/311-Calls-Historic-Data-2012-2018-/3iz8-nghx`.

Mapping basics

Mapping in Tableau is very simple and based on geographic data fields that can be identified by the globe symbol next to them. To create a map, select the geographic fields and any measure, and then click on the **Show Me** Window. As you can see in the following screenshot, Tableau automatically highlights the symbol map as the preferred visual:

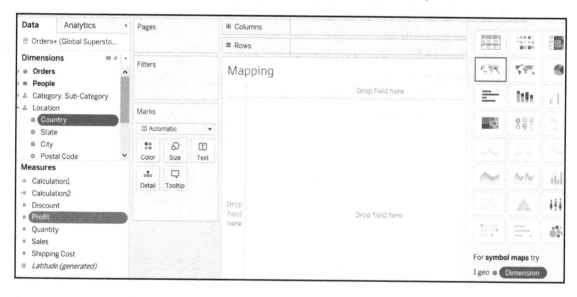

Once you click it, it will create the following screenshot. As you can see, for each country, the symbol marks a point at the geographic center of the location:

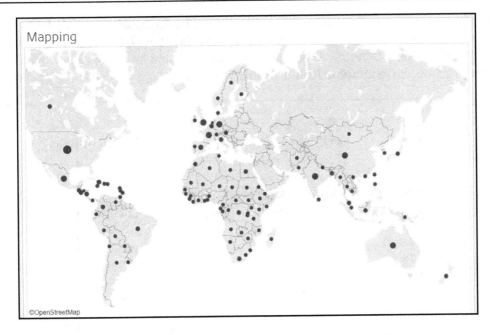

Symbol maps always plot marks at the geographic centers and can plot two measures at a time. Filled maps, on the other hand, use geographic locations to define the boundaries within which to fill and can only plot one measure at a time. Using the **Show Me** menu, if we now switch to filled maps, we can see the following screenshot:

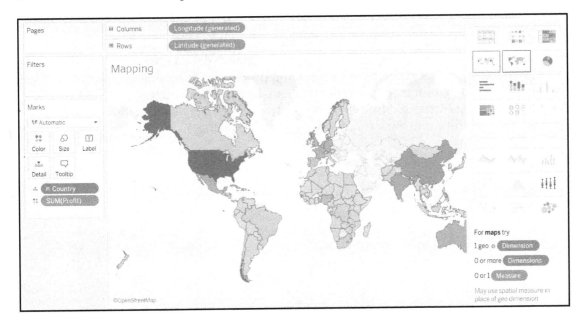

If there are no geographic fields automatically detected by your data, right-click the field you want to display. Click **Geographic Role | Appropriate Level.** For example, in the following screenshot, if Country is not automatically detected as a geographic field, we can right-click and select **Geographic Role | Country/Region**:

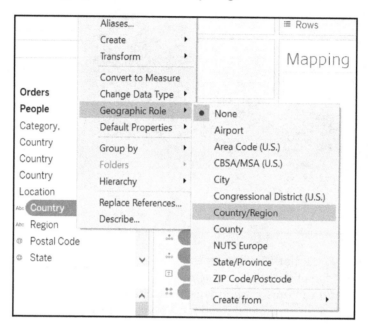

This will now turn the Country field into a **Geographic field**, which can be used in both **symbol maps** and **filled maps**. Both **symbol maps** and **filled maps** only differ in the number of measures they can show and how they visualize data. Other than that, both maps have the same shared common features and properties. From this section onward, we will use the common term **map** to refer to them, instead of differentiating between them. All of the properties discussed from here on apply to both map visuals. Now that we have clarified this, let's dive into the various **map navigation** features.

Map navigation

When the mouse is anywhere on the map, you will see the **Map Options** menu appear by default, as shown in the following screenshot:

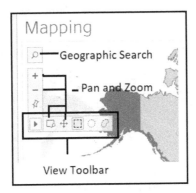

If you do not see these options, don't worry. On the **Menu Bar**, click on **Map** | **Map Options** and it will show the options to add to the screen. You can see in the following screenshot that we had only the option for **Show Map Scale** unchecked. Go ahead and check that:

You will notice at the bottom-right of the screen that, the map scale accuracy has appeared. The more you zoom into the map, the more your accuracy will increase. Having the distances scale easily allows us to look at distances in miles, kilometers, or any of your preferred units:

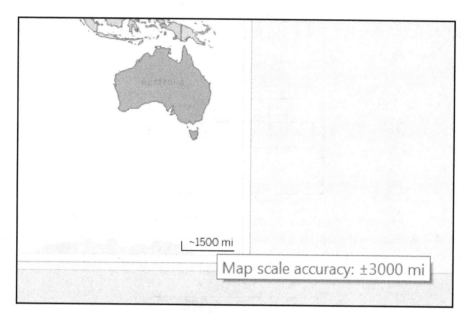

Now, let's look at each of the features in detail.

Pan and zoom

The pan and zoom features allow us to interact and inspect data on the map. We can focus on specific locations and move the map around to focus on key information.

Zoom in/out

The **Zoom In (+)** or **Zoom Out (-)** buttons can be used to zoom into the map. You can also use your mouse to zoom in/out as you would usually do. Alternatively, you can **double-click** to **Zoom In** and press *Shift* and **double-click** to **Zoom Out**.

Once you zoom in/out, the map gets fixed to that area in the view. To quickly go back to the default view, click on the **Reset Map** pin. For example, in the following map, we are zoomed in on Europe, and the moment we click on **Reset Map**, it will take us back to the wider world view:

Zoom area

To zoom in to a particular area on the graph, the Zoom Area option is also available.

Simply select the **Zoom Area** button from the toolbar and highlight the area you want to zoom into. In the following example, we are using the **Zoom Area** button to zoom into Canada and Alaska:

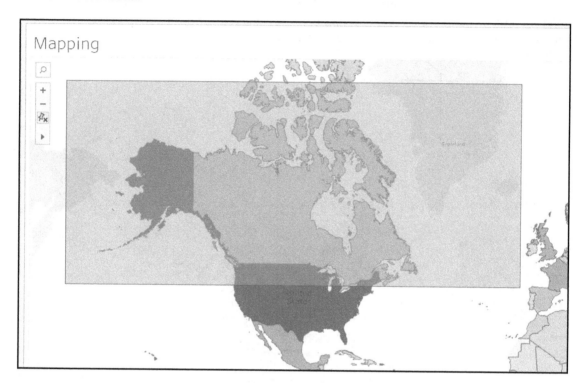

Pan

The **Pan** option can be found right next to the Zoom Area options. **Pan** allows us to move the map to focus on it or show the regions the way we want. To pan, just select the **Pan Option** and then move the map around to suit your needs. Alternatively, you can hold down the *Shift* key and move the map. For example, in the following map, the position has been moved from the default display to show—to start with—Asia in the left and moving up to Europe and Africa on the right:

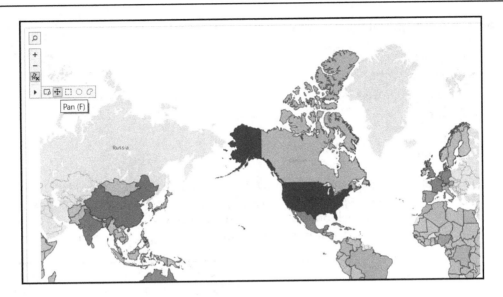

For pan/zoom, use the shortcuts to navigate faster. Double-click to zoom in, press *Shift* and double-click to zoom out (alternatively, use default mouse zooming), and press *Shift* and move the map to pan.

Geographic Search

Geographic Search allows us to quickly search locations on the maps. For example, in our map of the countries, if we wanted to quickly look for Nigeria, we could simply use the search box and type `Nigeria` in it. As you type, a list of all relevant locations appears in the suggestions for you:

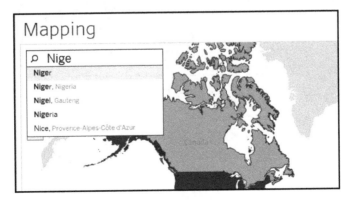

You can search for the following on the maps:

- Continent
- Country
- State or province
- County
- City
- Postcode

Once you type/select **Nigeria**, and press *Enter*, the map will zoom in to focus on it. You may notice that the map again gets pinned. Whenever you search/zoom/pan, the map will get pinned to that location. Just click on the reset button to reset to the default view. The following screenshot shows the result we obtain after searching for **Nigeria**:

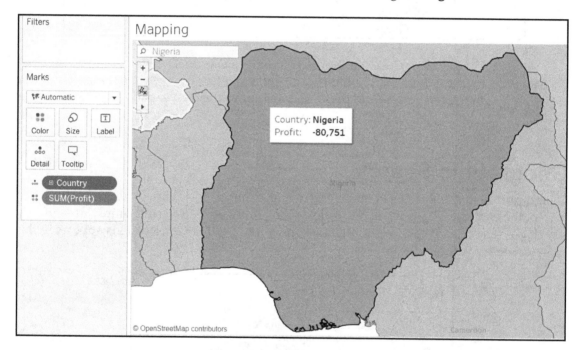

Marks selection

As with all graphs, you can select marks on the maps, and perform activities such as grouping/sets creation. Beyond the usual rectangular selections, maps have two other selection features, **Radial Selection** and **Lasso Selection**, respectively:

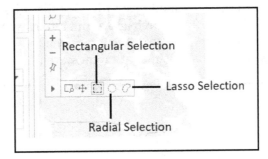

Rectangular Selection

Rectangular Selection is the default selection option available. Just drag the mouse on the screen to make a selection:

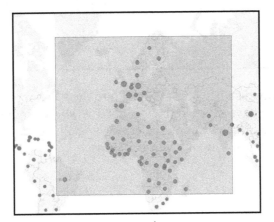

Radial Selection

Radial Selection is a super useful feature of maps. It allows us to select locations in terms of a circular radius, which, in turn, allows us to look at the location in a radial distance of a point or to calculate distances between locations.

For example, we want to find the combined profit for all of the cities within a 50-mile radius of New York City, USA. We first search and zoom into New York City, USA. Then, we select **Radial Search**. Now, keeping New York City in the center, we zoom out 50 miles from the USA. The following screenshot shows a radial search:

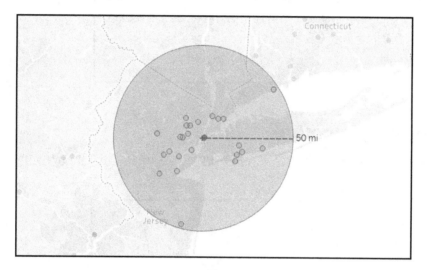

In case you do not see any distance marks, zoom into the location a bit more until they become visible. Once you have selected the locations, as shown in the preceding screenshot, you can see the summary for the locations selected as you would with a rectangular selection. Here, we can see the sum of profit is 79,534:

In this example, we used the radial select tool to define the locations which fall within a certain radius. Using the same principle, we can use this to find the radial distance between two locations. For example, if we had to search for the radial distance between San Diego and Los Angeles, we first filter on the two locations and then create a radial distance search between the two points. Choose any city as the center and extend the radius till you reach the other city. In the following screenshot, we kept Los Angeles as the center and extended the radius for 110 miles, until we reached San Diego. Hence, the radial distance between the two locations is 110 miles:

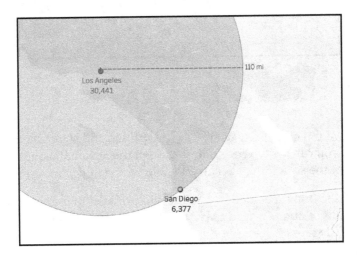

Lasso Selection

Sometimes, bounded ways of selection are not enough and we may need to select certain locations in an area but exclude others. In this case, **Lasso** (a freehand shape selection) is the best way to go. An example of this kind of selection can be seen in the following screenshot. Here, all western states that we want except Georgia are selected:

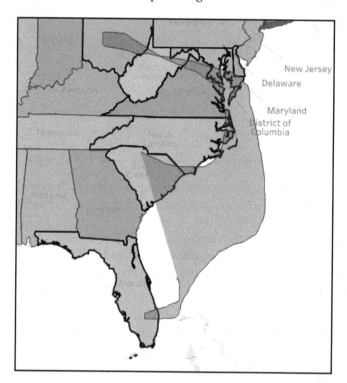

Scaling

To change the scale of the map, go to **Map** | **Map Options** and select the **Show Map Scale** option. Here, you can switch the scales between the automatic, metric system, or US system. Once you set the scales, they become visible on the lower-right side of the map.

Read the units specified in any question related to mapping very carefully. You may need to change the scale of the map before performing the next steps.

Map features – layering and custom territories

Now that we have learned how to create maps, let's look at how we can customize certain map details, such as the color of the map, what level of details it will display, and the territories shown within it.

Map Layers

To view the layers that can be added or removed from the map or how it will look in the background, select **Map | Map Layers**. In previous versions of Tableau, you would select **Map | Map Options.** You will get the following screen:

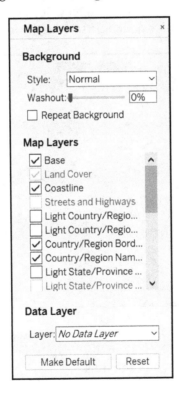

Here, you can select and change between the different backgrounds: **Normal**, **Light**, and **Dark**. Depending on the Tableau version, you may also have **Street**, **Outdoors**, and **Satellite Backgrounds** available:

As shown in the following screenshot, in **Map Layers**, you can add the details you want to see on the map. For example, after focusing on New Jersey, the map now shows **Zip Code**, **Metro Code**, and **Metro Boundaries** as can be seen in the following screenshot:

These layers help to add a deeper level of detail to the maps and allow you to customize what to view as per your needs. There are many map layers available for various regions. Explore each of them to see what you can add.

 Certain map layers are only available at certain zoom levels and will appear grayed out if you are not at that level. Zoom in to reveal further layers.

Beyond changing the map background and layers, Tableau also has many data layers available that can be used to overlay data on the map. To add a data layer, select a layer from the **Data Layers** menu. For example, to understand whether `Profit` in `State` of the US is linked to the median age of the people, we can overlay **Median Age** on the graphs.

Create a symbol graph showing `Profit` by each `State`, and zoom in on the USA. Under **Data Layers**, select the following:

- **Layer: Median Age**
- **By: State**
- **Using: Blue Green Sequence**

You will see the following graph:

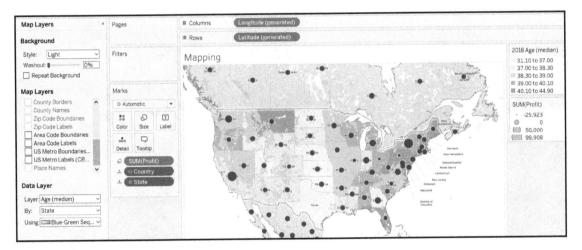

As an exercise, add a few data layers and change the level to view them. This will familiarize you more with the data layer options you have available.

Custom territories

Beyond defining what the map layers display, we can also create and show your own custom territory. There are two ways in which we can create our own territories:

- Grouping locations
- Geocoding a field using other geographic fields

Grouping locations

Assume you are looking at data at the country level and focusing on Europe as a continent. Instead of looking at each country individually, you want to look at the data in two sections, Eastern Europe and Western Europe. To achieve this, look at the locations on the map, and use the selection tool to select the territories. Once you have them selected, click on the grouping icon, as shown in the following screenshot:

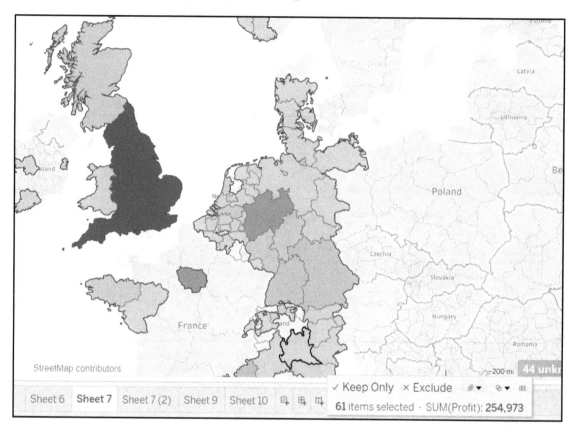

Selecting the groups will create a combined group for these locations. It will also add a Country & State grouping to the marks shelf. All of your selected locations are now grouped and will be colored the same:

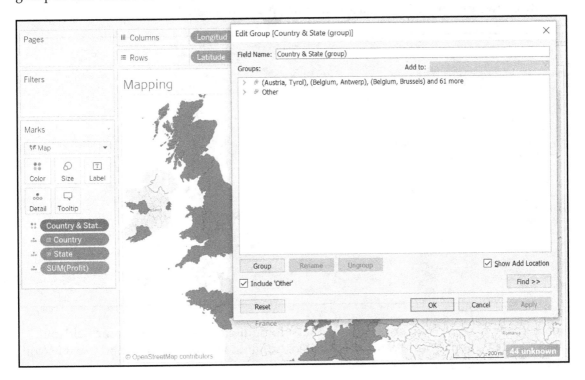

Continue and group locations as you want. Once you are done grouping, remove the field from the **Colors** shelf. From **Dimensions**, bring Country (group)1 to the **Marks** detail shelf, and move Profit back to colors. For example, in the following screenshot, based on **Countries**, two groups called **Group 1** and **Group 2** were created:

Another way to create similar groups would be to right-click on the geographic field and select **Create Group**. Once the group is created, bring it to the details shelf and use it as you would use any other geographic field.

Geocoding using other geographic fields

Another way to create custom territories is to geocode a custom location field present in the data based on other fields.

For example, we want to add the Region field to Location Hierarchy. To achieve this, right-click on the Region field. Select **Geographic Role** | **Create From** | **Country.** This adds the field to the location hierarchy and the globe shape denoting a geographic field appears next to it:

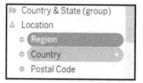

Bring the `Region` field onto the **Labels** shelf. You can see the custom location on the map now appear as shown in the following screenshot:

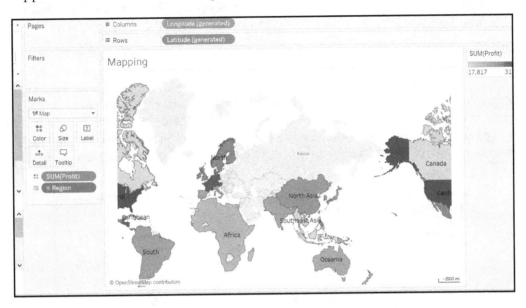

Using this method, you can view any custom territory that you have in your dataset.

Now that we have learned how to create maps and add geographic fields, we will move on to the next section where we will learn about modifying locations to help deal with erroneous or ambiguous location data.

Modifying locations

Once you define a field as a geographic field, Tableau automatically detects the locations of the places. Sometimes, however, Tableau will show **x Unknowns** in the right-hand corner of the screen. This could be because the location can be ambiguous, that is, multiple places having the same name, or the spelling could differ from what Tableau recognizes, for example.

The easiest way to fix most errors is to bring other data fields into the map details as well. For example, if you are only plotting cities, many countries can have the same city names. Adding a country and state can help to rectify such errors. If there is a hierarchy of locations, then Tableau automatically uses it to remove ambiguities. If, after doing this, there are still errors remaining, you can custom edit the locations to make them match.

Editing locations

To edit locations, either click on the right-hand corner on the **x Unknowns** value and it will open the **Edit Locations** window, or go to **Maps | Edit Locations.**

Click on **Country/Region.** This will show how the country or region is getting detected. Many times, this field is set to fixed for a particular country. So, if you are in the UK, your map could be set at the fixed field for the United Kingdom. Now, if you had a dataset with states from the USA, it would not match any location. To fix it, you would need to edit the location and set either the fixed **field** to be the **United States**, or if your dataset contains a Country field, then set it to be matched from that field. In the following example, you can see that the **Country/Region** field is mapped to the Country geographic field, which is good:

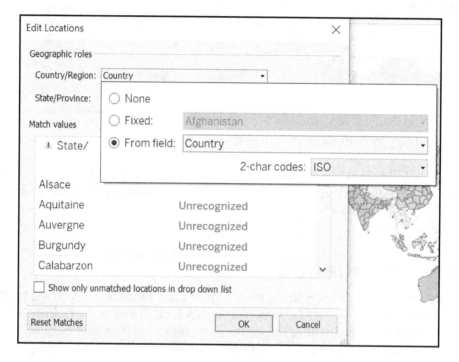

Close that dialog box and look at the ambiguous values to edit. You will notice that the unmatched locations are highlighted. For example, for **Lower Normandy**, we know this is the state of **Normandy**. Search for *Normandy* in the **Unrecognized** box. Once you search and find it, select it. This will now match the location, as can be seen in the following screenshot:

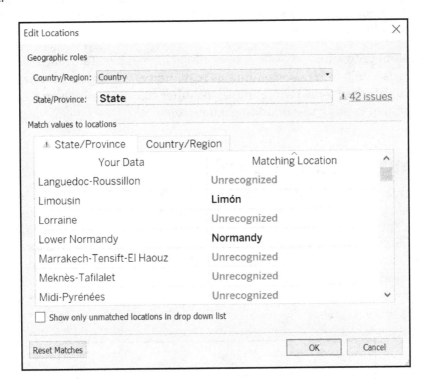

If you can't find matching names, but know the latitude and longitude of the location and when you are typing, you will see a message in the dialog box saying `Enter a Latitude and Longitude value`. If you don't see this, just type any number. Once you click on it, it will open a box where you can enter the **Latitude** and **Longitude** values alternatively, and click **OK**.

Once you are have mapped all of the locations you can, click OK. Now if you look at the lower-right corner, the number of **Unknowns** decreases. In this way, even if you have custom locations or different spellings, you can custom match them to appropriate locations to appear in the maps. So far, we have learned how to modify and match locations, and create custom geolocations. In the next section, we will go one step further and learn how to import custom geocoding into Tableau.

Importing and managing custom geocoding

Beyond providing standard geocoding for geolocations such as City, State, Country, Country/Region, Zip Code, Postal Code, and County, Tableau also allows us to custom import their own geocoded files. Custom geocoded files are useful if we have locations that Tableau can't map, for example, a street address, or if there is a custom geographic field that we want to define, and so on.

To create a custom geocoding, we need a `.csv` file to import into Tableau. This file must contain `Latitude` and `Longitude` columns as real numbers, with at least one decimal point in them. Other than these two columns, the other columns will depend on whether we are extending an existing role or adding a new role.

Extending an existing role

If your data contains many locations that do not get mapped easily using Tableau default hierarchies, instead of trying to correct every error manually, you can just extend the locations to include these missing values. The import file should contain the names matching the hierarchy you are extending and data for all levels above the location you are extending. For example, if you wanted to extend the `States` mapping to improve it, you will need to include the columns for `State/Province` and `Country` along with `Latitude` and `Longitude`. For example, if we want to add the following location to our data, we will first create a `.csv`, as follows:

	A	B	C	D
1	Country (name)	State/Province	Latitude	Longitude
2	XYZ	XYZ	15.69	23.24
3				
4				

To import data, select **Map** | **Geocoding** | **Import Custom Geocoding**:

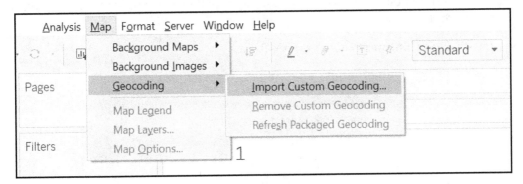

Select the folder where your `.csv` file is saved and click **Import**. Depending on the size of the default file and the geocoding to be imported, it will take a couple of minutes and then get imported.

Remember that, the highest level when extending geocoding is **Country**. There is no continent level. However, we can add new roles if we want to add geocoding up to the continent level.

Adding new roles

If, for example, we wanted to create a hierarchy for locations including a **Continent** as a geographic field, we can create a simple dataset as follows:

1	Continent	Country (N	latitude	longitude
2	Asia	India	20.6	78.96
3	Australia	Australia	-25.27	133.77
4	Europe	United Kin	55.37	-3.4
5				

Now, click on **Map | Import Custom Geocoding** and find the location of the folder. Click on **Import**. Depending on your files for geocoding, it will take a couple of minutes for the file to be imported.

Now, right-click on **Continent | Geographic Role**:

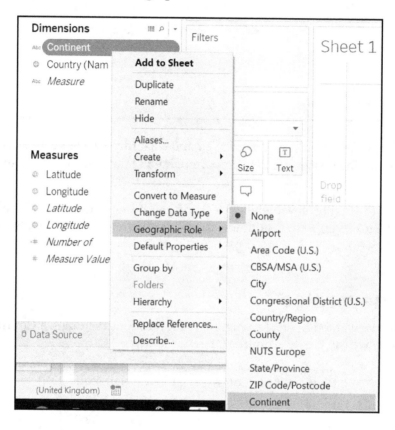

You will see that **Continent** appears as a role. You can select that to be the geographic type for Continent. To create a map from the custom mapping, select the Latitude and Longitude fields (not the generated ones) and the continent field, and create a map using the **Show Me** menu. Now, move the Continent field to **Labels** so you can see the labels on the Continent field. You should get a map like the following:

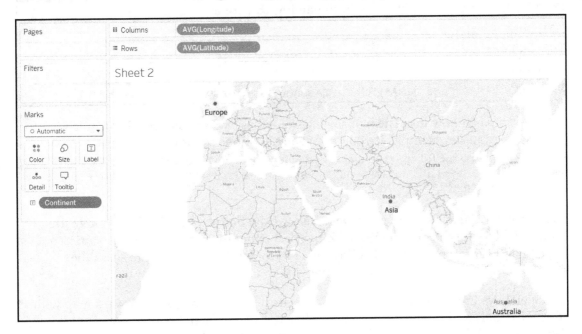

As you can see, all of the continents are plotted where we want them to be. Beyond adding geocoding, you can also import your own spatial files to plot maps. Let's look into them in the next section.

Connecting to spatial data

We can connect to, and import spatial data from, TopoJSON files, Shapefiles, MapInfo tables, GeoJSON files, KML files, and Esri File Geodatabases. Using these files, we can connect to point, linear, and polygon geometries. Currently, mixed geometries are not allowed in Tableau.

Each of the file sources listed earlier has certain restrictions on what the folder containing these files must include. These are listed in the following table:

File Source	Files Required in Folder
Esri Shapefiles	`.shp`, `.shx`, `.dbf`, `.prj`, and `.zip`
Esri Geodatabases	Either `.zip` containing `.gdb` or a `.gdb` file
KML files	`.kml`
TopoJSON	`.topojson` or `.json`
GeoJSON	`.geojson`
MapInfo	`.MAP`, `.DAT`, `.TAB`, and `.MID`, or a `.MIF`, or `.ID` file

For an example of how to create maps using shapefiles, we will use the file downloaded for London Wards as an example. If you haven't already done so, download the `London-wards-2018.zip` file (`https://data.london.gov.uk/download/statistical-gis-boundary-files-london/08d31995-dd27-423c-a987-57fe8e952990/London-wards-2018.zip`) and extract it.

To connect the file in Tableau, go to **Data** | **New Data Source** | **Spatial File**. Locate the extracted folder for the London Wards Zip. Select either the Esri folder or the `Mapinfo` folder. For this example, we are loading the ESRI folder. It will ask you to select the shapefile. Select the `london_ward.shp` file.

Once you have imported the file, you are now ready to create maps. To create a map with all of the details for London Wards, click on the `Geometry` field. You will notice that, Tableau has automatically detected it as a Geographic field. Bring this field to the **Detail Marks** tab. As soon as you do this, the autogenerated `Latitude` and `Longitude` marks appear and a graph is created. Zoom out and you will see the same as the following screenshot. As you can see in the following screenshot, all of the wards for London in the UK have been plotted:

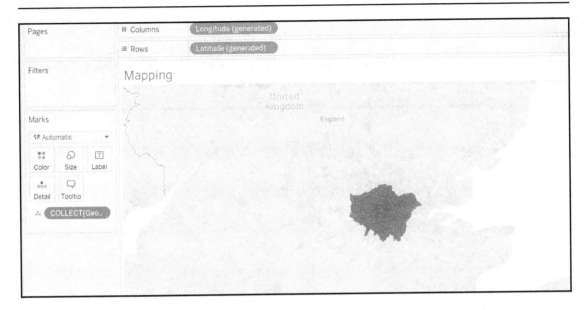

Now, to see the hectares per ward, bring the Name field in the details **Marks**, add the hectares field to the color, and your graph is created:

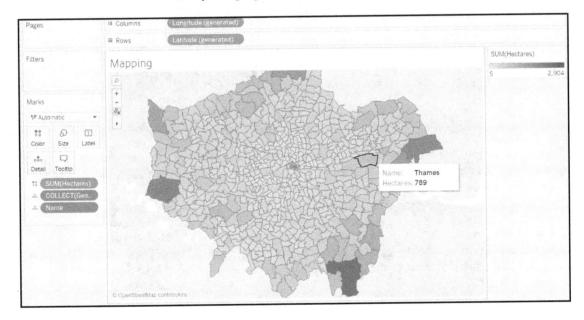

If you instead want to view the data at the district level, remove `Name` from detail and add `District` to the graph. In this way, you can see data at the district level. You can also make the map cleaner by removing any borders. Click on **Color | Border | None.** This will make the map cleaner, as shown in the following screenshot:

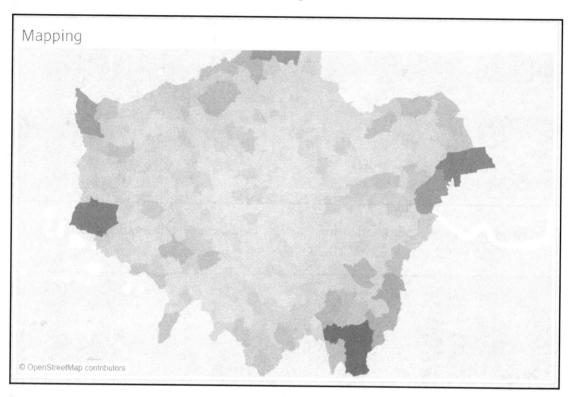

Sometimes, shapefiles only contain geometric details but not the measures you want to see; for example, if you wanted to inspect a dataset about the population of each ward. Not to worry. Shapefiles function as normal files and can be joined to any other files, even other shapefiles. As an exercise, join two shapefiles and use them to create a dual-axis map.

In this section, we learned how to import custom geocoding to enhance mapping capabilities. For some use cases, even custom geocoding may not meet our needs. For such cases, we can use background images to plot our data. Let's learn how to do this in the next section.

Using background images to plot spatial data

There may be situations when spatial data is not enough to accurately plot data on the map. In such cases, we can also use background images as a background. While this option allows for the most flexibility in how to plot, it also requires the most effort in defining the boundary and point coordinates.

For example, say you wanted to plot the house plan of your house and have the following data:

Location	Location ID	X	Y	Size
Room 3	1	15	20	100
Room 1	2	15	50	100
Room 4	3	40	20	125
Room 5	4	40	50	125
Porch	5	60	40	60

You also have this screenshot:

We add the screenshot data as the data source. To test how the appropriate positions would look, create a scatter plot with unaggregated measures. For the preceding example, plotting the X and Y values, we get the following:

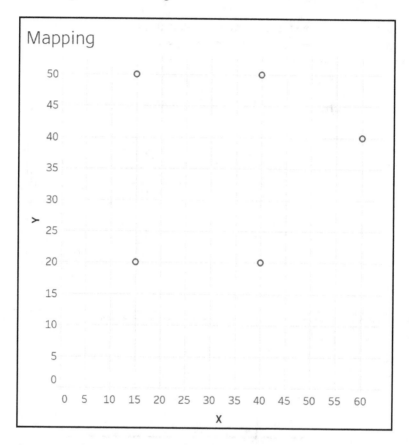

Once happy with where the X and Y points appear, click on **Map** | **Background Image** | **Dataset**. Select **Add Image**. Browse to where you saved the floor plan screenshot and click **OK**. Add in the details shown in the following screenshot:

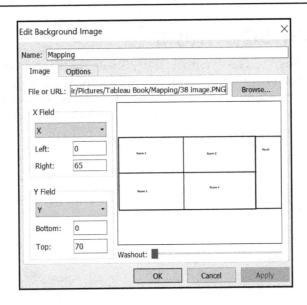

Once you have entered the limits for **X** and **Y** and which fields denote **X** and **Y**, go to **Options** and select **Always Show Entire Image**. Click **OK**. You will get the points plotted on the screenshot. Now, you can see where each of the points is plotted. Change the marks type to **Map** and then add in the measures you want to plot. This now behaves like a map:

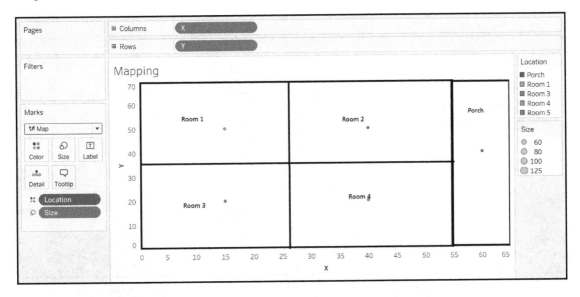

This technique can be used to plot static images from any map and plot measures on them.

Creating density maps

Density marks were added to Tableau in version 2018.3. These marks add another way of finding patterns in areas where there is a lot of overlapping data or the concentration of data is very high. Density marks find their best use in creating density maps, making it super easy to find trends in spatial data. Density maps work best with custom geocoded files, as they allow for detailed granular data to be added. Granular and precise data in a small range, along with smooth changes in measure values is the ideal use case for using density maps.

For this example, we will be using the 311 calls dataset. In case you have not yet downloaded it, download it here in a `.csv` format: `https://data.nola.gov/City-Administration/311-Calls-Historic-Data-2012-2018-/3iz8-nghx`.

Now, if we want to understand the distribution of calls by `Zip Code` for `LA`, and decide to plot a **Symbol Map**, after much zooming in, the following screenshot shows what it would look like:

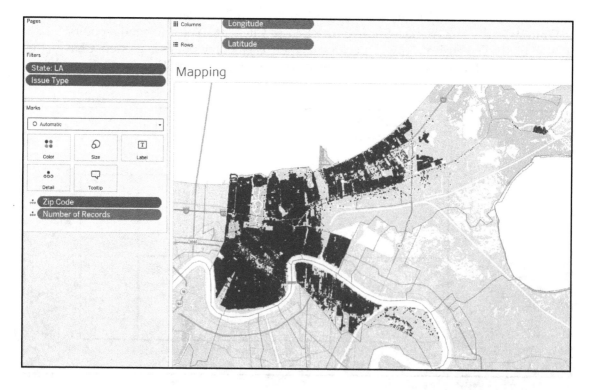

This doesn't give us much information. Looking at the map, it looks like all locations have almost equal calls, which isn't true. In cases like this, density maps become super useful. To convert this screenshot into a density map, in the **Marks** menu, change the mark type from **Automatic** to **Density**. You will see a certain pattern emerging, but it isn't very clear. To enhance it, it becomes important to have a proper color scheme. Click on the **Color** mark, and change the color to **Density Multi-Color Light**. Once the color is changed, we can see the pattern more easily as in the following screenshot. You can further change the intensity and opacity of the colors in the **Color** menu:

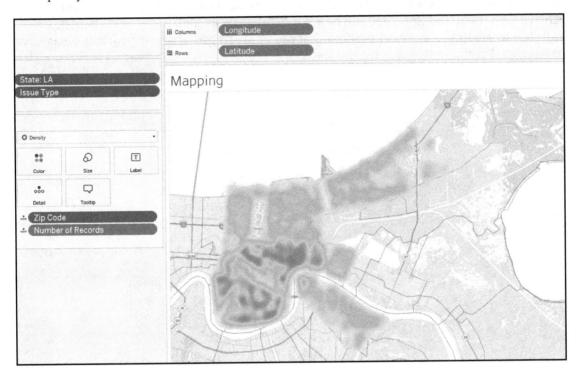

You can quickly see that the calls are concentrated in the center of the city and less toward the lakeshore. You can further filter and compare the different issue types and see how they differ in their concentration. You can further use the **Pages** shelf to see the trends across time for the issues. The density when using the pages shelf is calculated for the entire dataset, so the patterns can quickly be seen relative to time or other factors.

Summary

In this chapter, we detailed how to create, navigate, and customize maps. We learned how to identify the correct locations for mapping, enhance geocoding, and create our own custom geocoding and geographic fields. Furthermore, we covered spatial files, and how they can be leveraged to create nuanced maps for specific purposes. We also looked at adding background images to maps, creating custom maps, and creating density maps.

All of this will give you a firm understanding of the extent of customization you can achieve with maps and how they can be a powerful analysis tool. In the next chapter, we will start by creating simple calculations that can be leveraged across the various visuals we have learned about in this chapter and the last.

5
Understanding Simple Calculations in Tableau

In the previous chapters, you have learned much about visualizing data in various forms in Tableau. It is common to have cases where the data you want to visualize is not directly present in your dataset but can easily be obtained by applying transformations on the dataset or even aggregating the data in the dataset. For example, you may have the full address for a placed order, and you want to obtain only the country or city where the order came from. Alternatively, you may have data for each individual sale and you want to know the average of all sales. This and the subsequent two chapters will focus on calculations and how you can use these to answer such questions. This chapter will introduce calculations and cover simple calculations, while the next two will look at more advanced calculations.

The following topics will be covered in this chapter:

- Calculation basics
- Creating calculations and understanding their components
- Building arithmetic calculations
- Building string calculations
- Building date calculations
- Building logical statements
- Building grand totals and subtotals

Technical requirements

This chapter uses the following dataset:

- The Global Superstore dataset, which can be found at `http://www.tableau.com/sites/default/files/training/global_superstore.zip`.

Calculation basics

Calculations allow us to obtain more data points from the existing dataset and allow us to enhance our visualizations and analysis. Creating calculations in Tableau enables you to analyze data on the fly, without having to create overheads by transforming your original datasets every time you have a new idea about how you can analyze your data even further.

When to use calculations

Before we dive into calculations and how to create them, it is equally important to understand when to create calculations. Some examples of when calculations are useful are as follows:

- **Changing datatypes**: For example, you have data that is being represented as a string value.
- **Performing mathematical calculations**: For example, you want to divide two fields to obtain ratios or percentages or subtract fields.
- **To create logical groupings/labels**: For example, if you want to group people in those who can drive or not, you can create a calculation saying: if you are older than 18 and have a valid driving license, you can drive.
- **To create new fields from existing data**: For example, you want to create a country field by extracting a part of the address or a new date field from another date field.
- **Aggregating data**: For example, you want to view the sum, average, and median of distribution or subtotals and totals at the country and city levels for sales.

Now that we understand when to use calculations, we can discuss the three types of calculations available in Tableau.

Types of calculations

- **Simple calculations**: These calculations allow you to create new fields at either the same level of granularity as your dataset (row-level) or aggregate data at the granularity of the visual.
- **Level Of Detail (LOD) expressions**: LOD calculations are an extension of simple calculations but allow you to have more control over the granularity of the data you are working on. You have options to work to specify a FIXED level of granularity or INCLUDE data fields to the visualization granularity or EXCLUDE them.
- **Table calculations**: Table calculations only work at the level of granularity of the visuals. These allow you to build calculations at visual levels of top of your existing data or simple calculations.

The type of calculation you require will depend on the use case of your problem. If you already have all of the data you want to answer the questions, then you need table calculations. If you do not have all of the data you need, but the data needed will be at the same granularity as your dataset, you will need a basic calculation. Otherwise, it will be a LOD calculation.

Do not worry if you are a bit confused about the types of calculations. We will cover each type in detail in separate chapters. This chapter will cover simple calculations in detail while the next two will cover the other two calculation types. So, let's look at how to create simple calculations.

Creating calculations

To create a calculation, click on **Analysis | Create Calculated Field**. Alternatively, you can scroll to the end of dimensions/measures tabs and right-click in the white space there.

You should see the following calculations window:

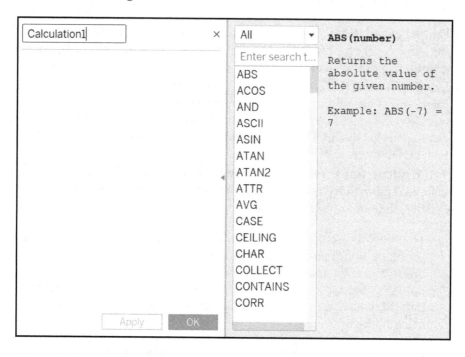

The top of the window, where it says `Calculation1`, is where you enter the name of your calculated field. The blank area underneath is where you enter your calculation. To the right side, you have a list of all of the available functions you can use and their syntax to quickly help you out. The tiny triangle icon to the right of the calculation editor can be used to toggle the functions window in/out.

Let's create a very simple calculation to see what our total profit would be if the average profit increased four times, and name this calculation `4x Profit`, as shown in the following screenshot:

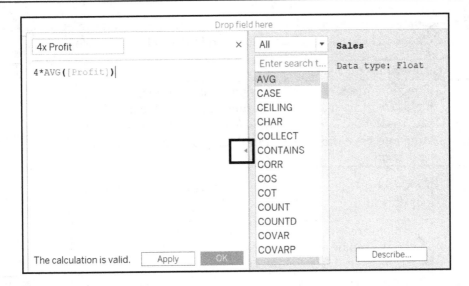

You will see, at the bottom of the calculation, the message: **The calculation is valid**. This means we can now click **OK** and the field will be created. The error checker in Tableau quickly displays error messages below if the calculation is invalid, allowing for easy troubleshooting.

Once you click **OK**, you will notice the field appears under **Measures**. Now, you can use this calculation as you would any other measure. Let's use it to show the results per **Segment**:

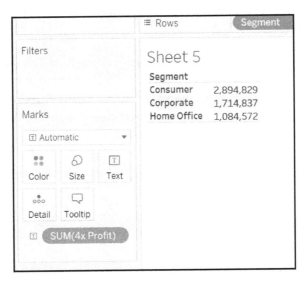

Like the previously discussed calculation, all calculations in Tableau can be a combination of six basic elements. These elements are described in the following table:

Components	Description	Example
Functions	Functions are used to transform the values or members of a field. There are many types of functions available in Tableau such as `Number`, `String`, `Date`, and `User`. Different functions have different syntax, inputs/data type expected, and so on.	In our example, `AVG()` was an example of a function.
Fields	Fields represent the dimensions or measures (columns) from our data source.	`[Profit]` was the field used by us.
Operators	Operators are symbols that denote some kind of operation. Operators can be one of the following: +, -, *, /, %, ==, =, >, <, >=, <=, !=, <>, ^, AND, OR, NOT, and ( ).	* in our example was the operator.
Literal expressions	These are constant values that do not change. These can be either Numeric, String, Date, Boolean, or Null.	4 was the literal used by us.
Parameters	Parameters, as we know, are dynamic values that can replace literals. These too can be used in the calculations.	
Comments	Comments are simple descriptions that you can add to the calculation fields. These are informational only and do not affect the actual calculation. The `//` symbols are used to add comments.	We didn't add a comment to our example, but we could have added something like `// To create 4 times profit value`.

Using the preceding combination of six elements, all calculations are created. Now that we understand the components better, we can look at the syntax of each component in detail in the following sections.

Functions syntax

There are many types of functions available in Tableau, such as `Number`, `String`, `Date`, and `User`. Different functions have different syntax and require different inputs for them to work. The list of all of the functions available to you in Tableau is available in the side tab of the calculated field window. Select `AVG()` from the functions list. Once you select any function, you will see three elements in the help window:

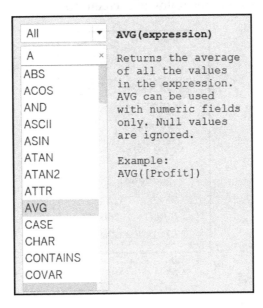

These elements are as follows:

- Syntax of the function: For `AVG`, it shows **AVG(expression)**, meaning that, to obtain the average, you need to write AVG(expression here).
- Explanation: Below the syntax, there is an explanation of what the function does.
- Example: This is an example of how the function can be used.

If you are unsure of how to use a function, copy and paste the example, and then replace the fields in it with your own fields. This ensures that the syntax remains correct.

You can use more than one function in a calculation and even nest them inside one another as long as they meet the syntax requirements. We will learn about some of the common types of functions later in this chapter.

Fields syntax

Fields are the columns in the data (and can be calculated fields too). A field should always be surrounded by square brackets, [ ], if they contain spaces or are not unique in name. It is best practice to surround fields with [ ]. Fields are shown in orange in Tableau. You can drag and drop the field directly into the calculation from the **Dimension** or **Measures** tabs. Alternatively, you can start typing the field name and Tableau will show you options to autocomplete fields, as shown in the following screenshot:

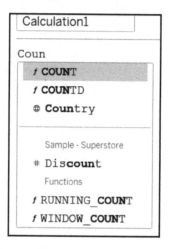

Operator syntax

Operators are symbols that denote some kind of operation. Operators can be of the following types:

- Mathematical operators: Mathematical operators are used for performing mathematical calculations. The operators are as follows:
    - **+ (plus)**: Plus can be used for addition (numeric and date fields) and string concatenation. For example, 4+2 will return 6 while Abc + Def will return AbcDef. We can use addition for dates as well, for example, adding #23-04-2019#+4 will give #27-04-2019#.
    - **- (minus)**: Minus can be used for the subtraction of dates and numeric fields, in a similar way to the + operator.

- *** (multiplication)** and **/ (division)**: This is used to multiply or divide numeric fields.
- **% (modulo)**: This returns the remainder of a division operator, for example, `5%2=1`.
- **^ (power/exponent)**: This returns the exponent value, for example, `2^3 =8`.

- Relational operators: These are used for comparing expressions and return TRUE, FALSE, or NULL values. Each operator can be used to compare numbers, dates, or strings. The operators are as follows:
  - **== or = (equals)**
  - **> (greater than)**
  - **< (less than)**
  - **>= (greater than or equal to)**
  - **<= (less than or equal to)**
  - **!= and <> (not equal to)**

- Logical operators: Logical operators compare both sides of the expression and return TRUE, FALSE, or NULL values. The logical operators are as follows:
  - **AND**: If both expression 1 and expression 2 are TRUE, then it returns TRUE; otherwise, it returns FALSE. If any of the expressions are NULL, then it returns NULL. AND follows the following rules for output:

Expression 1	Expression 2	Output
TRUE	TRUE	TRUE
TRUE	FALSE/NULL	FALSE/NULL
FALSE/NULL	TRUE	FALSE/NULL
FALSE/NULL	FALSE/NULL	FALSE/NULL

- **OR:** OR returns FALSE only if both the expressions are FALSE; otherwise, it will return TRUE. It returns NULL only if both values are NULL. It follows the following rules for output:

Expression 1	Expression 2	Output
TRUE	TRUE	TRUE
TRUE	FALSE/NULL	TRUE
FALSE/NULL	TRUE	TRUE
FALSE/NULL	FALSE/NULL	FALSE/NULL

- **NOT:** NOT is used to negate other Booleans or expressions. It follows the following rules of output:

Expression 1	Expression 2
TRUE	FALSE
FALSE	TRUE

Order of precedence of operators

The operators get evaluated in the following order of precedence:

1. – (negate)
2. ^ (power)
3. *, /, %
4. +, –
5. ==, >, <, >=, <=, !=
6. NOT
7. AND
8. OR

To change the order of precedence, we can use the final operator called parentheses, (). If you put something in parentheses, it gets executed first. If there are nested parentheses, then the innermost gets executed first and so on, for example, if we had the following expression to get evaluated: (1+2*5) = 11 , (1+(2*5)/2) = (1+10/2) =6.

Literal expressions syntax

Literal expressions are constant values that are represented as is. Literals are of the following types:

- **Numeric literals**: Numbers or floats such as 4.2 and 2
- **String literals**: Constant strings such as Hello
- **Date literals**: Represent dates as constants, such as #20-05-2019#
- **Boolean literals**: Represent Boolean values of TRUE or FALSE
- **Null literals**: Used to assign or compare against NULL

Parameter syntax

Parameters are simply placeholder variables. Parameters are represented with the color purple in Tableau. They can represent numbers, floats, strings, date/date-time values, or Booleans.

Comments syntax

Comments are represented using //. To add multiline comments, add // in every line.

Now that we understand all about the basic elements of what constitutes calculated fields and how to create them, let's dive into some calculations.

Building arithmetic calculations

To work with arithmetic calculations in Tableau, we can either use operators as discussed in the last section, work with one of the many **number functions** that are present, or make use of some of the **aggregation options**. This section will cover some of the important functions but it is not an exhaustive list. The *Further reading* section contains links to an A-Z list of functions maintained by Tableau.

Aggregation options

Aggregation options define how your data values are combined or aggregated. Simple aggregation works at the level of visual granularity.

What this means is the data is aggregated at the level of the dimensions in the visual. Without even studying it, we have used this logic in the previous chapters when we created visuals. Whenever we wanted to see the total **SUM(Sales)**, we would only bring the **SUM(Sales)** measure to our visual window. However, if we wanted to see the sales per segment, we would add the **Segment** dimension to our window and our sales would split up, as can be seen in the following screenshot:

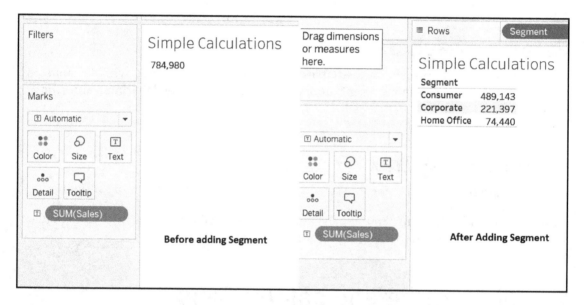

This same principle works with all the aggregations. To see the aggregation levels available, right-click on the measured field, select **Measure** (aggregation level) and it will show you what other options are available. For example, by right-clicking on the **SUM(Sales)** measure field, the following aggregation levels are available:

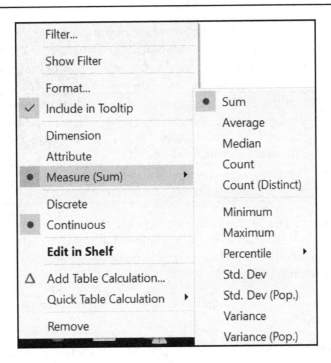

Similarly, if you want to use a dimension field to represent a measure value, you can bring it into the visual and right-click and select **Measure**, and then it will show the aggregation options available for the dimension.

Assuming a column in our dataset looks like 1, 1, 1, 2, 2, 3, 4, the various aggregation options and their results are as follows:

Sum	This adds the measure values, calculated by adding values = 1+1+1+2+2+3+4 = 14.
Average	This is the average of the measure values, calculated by adding values divided by the count of values = 14/7 = 2.
Median	This is the central value = 2.
Count	This simply counts the number of elements = 7.
Count (Distinct)	This is the count of distinct values, so no same value is counted more than once = 4.
Minimum	This the least value = 1.
Maximum	This is the highest value = 4.

Percentile	This shows what percentage of the values are less than this value. It has further options to look at the 5, 10, 25, 50, 75, 90, and 95 percentiles. Here, the 25th percentile would be 1, the 75th percentile would be 3, and so on.
Standard Deviation, Standard Deviation(Pop)	Standard deviation defines how much of the members are differing from the mean value. If you have an entire dataset, use the standard deviation population; if it is a sample, then use standard deviation. **Standard deviation (Pop)** = 1.07
Variance, Variance (Pop)	Variance is the square of standard deviation, so depending on population or sample, we use variance = 1.14 for this case.

The aggregations calculated in Tableau are sent back to the databases for querying. So, the general rule of thumb is if the database doesn't support a particular aggregation, Tableau will not be able to support it either. However, if you create extracts of the same data, then the aggregation will be supported.

As an exercise, look at all of the aggregation options for the `Profit` measure and the `Customer Name` dimension.

By simply using a combination of the preceding aggregation options and operators, many important calculations can be done. For example, `Cost` can be determined as `[Sales]-[Profit]`. Then, the average cost can be found with `AVG(Cost)`.

We can also calculate the `Profit to Sales` ratio as `SUM(Profit)/SUM(Sales)`. This will show up in decimals. To see it as a percentage, one way would be to multiply the calculation by 100. However, this will not show the % sign. To show the percentage sign, we need to format the results as a percentage. To do this, right-click on **Measure** and select **Format**. A side window will appear. Here, under **Default**, click on **Numbers** and then **Percentage**.

You can also include other things such as a suffix/prefix by using custom options. Once you are happy, you can close the side window.

Beyond the aggregations and operator use, we can look at other number functions available. They can be logically grouped into the following categories:

Trigonometric functions: These include the following:

PI	This returns the numeric constant value for pi, as 3.141592...., up to 16 decimal places. PI() is generally used within other trigonometric functions to specify the angles in radians.
SIN	This returns the sine of an angle. The angle must be specified in radians, for example, SIN(-PI()/4) =-0.7071.
ASIN	This returns the arc sine of a number in radians. This is the inverse of SIN, for example, ASIN(-0.7071)=-0.7854 (which is *-pi/4*).
ATAN2	This takes the two coordinate positions *y* and *x* as input and returns the arc tangent of two numbers in radians, for example, ATAN2(1,1) = 0.7854 i.e pi/4
DEGREE	This converts radians into degrees, so DEGREE(0.7854) =45..

** The COS, ACOS, TAN, ATAN, and COT functions are similar to SIN and ASIN.

Logarithmic and exponential functions: These include the following:

EXP	This returns *e* raised to the power of a number, for example, EXP(2) = e^2.
LN	This returns the natural logarithm of the number. The value is null for all zero and negative values, for example, LN(2) = 0.69 or LN(EXP(2))=2.
LOG	This returns a logarithmic value to the base of another number. If no base is specified, then it returns a logarithmic value to the base of 100, for example, LOG(1000) = 3 and LOG(4,2) = 2.
POWER	This returns a value to the power of another, for example, POWER (2,3) =2^3= 8.

Other mathematical functions: These include the following:

SQUARE	This returns the square of a number and is equivalent to Power (number, 2), for example, SQUARE(5) = 25.
SQRT	This returns the square root of a number and is equivalent to Power (number, 0.5), for example, SQRT(25) =5.
ABS	This returns the absolute value of a number, for example, ABS(-7) =7. It's very useful when you work with quantities or deviations where the actual values are more important than the sign of the numbers.

CEILING	This rounds a number to the nearest integer greater or equal to the number. This is useful when doing capacity planning kind of problems, for example, if you had to assign resources to a project to get work completed and the result was 3.2. If you simply round the number, your result would be 3. But you actually have more work, so it makes more sense to have four resources than three and plan based on that, for example, CEILING(3.2) = 4.
FLOOR	FLOOR does the reverse of CEILING. It returns the greatest integer smaller or equal to the given number, for example, FLOOR(3.2) =3.
ROUND	This rounds the number to the nearest integer or the specified decimal values, for example, ROUND (3.2)=3, ROUND(3.7) = 4, and ROUND(3.1421,2) = 3.14.
SIGN	This returns the sign of the number, 1 if positive, 0 if zero, and -1 if negative, for example, SIGN(-3)=-1 and SIGN(4) =1.
ZN	This returns the expression if it is not null; otherwise, it will return 0. This is useful if we want to calculate averages, without ignoring NULL or to display 0s instead of nulls.
DIV	This returns the quotient of a division operation, for example, DIV(7,2) =3.
HEXBINX, HEXBINY	Both of these functions are used to map an x, y coordinate to the nearest hexagonal bin. HENBINX maps to the nearest x coordinate while HEXBINY maps the nearest y coordinate. The bins have side length 1, so the inputs need to be scaled accordingly.

Now that we are familiar with the various aggregation options and number functions that can be used to create numeric calculations, let's move on to the next section where we will learn about string calculations.

Building string calculations

Similar to numeric calculations, many string functions exist to allow for various calculations. Let's look at some of the key string calculations and how they can be used.

Functions related to obtaining substrings from a string

One of the most common use cases when dealing with strings is that we want only parts of the string and not all. Many functions help us to do that. Let's have a look at what functions we can use.

LEFT: This follows the syntax LEFT (string, num_chars).

Using LEFT, the num_chars specified starting from the start of a string is returned. This becomes very useful for grouping.

For example, we want to find the customers who have ordered the most, based on what letter their name starts with. We could create a calculation as follows: LEFT([Customer Name,1). This will return only the first character of the string. We can then use this and count the number of orders to clearly see which category ordered the most:

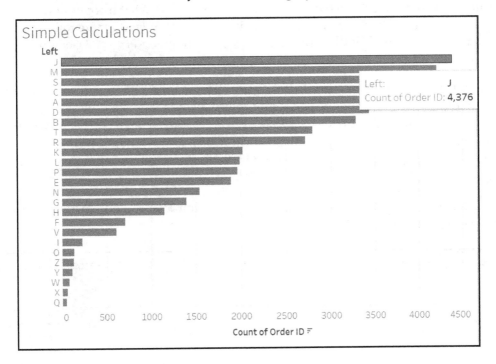

RIGHT: This follows the syntax RIGHT(string, num_chars).

Using RIGHT, the num_chars specified starting from the end of a string is returned.

Similar to the first example, if you wanted to find the last letter of the names of the people who ordered, you would use RIGHT([Customer Name,1).

MID: This follows the syntax MID (string, start, [length]).

It returns the characters from string, starting from the position specified by the start value. The first character of the string has the starting position of 1. length is optional to specify, and if it is specified, it will return up to that many characters.

Look at the following example:

```
MID("Hello",2) = ello
MID("Hello",2,3) = ell
```

SPLIT: This follows the syntax `SPLIT (string, delimiter, token number)`.

Sometimes, we don't know the exact position we want to create a substring from but might have a delimiter to specify it.

For example, in our dataset, we have a customer full name, so what if we only wanted to obtain the first name? We know the names are in the format of **First Name** followed by space character and then **Middle + Last Name**. So, our delimiter is " ". Based on the delimiter, your string is divided into equal tokens.

For example, if the string was `Alex Young`, your string would be broken by the delimiter into two strings. Token 1 would be `Alex`, and Token 2 would be `Young`. So, `SPLIT("Alex Young", " ",1)` would return `Alex`, while `SPLIT ("Alex Young"," ",2)` would return `Young`. If you use negative numbers, it counts from the right in a string. So, `SPLIT("Alex Young"," ", -1)` would be `Young`, and `SPLIT ("Alex Young"," ",-2)` would be `Alex`.

Now, back to our example—if we wanted to find the **First Name** of our customers, we would create a calculation as follows:

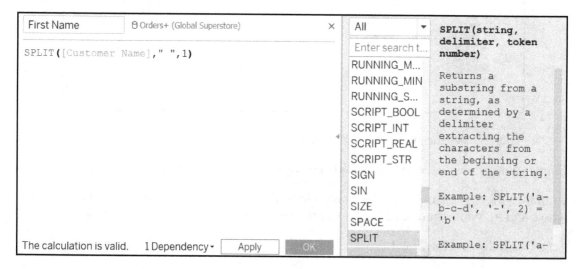

Now, we count the people with that as their first names, to find the most popular names, as shown here:

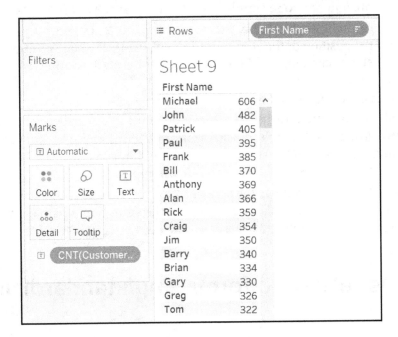

This first logical subset of string functions allows us to obtain substrings from a string. In the next section, we shall learn about functions that deal with the position of occurrence or existence of a substring within a string.

Functions related to finding a substring within a string

Sometimes, we don't want to obtain substrings, but just check whether certain substrings exist in strings or even obtain their position of occurrence. For this, the following functions are useful:

- CONTAINS: This follows the syntax CONTAINS(string, substring). CONTAINS returns true if the string contains the substring within it, for example, CONTAINS("Tableau", "Table") = TRUE. For example, to find how many people have names containing the letter E, we can then create the calculation as CONTAINS([Customer Name], "e") and see the count of TRUE.

- `ENDSWITH`: This follows the syntax `ENDSWITH(string, substring)`. This returns true if the string ends with the substring provided, and trailing white spaces are ignored, for example, `ENDSWITH("hello", "lo")=TRUE`.
- `FIND`: This follows the syntax `FIND (string, substring, [start])`. It will return the position of the string within a substring. If a start position is specified, then it starts searching for the substring after the start position. For example, `FIND("hello","lo")` would return 4.
- `FINDNTH`: This follows the syntax `FINDNTH(string, substring, occurrence)` and returns the nth position of the nth occurrence of a substring with a string. For example, if a string is `abcabcabc` and we want to find the third occurrence of `abc` in the string, we would find it using `FINDNTH("abcabcabc"."abc", 3)`. It will return 7.
- `STARTSWITH`: This follows the syntax `STARTSWITH(string, substring)`, similar to `ENDSWITH`. This displays true if the string starts with the other substring, for example, `STARTSWITH("hello","he")=TRUE`.

Functions related to formatting/standardizing a string

Often, strings do not all follow a consistent format. There could be leading or trailing spaces in strings or them having different cases. All of these will lead to the strings to be considered distinct and separate. For example, if there was a string called book and another string called BOOK, they would be considered different. Using the following functions, we can standardize the string in our dataset:

- `LOWER`: This follows the syntax `LOWER(string)`. It will return the string in all lowercase, for example, `LOWER("Book") = book`.
- `UPPER`: This follows the syntax `UPPER(string)`. It will return the strings in all uppercase, for example, `UPPER("Book")= BOOK`.
- `TRIM`: This follows the syntax `TRIM(string)` and removes both leading and trailing spaces from a string, for example, `TRIM(" Book ") = Book`.

Similar to `TRIM`, there are `LTRIM` and `RTRIM`, which follow the same syntax but only remove spaces from the left of the string or the right of the string.

Other important string functions

- LEN: This follows the syntax LEN(string). Length is used to find the number of characters in a string. It counts the number of spaces as a character within a string. For example, LEN("Hi There") is 8: 2 for Hi, 1 for space, and 5 for There.
- REPLACE: This follows the syntax REPLACE(string, substring, replacement). REPLACE is used to replace every occurrence of the substring in a string with the replacement, for example, to replace occurrences of special characters such as / or ' in the string, such as Replace([Customer Name],"/","").

Another example would be if someone changed their name. You could replace their name with the new one. Let's replace Aaron Bergman's name with Aaron B. Create a new calculation using REPLACE as follows: REPLACE([Customer Name], "Aaron Bergman", "Aaron B"). The result of this calculation can be seen in the following screenshot:

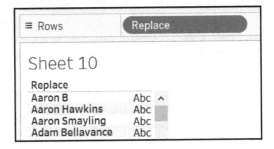

Now that we have made ourselves familiar with the important string calculations, let's look at date calculations in the next section.

Building date calculations

Date calculations allow us to perform operations on dates, such as adding or subtracting dates and obtaining parts of dates. Let's look at some of the key functions in the following sections.

Obtaining the current date/time

Today() returns the current date in Tableau and NOW() can be used to return the current date-time. A common use case of this is to find the time taken between an event occurrence and today.

Obtaining parts of a date

- DAY(), MONTH() and YEAR(): They share the syntax of function (date). They can be used for obtaining the day, month, and year part of the date as integers respectively. For example, DAY(#24-05-2019#) returns 24.
- DATEPART: It follows the syntax: DATEPART(date_part,date,[start_of_week]). If the start of the week is not mentioned, then it is determined based on the start day defined in the data source. For example, DATEPART(week,#24-05-2019#) returns 21.
- DATENAME: The syntax remains the same as DATENAME as DATEPART(date_part,date,[start_of_week]). It is very similar to DATEPART. The key difference is that it will return the values as a string. For example, DATENAME("month",#24-05-2019#) returns May.
- DATETRUNC: The syntax is the same as DATEPART and DATENAME, as follows: DATETRUNC(date_part, date,[start_of_week]). It allows us to not just obtain a date_part but rather truncate the date to that date_part. The syntax is the same as DATEPART and DATENAME, as follows: DATETRUNC(date_part, date,[start_of_week]). For example, DATETRUNC("month",#24-05-2019#) returns 01-05-2019 00:00:00.

Other date calculations

- ISDATE: This follows the syntax ISDATE(string). It returns TRUE if the string is a date otherwise, it returns FALSE, for example, ISDATE("24-05-2019")= TRUE.
- DATEPARSE: This follows the syntax DATEPARSE(format, string). It is used to convert a string into DATE in the format specified. For example, DATEPARSE("dd-MM-yyyy","24-05-2019) returns 24-05-2019 as a date.

- DATEADD: This follows the syntax DATEADD(date_part, interval, date). It adds the interval to date_part specified of the date. DATEADD is one of the most commonly used date functions.

Suppose there was an issue in the system and all of the order dates captured were wrong. They were actually a month before they are showing in the calculation. To get the right order dates, we create a calculation for Correct Order Date as DATEADD("month",-1,[Order Date]). Now, if we place the dates next to each other, we will obtain the following:

- DATEDIFF: This follows the syntax `DATEDIFF(date_part, start_date,end_date,[start_of_week])`. It returns the difference between the two dates in terms of the units of `date_part`. For example, if we wanted to calculate the time to ship orders after they are ordered in months, we can calculate `Shipping Time` as `DATEDIFF("month", [Order Date],[Ship Date])`. Once created, if we look at the total time spent in months across all shipping categories, we get the following:

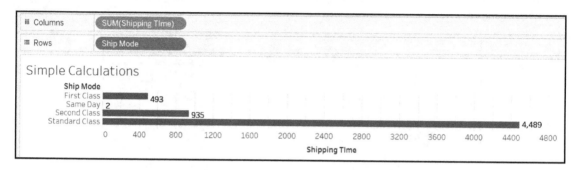

As you can see, same-day delivery is super-fast, so even after combining all of the orders, shipping only took 2 months. On the other hand, 4,489 months was spent in shipping orders by standard class.

In the past few sections, we have covered numeric, string, and date calculations. In the next section, we will focus on building logical statements. Logical statements work with numbers, strings, and dates and can be used in combination with the calculations we have learned so far.

Building logical statements

Logical functions allow you to check conditions and see whether they are true or false. We will take a look at the various categories of logical functions over the coming sections.

Case statements

Case statements make use of the following syntax: `CASE <expression> WHEN <value1> THEN <return1> WHEN <value2> THEN <return2> ... ELSE <default return> END`.

In case statements, the value of the expression is matched to each of the values and whenever a match is found, the return value corresponding to it is returned. If no value matches the expression, then the default else value is returned. If there is no default value, null values will be returned.

Case statements are very useful when you have to compare the same expression against multiple values. An example would be if we wanted to assign numbers to some of the markets. We can create a calculation as shown in the following screenshot:

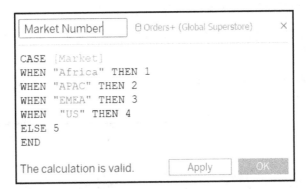

Now, if we place both **Market** and **Market Number** next to one another, we can see the groups:

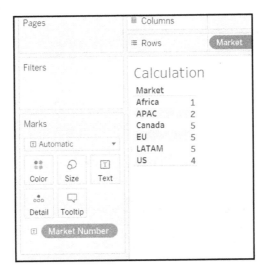

As an independent exercise, create a case statement giving each day of the week a number.

IF statement

An IF statement has the following syntax: IF <expr> THEN <then> [ELSEIF <expr2> THEN <then2>...] [ELSE <else>] END.

Using an IF statement, we can test a series of conditions, and based on whether the condition is true, the values are returned; otherwise, the next condition is tested. This continues until no condition is true, in which case, the default condition's value is represented; otherwise, it is returned. If there is no default condition, then null is returned.

Within IF statements, multiple conditions can also be combined using OR and AND operators.

For example, if we wanted to group sales into categories of high, medium, and low, we could create a calculation such as the following:

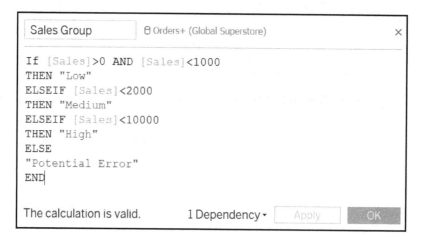

Here, you can see we have grouped any sales that are greater than 0 and less than 1,000 dollars as being in the category of low, anything up to 2,000 dollars is medium, from 2,000-10,000 is high, and all other values we assume are potential errors, either from the sales value being too high or being under 0, which we might need to recheck.

Now, counting the number of order IDs by each **Sales Group**, we can see that the bulk of the orders are for the **Low** category, followed by the **High** category, and there are only five potential error cases, as shown in the following screenshot:

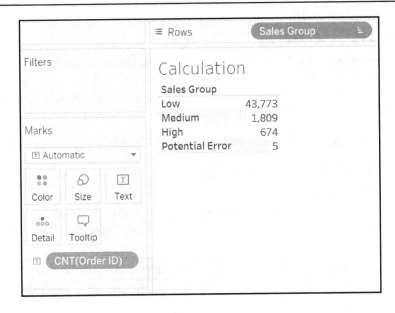

As an exercise, create similar calculations for the profit ranges.

IIF

IIF is similar to IF for one condition. It follows the syntax: IIF(test, then, else, [unknown]). Here, it will test a condition and if the condition is true, the statement returns the then value; otherwise, it returns the else value. If the else value is not specified, NULL will be returned, for example, IIF([Sales]>0,"Valid","Invalid").

IFNULL and ISNULL

Both IFNULL and ISNULL are used to test whether an expression is null or not.

IFNULL: It follows the syntax: IFNULL(expr1,expr2), and it returns expression 1 if the value is null and expression 2 if it is not. For example, IFNULL([Sales],0) will return the value of Sales where it is not null, else return 0.

ISNULL: ISNULL follows the syntax: ISNULL(expr). It returns TRUE if the expression is NULL. For example, ISNULL([Sales]) will return true if Sales is null.

Other functions

Beyond the functions discussed so far, there are some other important functions that are useful and available in Tableau. One of those is the type conversion functions. Type conversion functions are useful for converting one data type into another, for example, from an integer into a string or from a float into an integer.

All of the following functions follow the common syntax of `Function(expression)`:

DATE	It is used to obtain a date from numbers or strings or date expressions, for example, `DATE("25/05/2019")` returns `#25-05-2019#`.
DATETIME	Very similar to `DATE`, this function returns the date and time, for example, `DATETIME("25 May 2019 13:40:00")` returns `#25-05-2019 13:40:00#`.
FLOAT	This is used to cast to floating-point numbers, for example, `FLOAT(2)=2.000`.
INT	This is used to cast its argument to integers, for example `INT("22")=22` or `INT(22.2)=22`.
STR	This is used to cast values to a string, for example, `STR(22)` results in a string, `22`.

For example, if there is number field `12` and another number field, `22`, and we want to obtain the concatenated field `1222`, we can convert them into strings and back into numbers as `INT( (STR(12)+STR(22))` and it will return `1222` as a number. Type conversions can help many times when we need to create complex calculations and need the output of one field to be in the correct format to be the input of another.

User functions are another set of useful Tableau functions. These are useful to create row-level filters and security to limit the fields that are visible if your dashboard is published to Tableau Online or Server. Tableau also allows for some regular expression functionalities in functions such as `REGEXP_MATCH` or `REGEXP_EXTRACT`, which can be used to create some advanced string matching. Also, in the next chapter, we will study some advanced table calculation functions that haven't been discussed so far.

One last thing we will discuss in this chapter will be totals and subtotals and how they can be used.

Building grand totals and subtotals

Beyond showing the values from calculations, sometimes, we also want to show the values of the totals or subtotals in the same window as these values.

For instance, we have the following graph for **SUM(Sales)** split by **Category** and **Sub-Category** across segments:

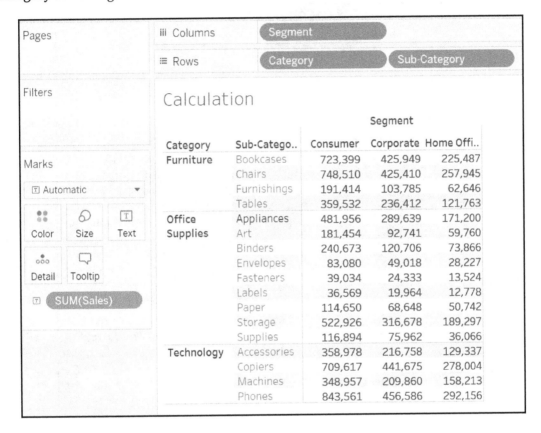

Now, if we want to add the subtotals and the grand totals for both rows and columns, we can do the following:

1. Go to **Analysis > Totals**.
2. Select **Show Row Totals | Show Column Totals**. This will show the graph as follows:

iii Columns — Segment

≡ Rows — Category — Sub-Category

Calculation

Category	Sub-Catego..	Segment Consumer	Corporate	Home Offi..	Grand Tot..
Furniture	Bookcases	723,399	425,949	225,487	1,374,835
	Chairs	748,510	425,410	257,945	1,431,865
	Furnishings	191,414	103,785	62,646	357,845
	Tables	359,532	236,412	121,763	717,708
Office Supplies	Appliances	481,956	289,639	171,200	942,794
	Art	181,454	92,741	59,760	333,955
	Binders	240,673	120,706	73,866	435,244
	Envelopes	83,080	49,018	28,227	160,325
	Fasteners	39,034	24,333	13,524	76,891
	Labels	36,569	19,964	12,778	69,311
	Paper	114,650	68,648	50,742	234,040
	Storage	522,926	316,678	189,297	1,028,901
	Supplies	116,894	75,962	36,066	228,923
Technology	Accessories	358,978	216,758	129,337	705,073
	Copiers	709,617	441,675	278,004	1,429,296
	Machines	348,957	209,860	158,213	717,031
	Phones	843,561	456,586	292,156	1,592,304
Grand Total		6,101,204	3,574,126	2,161,010	11,836,341

3. Now if we want to see the subtotals too, we can select **Add All Subtotals** from **Analysis | Tools**. This will show the following:

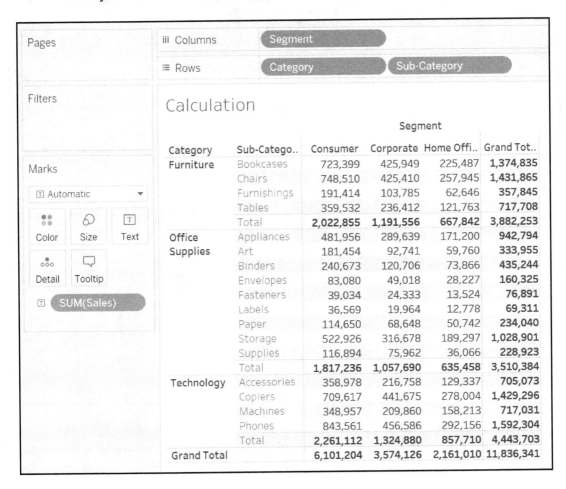

If there is more than one dimension for which the subtotals are being calculated, then we can right-click on the dimensions to select or unselect, depending on whether we want the totals to be calculated or not.

For example, adding city to the previous and adding all subtotals creates the following:

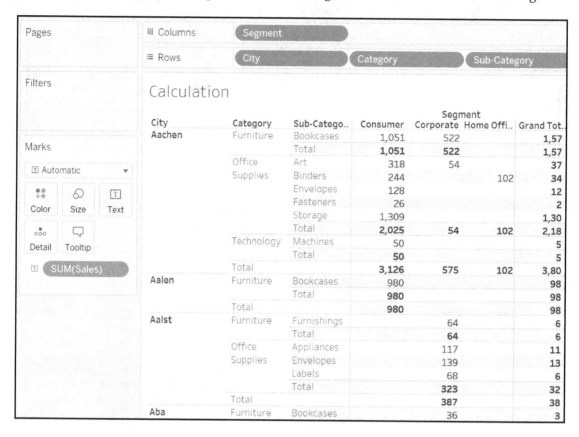

Now, if we do not want to see the subtotals at the level of **Categories**, then right-click on **Category** in the **Rows** shelf and uncheck **Subtotals**, as shown in the following screenshot:

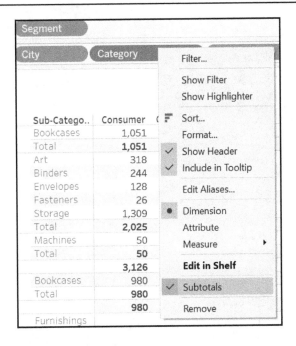

This will remove the subtotals from the level of **Category**. Another way to create totals and subtotals is to use the **Analytics Window | Totals**.

Summary

In this chapter, we have learned how to create simple calculations. We looked at the format and syntax requirements for the various elements of calculations. Following that, we looked in detail at some of the important functions and examples of number, string, date, and logical functions. Lastly, we also learned how to add totals and subtotals to our calculations. In the next chapter, we will learn about more advanced table calculations, where we will use the results of the calculations learned in this chapter to build on further calculations.

Further reading

To look at a list of all available functions in Tableau, go to the following link: `https://help.tableau.com/current/pro/desktop/en-us/functions_all_categories.htm`.

Section 3: Advanced Tableau 3

This section includes advanced Tableau topics such as table calculations, level of detail expressions, and Tableau analytics capabilities such as trend lines, forecasting, and clustering. In addition, you will learn how to build and use dashboards. Finally, you will practice with sample exams that closely resemble the actual exam.

This section comprises the following chapters:

- Chapter 6, *Tableau Table Calculations*
- Chapter 7, *Level of Detail Expressions*
- Chapter 8, *Leveraging Analytics Capabilities*
- Chapter 9, *Building Your Dashboards*

6
Tableau Table Calculations

In the previous chapter, we learned how to create some simple calculations in Tableau. However, sometimes we might want to use the results of those calculations to create new insights. For instance, at this point in the book, we can use the knowledge we have gained thus far to create fields to show the total number of sales by customer and add calculations to show the average sales for a line item, but we can't use the results of the sales by customer to show the average overall sales by customer. This is where **table calculations** come in, enabling us to use the results of our prior calculations as input for new ones.

The following topics will be covered in this chapter:

- General table calculations and background
- Creating quick table calculations
- Customizing table calculations
- Setting up manual table calculations
- Practical examples

Technical requirements

This chapter uses the Global Superstore dataset, which can be found at `http://www.tableau.com/sites/default/files/training/global_superstore.zip`.

General table calculations and background

A table calculation is a way to take the results of usual calculations, as defined in the previous chapters, and perform additional calculations based on those results (and not on the underlying data).

Let's take an example of a table calculation that looks at the average of SUM(Profit) by Year (Order Date) (we will learn how to create such a calculation later in this chapter):

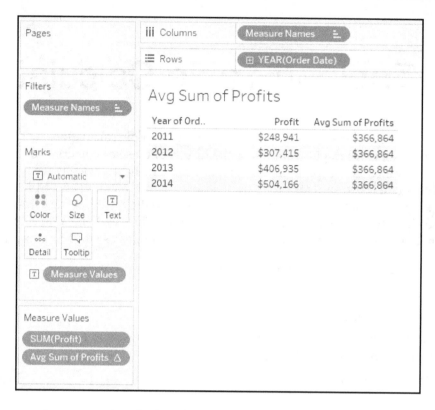

In this instance, the average is calculated by looking at the aggregated marks (in this case, (**$248,941+$307,415+$406,935+$504,166**)/4 = **$366,864**), not by averaging the profits in the underlying data.

There are two main components to a table calculation in Tableau. The first element is the calculation that we want to perform on those marks (in this case, a straight average on the marks). The second is the **scope** (or **partition**), which we will look at in the next section.

Structure of a view

A Tableau worksheet view can be broken down into three main levels, as shown in the following screenshot:

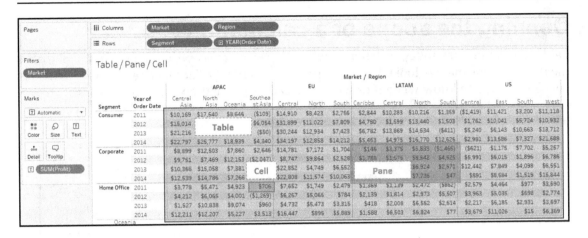

While the **Table** represents the entire view, a **Pane** is the part of the view corresponding to an intersection of dimensions in the rows and columns that is delimited by a **dividing line**. For instance, in this example, there are 12 panes because there are 4 divided column sections and 3 row sections, and therefore, there are 12 intersections.

Lastly, the **Cell** is the smallest intersection of dimensions, and there are 180 of them in the preceding view. In this case, the cell consists of one single mark (a text value), but a cell can include multiple marks, as shown in the following screenshot:

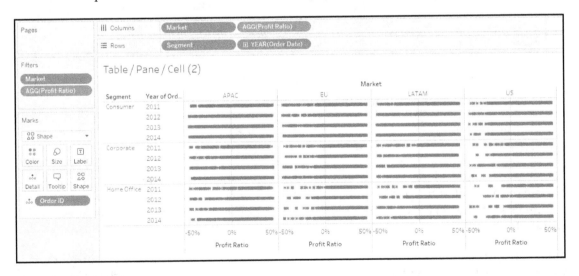

Let's see how these different partitions interact with table calculations.

Defining the scope of a calculation

Table calculations are always calculated within a particular scope, which is usually one of the three options that we looked at in the previous section (a **Table**, **Pane**, or **Cell**); this enables Tableau to know when if or when to reset the calculation at a certain point.

Let's use our previous example and introduce Segment:

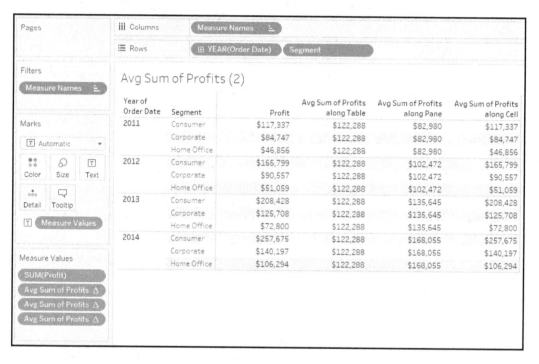

In this case, the same calculation can take one value for the entire table (**along Table**), or be calculated within every pane (**along Pane**) or every cell (**along Cell**).

Some options also include a direction: **Down**, **Across** (which resets when you get to the bottom or the right of the partition) or combinations, such as **Across, then Down** (which continues with the next row, rather than stopping at the end of the current one, while within the scope).

Finally, table calculations are sometimes computed relative to another cell. For instance, if we are calculating a percentage difference, we have to specify which cell is the reference for the calculation. This can be within the scope, the first or the last, the previous or the next, or the cell corresponding to a specific value of a dimension (for example, relative to the value associated with the year 2011).

To summarize, table calculations are further computations on the aggregated results of our simple calculations, defined within a certain scope. Now that we have some context for table calculations, let's start to set some up.

Creating quick table calculations

The easiest way to create a table calculation is to start with the **Quick Table Calculations** options.

Every pill representing a measure (including a count or distinct counts of dimensions), whether discrete or continuous, holds the **Quick Table Calculation** option in its own menu:

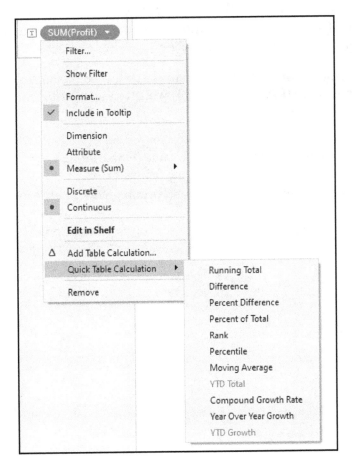

Using one of the options presented here will replace the current aggregation with a table calculation, and the pill will then include a Δ sign to signify that the calculation is now a table calculation. Let's go through the different options available.

Different options for quick calculations

There are 11 options in total to create quick table calculations:

- **Running Total** progressively sums the aggregated marks within the partition and along a direction (across or down).
- **Difference** is the absolute difference between the mark and a reference mark: (Mark - Reference).
- **Percent Difference** states the relative difference: (Mark - Reference) / Reference.
- **Percent of Total** shows the contribution of the current mark to the total aggregation of marks within the scope.

> **Percent of Total** calculations can also be turned on via **Analysis |**
> **Percentage Of | ...**, although this will affect all measures.

- **Rank** ranks the cells based on their value (with different options for how to differentiate between cells with equal values).
- **Percentile** represents how many cells within the scope are lower than the current value.
- **Moving Average** averages a set number of previous and next values.

Finally, there are four time-based quick table calculations:

- **YTD** (Year To Date) **Total** is a running sum that restarts every year.
- **Compound Growth Rate** computes the growth rate r relative to the first value so that $n^{th}value = (1+r)^{n-1} \times 1^{st}value$. This is used to decide what the growth factor would have been, had the evolution been perfectly steady.
- **Year Over Year Growth** calculates a percentage difference compared to the same period in the previous year.
- **YTD Growth** creates a percentage difference compared to the **YTD Total** in the previous year.

It is important to note that **YTD** calculations require a discrete date field with granularity strictly finer than a year (for instance, Year, Quarter, Month, or Year, Month), while the **Year Over Year Growth** requires a discrete date field that can be a year or finer.

It is possible to drag a pill that includes a table calculation back into the **Data** pane to create a calculated field based on the current definition of the table calculation. Editing a table calculation created this way helps you understand how Tableau performs the calculation under the hood.

If at any point you want to revert to the original calculation, you can use the **Clear Table Calculation** option when right-clicking the pill.

Now that a quick calculation has been turned on, let's see how we can change the different parameters to take control of this out-of-the-box calculation.

Customizing table calculations

One of the first things that users want to do after creating a quick table calculation is to update the scope of the calculation, as the default choice was not necessarily what they had in mind.

Adapting a % Difference Calculation

Let's plot `Profit` by `Year(Order Date)` in rows and `Quarter(Order Date)` in columns, create a quick calculation for **% Difference**, and add `Profit` back into the view by double-clicking on the field in the **Data** pane (as the table calculation will take over the original `Profit` field, and it is not possible to add the same calculation twice):

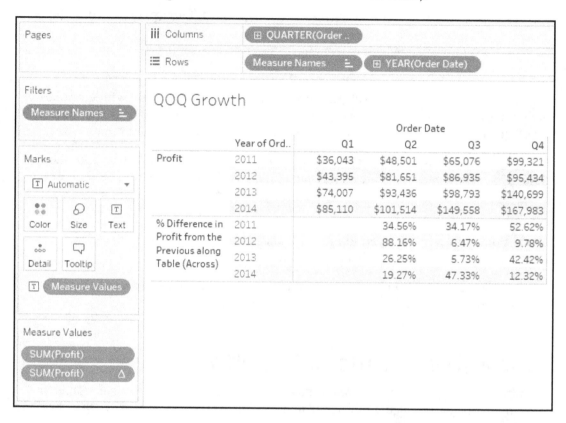

Tableau's default choice was to compute this table calculation along **Table (across)** and relative to the **Previous** value, which shows us quarter-over-quarter growth, but not between Q4 and Q1. When Tableau runs across the table, its instructions are only to go across. When it can't go any further, it will reset and restart at the next row. If we wanted to see the growth relative to the first quarter of 2011 instead, we would need to perform two actions, which we will look at in the following sections.

Defining a percent difference versus the first cell in the partition

First, we should change the calculation so that it's relative to the **First** rather than the **Previous**. This can be achieved by right-clicking the pill under the **Relative to** option, as shown in the following screenshot:

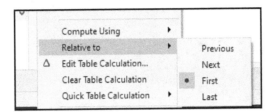

This will make it so that each line compares the current value to the first in the line (in this case, the **Q1** of the given year). If we want it to compare all lines to the first value of the first line (that is, **Q1 2011**) instead, we can change **Compute Using** to **Table (Down then Across)** in the same pill menu.

 Sometimes, some of the options for **Compute using** (for instance **Pane (across)**) will not appear. That is because that option is not relevant to your current view, and is probably already covered by another choice, for example **Table (across).**

In this instance, you can also choose **Down then Across:** as we are comparing with the first value in the table and not the previous or next, the order is less important:

Growth vs Q1 2011					
			Order Date		
	Year of Ord..	Q1	Q2	Q3	Q4
Profit	2011	$36,043	$48,501	$65,076	$99,321
	2012	$43,395	$81,651	$86,935	$95,434
	2013	$74,007	$93,436	$98,793	$140,699
	2014	$85,110	$101,514	$149,558	$167,983
% Difference in Profit from the First along Table (Across then Down)	2011	0.00%	34.56%	80.55%	175.56%
	2012	20.40%	126.54%	141.20%	164.78%
	2013	105.33%	159.23%	174.10%	290.36%
	2014	136.13%	181.65%	314.94%	366.06%

All calculations are now relative to Q1 2011, which is what we wanted.

Using a different order

If we changed the options to **Compute Using Table (Down then Across)** and **Relative to Next**, we could get drastically different results:

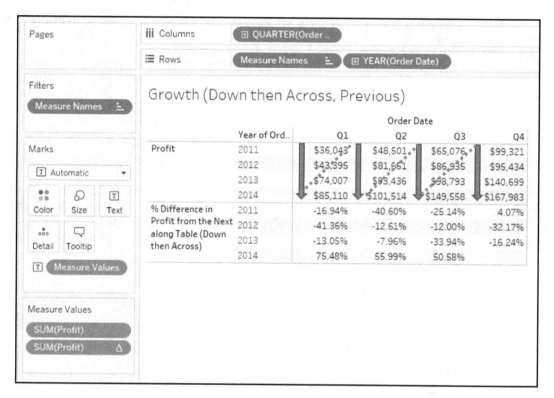

Because we are going **Down then Across**, we are calculating a percentage difference for all quarters compared to the next year (going down takes us through the years for a given quarter). The exception is for Q1–Q3 2014, where we would get the difference compared to the next quarter in *2011*; because there is no following year for the given quarter, we are going across to the first year of the following quarter. In this case, we are comparing **$85,110** in Q1 2014 to **$48,501** in Q2 2011.

We cannot stress enough that the order is very important if we want to get meaningful results.

It is also possible to change those options from the **Edit Table Calculation** window, which you can find when right-clicking the pill.

Now that we've learned how to create quick table calculations, let's see if you can get more depth by creating manual table calculations, which will, for instance, allow us to compute an average of all the marks in the view.

Setting up manual table calculations

While it is possible to create some table calculations easily with the quick options, there are times when an off-the-shelf calculation cannot fit your needs. In this case, you need to create a manual table calculation. This is done by creating a calculated field.

As a reminder, you can create a calculated field by any one of the following three methods:

- Go to **Analysis | Create Calculated Field...** in the menu bar.
- Right-click any field in the **Data** pane and use the **Create | Calculated Field...** option.
- Click the arrow next to the search icon in the **Data** pane, close to **Dimensions**, and use **Create Calculated Field...**.

There, you can define your function manually and choose **Default Table Calculation** options once the calculation is valid. Let's go over the three main types of functions that are available to users.

Creating functions similar to quick table calculations

There are two ranges of functions available that work in a very similar way to some of the quick options.

The first range is the RUNNING functions, including RUNNING_SUM, RUNNING_COUNT, and so on. These functions aggregate the results that are in cells in the current partition by starting with the first one and running along, updating the calculation and aggregating the results for each new cell. While the running sum is the most obvious example, and is one of the available quick calculations, it can sometimes be useful to use another running function to provide results. For instance, the RUNNING_MAX function is useful when keeping track of a record, as the function will update to the largest value up to the point of the calculation.

When creating a table calculation, it is imperative that you use an aggregation inside of the function, as the syntax checker will remind you.

For instance, if we wanted to keep track of our record line profit, we could create `Record Line Profit` as `RUNNING_MAX(MAX([Profit])` and add it to a view with `MAX(Profit)` by `Year (Order Date)` and `Quarter (Order Date)`. This will show the record to date for the largest line profit (**$2,939** until Q2 2011, then **$4,630** until Q3 2013, and so on).

The second type of function that should be familiar is the `RANK` functions, including `RANK`, `RANK_DENSE`, and so on. These functions will, as their name suggests, rank the results in the cells based on a given order (either descending (the default) or ascending, as defined by the second argument of the function). Here is a quick summary of how the different functions will rank the same set of data (10, 10, 15, 20) in ascending order:

Function	How 10, 10, 15, 20 are ranked in ascending order	Comment
RANK	1, 1, 3, 4	Same rank (highest) for equal values
RANK_DENSE	1, 1, 2, 3	Same rank (highest) for equal values; no gap
RANK_MODIFIED	2, 2, 3, 4	Same rank (lowest) for equal values
RANK_UNIQUE	1, 2, 3, 4	Unique rank
RANK_PERCENTILE	50, 50, 75, 100	Percentile rank (% of values equal or below this)

Using the Lookup function

When Tableau computes a table calculation for **Percent Difference** against the previous value, it actually uses one base table calculation function inside a more complicated calculation. If you wanted to drag and drop a **Percent Difference** calculation into the **Dimensions** pane and later **Edit** that calculation, the resulting formula would look something like the following (simplified for our purposes):

```
( (SUM([Sales]) - LOOKUP(SUM([Sales]), -1) ) / LOOKUP(SUM([Sales]), -1)
```

Here, we can see that we are making the most of a function called LOOKUP (expr, offset), which returns the value of the calculation specified by expr in a given cell, and more specifically of LOOKUP (expr, -1) to grab the results of the expression in the previous cell.

When specifying the offset in the second part of the function to tell Tableau which cell to refer to, we can use simple numbers *relative* to the current cell, with negative numbers representing previous cells and positive ones representing the next cells. In the last example, we used -1 for the previous cell, but it could also be 2 for the cell that is two rows after the current one. If there would be no such cells (because they would be out of bounds), the result would be NULL.

> Because the results of these can be NULL, Tableau generally uses a function called ZN (expr), which returns the results of the expression if it is not NULL, and 0 otherwise. This would be the case when looking at the **Percent Difference** formula.

Finally, we also have the option of using FIRST() and LAST() for an *absolute* position, to specify that we are after the results that are in the first or last row of the current partition. For instance, LOOKUP (SUM([Sales]), LAST()-1) would return the sales in the second to last row of the partition.

Defining Window functions

The last type of function that is very useful in Tableau, and especially in the exam, are Window functions. These are a set of functions that includes WINDOW_SUM, WINDOW_COUNT, WINDOW_AVERAGE, and so on. These functions all work in a similar manner. The basic syntax for these functions is WINDOW_SUM(expr, [start,end]).

There are two main ways to use these functions. The first is to use the calculation without specifying a start or an end in the second part. In this case, the function will perform the specified aggregation, for instance SUM, against all rows that are currently in the partition (as defined by the **Compute using** option when right-clicking the pill). We will use this technique in the second practical example at the end of this chapter.

Additionally, we can, of course, specify the start and end, which will calculate the specified option only within the desired range. For instance, WINDOW_AVG(expr,-1,1) will average the results of the previous, current, and next cell. We just created a moving average for three periods!

As was the case with LOOKUP, we can also make the most of the FIRST() and LAST() functions. For example, WINDOW_SUM(expr,FIRST(),0) will sum all cells between the first and the current cells. We just set up a running sum!

With this last set of useful manual alternatives, our exploration of the different options to create table calculations draws to a close. Let's now practice our newly acquired talents with some exercises.

Practical examples

Before concluding this chapter, let's go over two quick examples that are based on questions that were used in real exams.

Moving average

Using Global Superstore, as of June 2012, what is the sum of the sales of the previous twelve months and the following twelve months, excluding the current month?

To do this, we start by plotting SUM(Sales) by Month(Order Date). Then we create a quick table calculation for **Moving Average** by right-clicking the pill.

 To add Month(Order Date) as shown in the following screenshot, you can drop Order Date in rows, then click on the pill menu for the second **Month** option (the one that reads a month and year) and change the pill to **Discrete** (in the pill menu).

The default calculation averages the values of the month in focus and the two previous ones, but we can go to **Edit Table Calculation** in the pill menu to specify that we want a **Sum** for the previous 12 values, and the next 12 values and untick **Current value** to exclude it from the calculation.

Then we add SUM(Sales) again alongside the calculation:

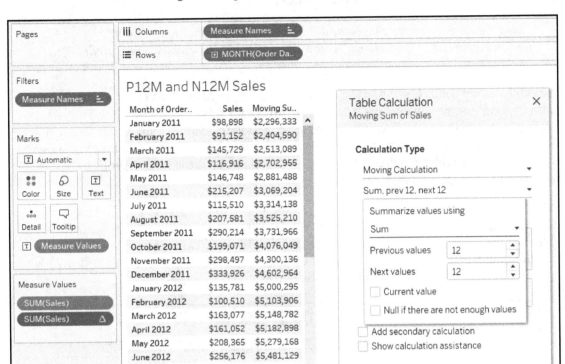

From there, we can immediately see that the required sum was **$5,481,129** for June 2012.

Dropping the calculation in the data pane tells us that we could also have defined a manual table calculation that read
WINDOW_SUM(SUM([Sales]), -12, -1) +
WINDOW_SUM(SUM([Sales]), 1, 12),
which sums Sales for the previous 12 values (offset -12 to -1) and the next 12 values (offset 1 to 12).

Difference in average profit

Using Global Superstore, what is the difference between the average profit for **Furniture** *orders for customer* **Aaron Bergman** *and the lowest average profit worldwide for any customer/category combination?*

We can first plot the average `Profit`, slicing by `Category` and `Customer`. In this case, we want to compare the **$79** average profit in **Furniture** for this customer with the lowest average profit in the table. Because of the number of marks (more than 2,000), this is not a very easy task if we are just using the tools that we have learned about so far. Just showing `MIN([Profit])` will not help us, since this will just show us the lowest profit for a line item, not the lowest customer average.

Let's define `Lowest Average Profit` as `WINDOW_MIN(AVG([Profit]))` by creating a calculated field and adding it to the view. By default, the calculation shows the lowest value for the customer because the **Compute using** is set as **Table (across)**, which means that the calculation restarts for every row. Changing this to **Table (across then down)** will ensure that the calculation encompasses the entire table:

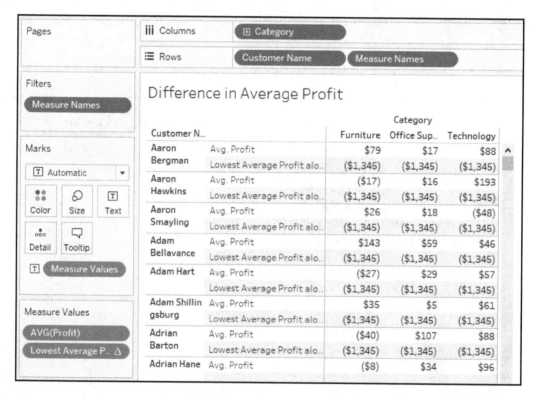

It is now easy to calculate that the required difference is **$79 - ($1,345) = $1,424**. Should we not feel in the mood for this simple calculation, we can also define `Lowest Average Profit` as `AVG([Profit]) - WINDOW_MIN(AVG([Profit]))` instead, which will display the result immediately.

With this, we conclude this chapter on table calculations, having run through two examples illustrating some of the simple and more advanced options available.

Summary

In this chapter, we covered table calculations, which enable us to use the results of our prior calculations as input for new ones. We learned how to create simple calculations with the click of a button, how to change their scope and customize them, and how to use them to create new and more complex calculations. After learning about simple aggregations in the previous chapter, this chapter serves as a good introduction to Tableau's most daunting element when coming from Excel or other BI tools: level of detail calculations. These will be covered in the next chapter, where we will learn how to make use of information that is not visible in the current views.

Questions

Answer the following questions to test your knowledge of the information in this chapter.

Q: Is it true that table calculations take into account the underlying data and can help create weighted averages?

A: No, table calculations use the results of prior aggregations as input for new ones, so a table calculation for an average will do a straight average of the results within the scope, not a weighted average. For an example, please refer to the first section of this chapter.

Q: One of the options for quick table calculations is **Total Sum** of all values. True or False?

A: False. The different options are listed in the chapter, although you could use one of the manual `Window` functions to achieve this result.

Q: Table calculations can also be created on dimensions. True or False?

A: True. You can create table calculations on counts and distinct counts of dimensions.

Further reading

You can check out the following links for more information about the topics that were covered in this chapter:

- **Different types of addressing**: `https://help.tableau.com/current/pro/desktop/en-us/calculations_tablecalculations.htm#table-across`
- **Using specific dimensions**: `https://help.tableau.com/current/pro/desktop/en-us/calculations_tablecalculations.htm#specific-dimensions`
- **Top 10 Table Calculations**: `https://www.tableau.com/about/blog/2019/11/top-10-tableau-table-calculations`
- **Table Calculations White Paper**: `https://www.tableau.com/sites/default/files/pages/table_calcs_in_tableau_6.pdf`

Level of Detail Expressions

In the previous chapter, we covered table calculations, which are extremely useful when we want to aggregate information using exactly the data that is in the view, but sometimes we want to use more (or less) than the information that can be seen on the screen. For instance, if you want to show the average spend by customer, you don't want to show all customers and their value to compute an average. This is where **Level of Detail (LOD)** calculations, which we will introduce in this chapter, can be used, because they help us change the level of aggregation.

The following topics will be covered in this chapter:

- Tableau's order of operations
- FIXED LOD calculations
- INCLUDE LOD calculations
- EXCLUDE LOD calculations
- Data source constraints for LOD

Technical requirements

This chapter uses the Global Superstore dataset, which can be found at http://www.tableau.com/sites/default/files/training/global_superstore.zip.

Tableau's order of operations

Before delving deeper into LOD calculations, it is first important to understand Tableau's order of operations, as this will guide our conversation, seeing where this new topic fits in.

Surprising results

Especially when coming to Tableau from Excel or other BI tools, one is sometimes at a loss when dealing with Tableau's order of operations. What can seem intuitive is not always what is reflected. Applying the wrong type of filter, or not using the proper calculation, will result in meaningless results.

The following is one such scenario. In the Global Superstore dataset, we create a data source filter for `Country` to show United Kingdom orders only, a dimension filter for `State` Wales and a **Top 10 Customer Names by Sales** filter.

 As a reminder, you can set up a **Top** filter by using the **Top** option of the **Filter** window, and in this case selecting **By Field**, **Top 10**, **Sales**, and **Sum**.

Why should there be only one customer in the results when we have set a filter for the top 10?

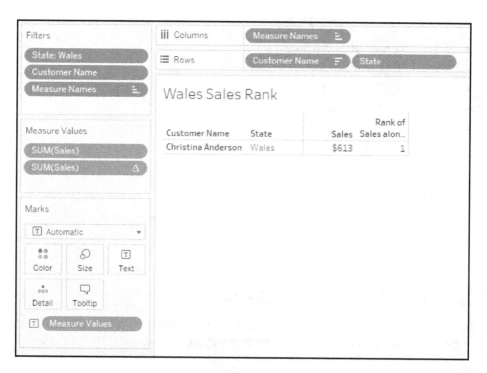

We will determine why we're not seeing the desired top 10 customers using the order of operations in the next section.

The order

In order to interpret this, let's look at the infamous order of operations with the elements that we are already familiar with at this point in the book:

1. Extract filters
2. Data source filters
3. Context filters
4. Sets, conditional, and top N filters
5. Dimension filters
6. Data blending
7. Measure filters
8. Totals
9. Table calculations

Operations in Tableau are performed in this order, starting from the top and making their way down.

First, we have **data source** or **extract** filters (depending on the type of connection used, whether **Live** or **Extract**), as described in Chapter 1, *Building Your Data Model*. These affect the entirety of your dataset at workbook level, before any specific filters that can be applied at worksheet level. As far as Tableau computation is concerned in the workbook, the filtered-out data doesn't even exist.

Context filters are similar to data source or extract filters, but are view-specific. They are generally used to speed up processing, because they can further reduce the scope of data, as if creating a temporary subset of it before generating the view. These are mainly useful to improve the performance of a view that will be category-specific (for example, sales of Copiers only), within a very large dataset that can't be filtered at workbook level.

Context filters can be created by selecting an existing dimension filter in the filters pane, and clicking the **Add to context** option. The blue pill will turn gray to signify that the filter is now a context filter.

Sets, dimension, and *measure* filters (including *conditional* and *top N* filters) have been described at length in Chapter 1, *Building Your Data Model*, and Chapter 2, *Working with Worksheets*, as is the case for *data blending* in Chapter 1, *Building Your Data Model*. Please refer to these chapters to clear up any remaining doubts on these subjects.

With the order of operations as it currently stands, it's worth realizing that table calculations (as described in the previous chapter) come last in the order, after totals (which represent the usual calculations used in Tableau). For example, if we are using a rank table calculation on **Customer Name** in a given **State**, the rank will include orders in that state and that state only, as table calculations come after dimension filters. The biggest customer in the dataset might just be the 10th customer in a particular region.

Now that we know about the order, let's go back to our previous example.

Explaining the surprising results

We now hold the tools to understand why only one customer shows up:

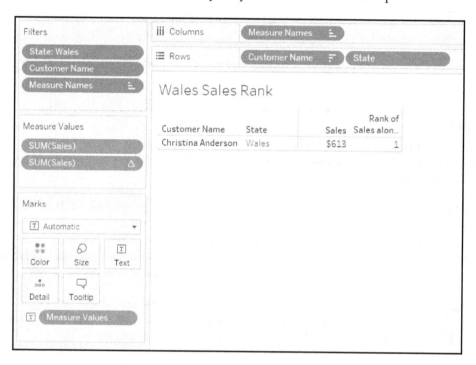

If we take a look at the order of operations, the top N filter comes before the dimension filter (in this case, for `State` Wales), but after the data Source filters (here, `Country` United Kingdom).

The sales shown in the results are therefore sales in Wales for customers that are in the top 10 *UK-wide*, not just in Wales. Nine of those customers have no sales in Wales, just in the other parts of the UK, and don't appear in our results.

If one wanted to see the top 10 customers in Wales for sales occurring there only, it is possible to promote the filter on `State` to be a context filter, moving it back up in the order of operations:

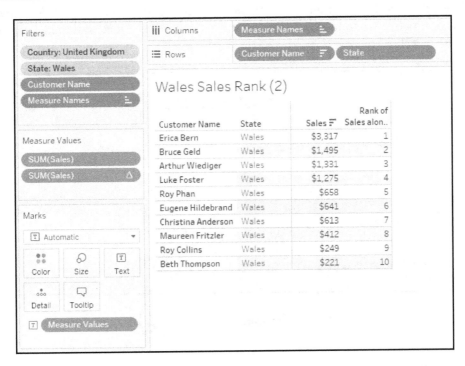

Now that we've covered the order of operations, let's dive into LOD functions, which are going to allow us to change levels of aggregation.

FIXED LOD calculations

`FIXED` is the first of three LOD calculations we will study in this chapter. It is used to make a calculation regardless of any dimension or measure filters that are applied in the workbook. The syntax of `FIXED` is the following: `{FIXED [dim1[, dim2]...] : aggregate-expression}`, with `[dim1[, dim2]...]` a list of dimensions along which the aggregation is to be calculated.

Please note the use of curly brackets. The syntax will be the same for all three LOD expressions we describe in this chapter.

For instance, let's look at the date of first order for a given customer. While a `MIN([Date])` calculation will give the first date *in the filtered dataset* with **Customer Name** used as a row or column, `{FIXED [Customer ID] :MIN([Date])}` will give the first date for a customer *in the entire dataset*, filters notwithstanding, for each `Customer ID`. As a result, if we look at orders in 2013 in the Global Superstore dataset, we notice that the `First Order Date` can be in 2011:

Let's now take a look at how this will be affected by the order of operations.

Order of operations

The place of this calculation in the order of operations is therefore the following:

1. Extract/data source filters
2. Context filters
3. Sets, conditional, and top N Filters, `FIXED` LOD calculations
4. Dimension filters
5. Data blending
6. Measure filters
7. Totals
8. Table calculations

Let's consider three examples to understand how to use this calculation.

Example 1 – lifetime sales value

Using the Global Superstore dataset, we want to represent the lifetime sales value of our low-profit subcategories in 2013.

We define a new calculated field, `Lifetime Sales Value`, as `{FIXED [Subcategories] : SUM([Sales])}`. This will calculate the total sales by subcategory, regardless of any dimension filters set. Therefore, if we filter for orders placed in 2013 as a dimension filter, and compute `Profit Ratio` (defined as `SUM([Profit]) / SUM([Sales])`), `Sales`, and `Lifetime Sales Value`, we have the following:

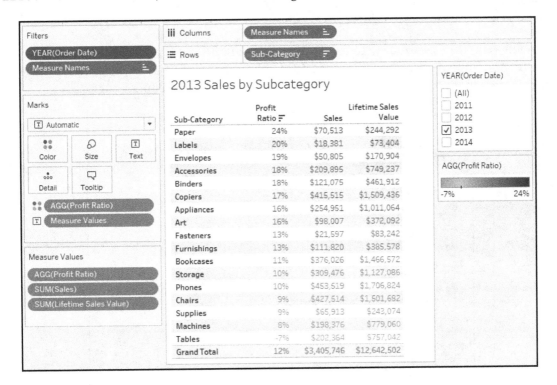

While the **Tables** subcategory is not profitable in 2013, with sales of $202,364, it generated $757,042 in sales across the whole dataset.

Example 2 – contributions

Using the Global Superstore dataset, we want to see the contribution of units ordered by country in the LATAM market, against both that region only and the whole company.

The list of dimensions in the `FIXED` syntax is optional. We can therefore define `Total Quantity` as `{FIXED:SUM([Quantity])}`. This will be the equivalent of having a quantity that is equal to the total units for each calculation. This will be a value that will never change regardless of the level of aggregation of our view.

We can then define `Worldwide Qty Contribution` as `SUM([Quantity])` / `ATTR([Total Quantity])` (as `Total Quantity` needs no aggregation).

 Here, we use `ATTR`, because otherwise we would get an error due to mixing aggregates and non-aggregates.

Showing `Quantity`, a window calculation for **Percent of Total** for `Quantity` that we can call `Region Qty Contribution` (along **Table (down)**) and the newly defined `Worldwide Qty Contribution`, and filtering for market **LATAM**, we get the following:

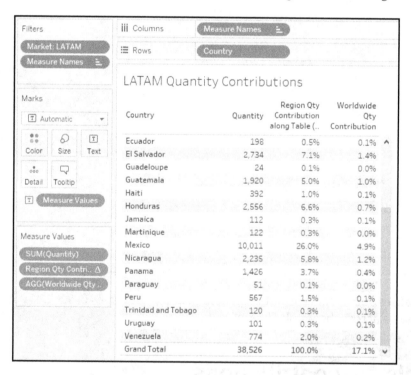

The results are different between the last two columns here because the table calculation only considers data in LATAM (because it comes after dimension filters in the order of operations), while the LOD calculation considers the entire dataset.

If we want to go a level further, we can make this a map view: remove the first two measures to keep only `Worldwide Qty Contribution`, click on **Show Me > Maps**, and finally choose the **Analysis > Show Mark Labels** options:

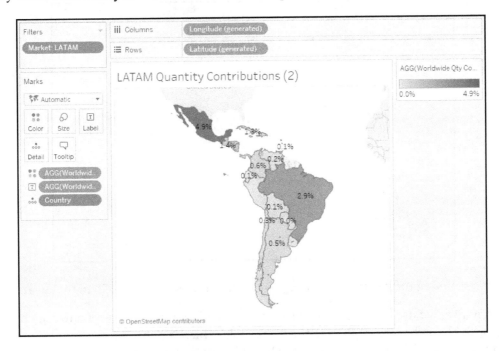

If we further filter the countries, we will still see their contribution to the worldwide market, contrary to a table calculation, which will consider only the filtered dataset.

Example 3 – cohorts

Using the Global Superstore dataset, we want to see how many sales were generated in 2012 for customers (`Customer ID`) making their first purchase (`Order Date`) in that year. This is what is usually called a **cohort analysis**, and is often seen in the exam.

For each customer, we first have to define their earliest date of purchase. To do so, we create a calculated `First Order Date` field as `{FIXED [Customer ID] : MIN([Order Date])}`. This will take the earliest `Order Date` in the entire dataset for each `Customer ID`.

We can then create a visualization with `Year([Order Date])` as columns, `Year([First Order Date])` as rows, and `SUM([Sales])` as measures. This gives the following:

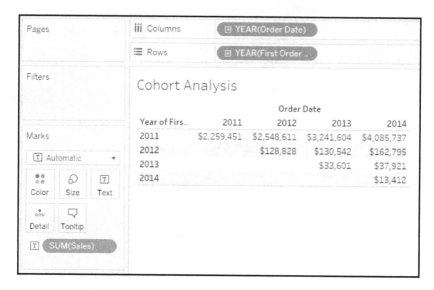

Customers making their first order in 2012 have therefore spent $128,828 in that year.

To summarize, we use the `FIXED` LOD to make a calculation regardless of any dimension or measure filters that are applied in the workbook, which is helpful for contributions, cohorts, or any calculation that has to take the entire dataset into account. Let's carry on with the second LOD calculation.

INCLUDE LOD calculations

The `INCLUDE` LOD calculation is used to add a layer of aggregation that will not be used as part of the dimensions. For instance, you might want to see the average customer's lifetime value in different markets. Under normal circumstances, you would need to first aggregate at customer level, and then use the results of that aggregation to compute an average. In the SQL world, we would use a subquery. Simply averaging all sales will not yield the same results, as it will be computed at the line item level and will therefore give the average value of a line item.

We can understand this by saying that we want to aggregate at a level that includes both the dimensions already in the view and another set of additional dimensions. This means that we have data that is more granular than what will be shown in the view, and therefore that we will need to further aggregate the results of that calculation to show them in the view. While the results of a FIXED calculation don't need to be aggregated, the results of an INCLUDE statement do.

As a reminder, the syntax is similar to FIXED statements: {INCLUDE [dim1[, dim 2]...] : aggregate-expression}. While the dimensions are technically optional parameters, there is no gain in using an INCLUDE function in that case, it is just computing the usual aggregation with no added granularity.

As for FIXED, it's important to see where this sits in the order of operations to optimize its use, before we carry on with examples.

Order of operations

This particular LOD function, as well as the EXCLUDE LOD calculation that will shortly follow, comes between data blending and measure filters. They are thus computed later than the FIXED calculation:

1. Extract/data source filters
2. Context filters
3. Sets, conditional, and top N filters, FIXED LOD calculations
4. Dimension filters
5. Data blending
6. INCLUDE and EXCLUDE LOD calculations
7. Measure filters
8. Totals
9. Table calculations

Example 1 – average customer lifetime value

Using the Global Superstore dataset, for the **Technology** category, we want to see the average lifetime sales value of customers, split by Segment and Market.

If we just calculate a straight AVG([Sales]), we get the following:

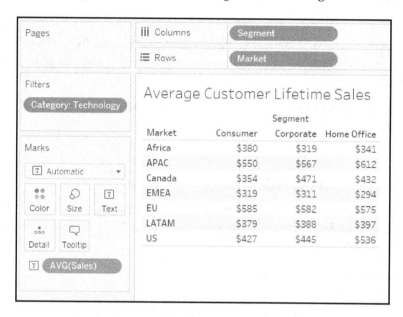

However, that is representing the average sales to customers *at the line item level*, not the lifetime value. If customer A has two orders for $100 and $200 and customer B has a sale for $300, the average sale is $200, but the average lifetime sales value is $300, as both customers have a lifetime value of $300. Here, we need to first compute the sales at customer level, and then average the results.

The dimension we're missing in the view is Customer Name. We will therefore create an INCLUDE statement as {INCLUDE [Customer Name]:SUM([Sales])}, which will create an intermediary calculation at customer level. The results of that calculation can then be aggregated using an AVG to yield the correct results:

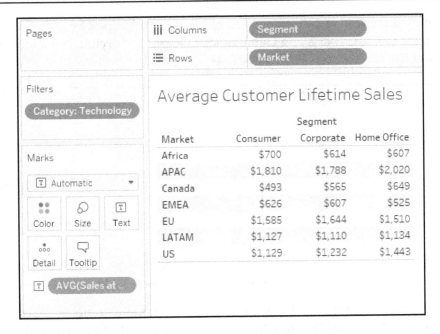

It is worth noting that if we are always going to average the lifetime sales value of a customer, we can enclose the INCLUDE statement in an AVG inside the **Calculated field**, and Tableau will recognize how to aggregate this without needing to specify it every time: AVG({INCLUDE [Customer Name]:SUM([Sales])}).

Example 2 – median of average days to ship by customer

The Global Superstore company is worried that some orders are being shipped late, and about the impact it might have on its customers. Let's look at Average Days to Ship by Customer Name for late orders.

If not already defined in the workbook, Average Days to Ship is calculated as DATEDIFF('day',[Order Date],[Ship Date]), and Ship Status as IF [Days to Ship (Actual)] > [Days to Ship (Scheduled)] THEN "Shipped Late"
ELSEIF [Days to Ship (Actual)] = [Days to Ship (Scheduled)] THEN "Shipped On Time"
ELSE "Shipped Early" END.

As seen in previous chapters, we can create a quick distribution plot by Segment and Market, using Customer Name as a **Detail** mark to see each individual customer, filtering for orders where Ship Status is **Shipped Late**:

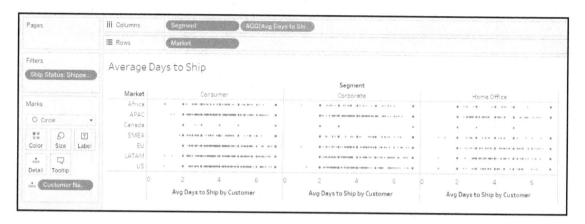

While it is sometimes worthwhile to see each customer, a top-line number for each quadrant can be a good indicator of performance. Let's choose the median as one such indicator. We now need to remove Customer Name as a dimension, but still keep it in the calculation to find the median.

Here, we can define MEDIAN({INCLUDE [Customer Name] : AVG([Days to Ship (Actual)])}).

Let's deconstruct this, starting from the right. Look at average days to ship. The view includes **Segment** and **Region**, so the aggregation would normally be performed at that level. However, we want to calculate this at customer level, so we create the INCLUDE statement, specifying that we want to add Customer Name to the list of dimensions even though it is not part of our view. Having results that are now too granular to be shown in the view, we choose to finally aggregate by taking the median of those results. If we create a quick view of that measure by Segment and Market, using the **Measure Values** as **Color** and the **Analysis > Show Mark Labels** option, we get the following:

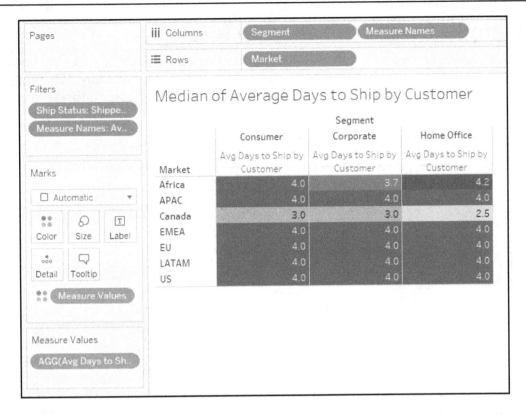

Median of Average Days to Ship by Customer

	Segment		
	Consumer	Corporate	Home Office
Market	Avg Days to Ship by Customer	Avg Days to Ship by Customer	Avg Days to Ship by Customer
Africa	4.0	3.7	4.2
APAC	4.0	4.0	4.0
Canada	3.0	3.0	2.5
EMEA	4.0	4.0	4.0
EU	4.0	4.0	4.0
LATAM	4.0	4.0	4.0
US	4.0	4.0	4.0

To summarize, we can use the INCLUDE LOD to first aggregate a level that is higher than the view, including some dimensions that are not present in it, that we can then aggregate back to the view level. This is useful when trying to extract and summarize order-level data from a dataset of item-level data. Let's study one last LOD calculation before closing off this chapter.

EXCLUDE LOD calculations

While INCLUDE LOD calculations enabled us to calculate along the view dimensions and the further dimensions specified, EXCLUDE LOD calculations enable users to make calculations omitting one of the dimensions that have been used in the view. For instance, we can use EXCLUDE to calculate the total sum of profits for one category across regions, even if Region is used as a row. This is especially useful when dealing with contributions to a total.

Example 1 – contribution to total

Using the Global Superstore dataset, we want to show contributions to total profit for the South region of the EU market, slicing by country, category, and subcategory. What is the contribution of the **Fasteners** subcategory in **Italy** to the overall Fasteners business in the South?

We can first plot profit by `Country` and `Sub-category` in the South, adding totals:

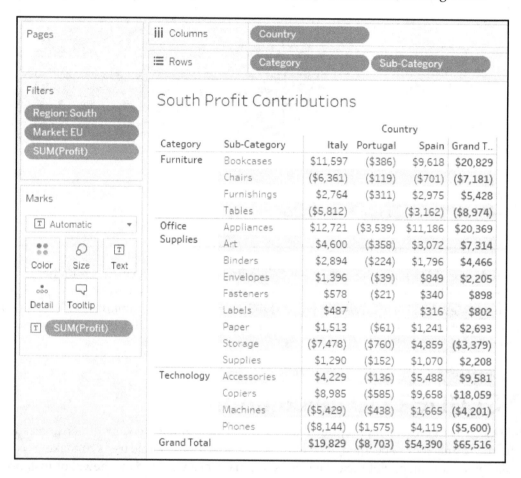

In the case of **Fasteners** in Italy, we want to see that it represents $578/$898 = 64% of the profit.

We have two ways of calculating that contribution. We can add a quick table calculation for **Percent of Total** for SUM(Profit), with computation along **Table (across)**.

We can also use an LOD, calculating the overall profit for a subcategory as {EXCLUDE [Country]: Sum([Profit])}, which will remove the dependency on Country, but not on Sub-category. As a result, we can further define SUM([Profit]) / ATTR({EXCLUDE [Country]: Sum([Profit])}) as the contribution of one country to the overall region:

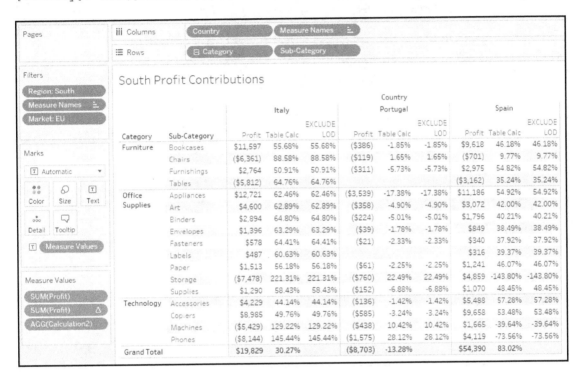

As expected, both calculations yield the same results. We can also roll up to category or drill down to product name without having to redefine the field. Regardless of how we slice the data, we will always show contributions to the overall region.

The only difference between those two calculations resides in the order of operations. While EXCLUDE LOD calculations come before measure filters, table calculations come after. As a result, if we filter on measures, the table calculations will reflect only the values in the table, while the EXCLUDE LOD calculation will continue to show the same results.

For instance, if we filter on SUM(Profit) to show only profitable quadrants (that is, SUM(Profit) > 0), we get the following:

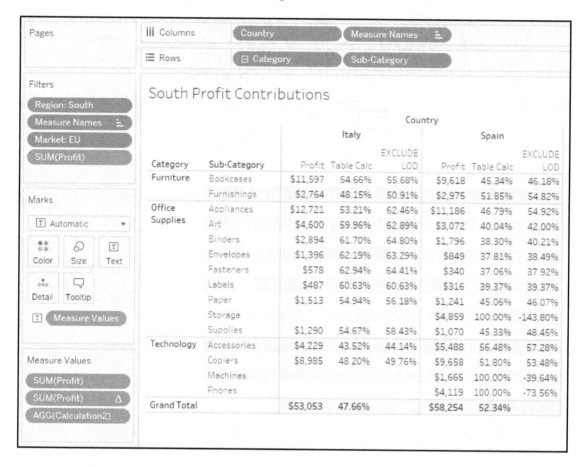

We can see that the EXCLUDE LOD calculations have not changed, while Table Calc now reflects only the data shown on the screen.

Example 2 – difference in average profit

Using the Global Superstore dataset, for profitable orders, we want to know the difference between the average profit per line by category and market, compared to the average for the entire category. For example, what is the difference between the average profit for Office Supplies orders in Africa and the average profit for any order in Africa?

We can first define `Order Profitable?` as `IF {FIXED [Order ID]:SUM([Profit])}` `> 0 THEN 'Profitable' ELSE 'Not Profitable' END`, which will calculate the overall profit for each Order ID and make for a quick filter.

We can then plot the average `Profit`, slicing by `Category` and `Market`, filtering for profitable orders, turning on **Grand Total** for rows:

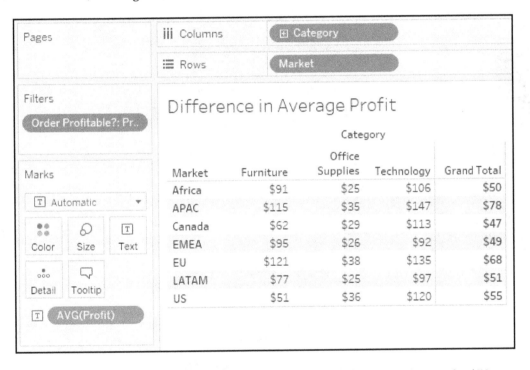

In this case, we want to compare the $25 average profit in Office Supplies to the $50 average profit for orders in Africa.

Thus, we can define `{Exclude [Category]: AVG([Profit])}` as the average profit omitting the `Category` dimension (which is equal in this view to the **Grand Total** for a given market), and a further calculation for `AVG([Profit]) - ATTR({EXCLUDE [Category]: AVG([Profit])})` will show us the required difference:

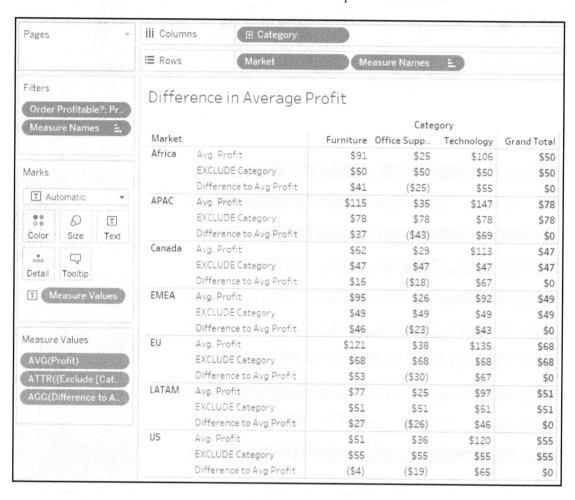

Market		Furniture	Office Supp..	Technology	Grand Total
Africa	Avg. Profit	$91	$25	$106	$50
	EXCLUDE Category	$50	$50	$50	$50
	Difference to Avg Profit	$41	($25)	$55	$0
APAC	Avg. Profit	$115	$35	$147	$78
	EXCLUDE Category	$78	$78	$78	$78
	Difference to Avg Profit	$37	($43)	$69	$0
Canada	Avg. Profit	$62	$29	$113	$47
	EXCLUDE Category	$47	$47	$47	$47
	Difference to Avg Profit	$16	($18)	$67	$0
EMEA	Avg. Profit	$95	$26	$92	$49
	EXCLUDE Category	$49	$49	$49	$49
	Difference to Avg Profit	$46	($23)	$43	$0
EU	Avg. Profit	$121	$38	$135	$68
	EXCLUDE Category	$68	$68	$68	$68
	Difference to Avg Profit	$53	($30)	$67	$0
LATAM	Avg. Profit	$77	$25	$97	$51
	EXCLUDE Category	$51	$51	$51	$51
	Difference to Avg Profit	$27	($26)	$46	$0
US	Avg. Profit	$51	$36	$120	$55
	EXCLUDE Category	$55	$55	$55	$55
	Difference to Avg Profit	($4)	($19)	$65	$0

In this case, we can see that orders for Office Supplies in Africa are $25 less profitable than the average order line in this market. Again, we can change the dimensions without having to change the definition of our field, for instance by `Segment`, as long as we keep slicing by `Category`:

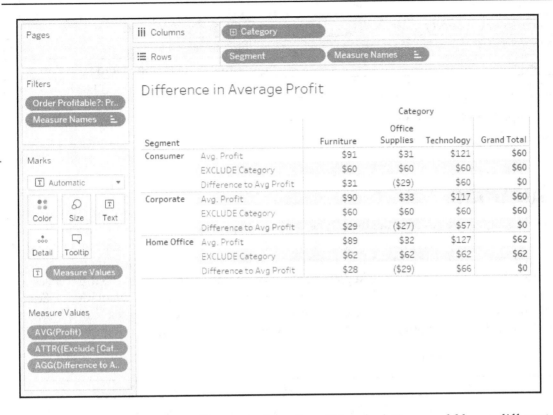

However, if we were to remove **Category** altogether, this calculation would be no different to a simple AVG([Profit]), and would lose its value.

Data source constraints for LOD

While LOD calculations are in general supported in Tableau, there are a few constraints on certain data source types. At the time of writing, here are the most notable exceptions to the rule:

Data source	Support
Google Big Query	Supported for standard SQL, not supported for legacy SQL
Microsoft Access	Not supported
Microsoft Jet-based connections (legacy connectors for Microsoft Excel, Microsoft Access, and text)	Not supported

Microsoft SQL Server	SQL Server 2005 and later
Mongo DB	Not supported
Oracle	Supported version 9i and later
PostgreSQL	Supported version 7 and later

A complete and up-to-date version of this list can be found at `https://help.tableau.com/current/pro/desktop/en-us/calculations_calculatedfields_lod_constraints.htm`.

Summary

In this chapter, we covered the three types of LOD expressions available in Tableau (`FIXED`, `INCLUDE`, and `EXCLUDE`) and studied how we can use them to aggregate data at a level that is either more granular (in the case of `INCLUDE`) or less granular than the dimensions already in the view. We also looked at the order of operations to explain the differences between these calculations and the ones seen previously (such as table calculations). For instance, we now hold the tools to calculate contributions to a total, create cohorts based on first order date, and aggregate customer-level information starting from item-level data.

Here is a quick reminder:

	FIXED	INCLUDE	EXCLUDE
Order of operations	Before dimension filters	After dimension filters	After dimension filters
Purpose	Calculate across the dataset along selected dimensions	Calculate results using a dimension that is not part of the view	Calculate results excluding one of the dimensions that is part of the view

This chapter closes a three-chapter journey into the different calculations that we can use in Tableau, and we are now ready to use some of the analytical tools to add some insights to our worksheets.

Questions

Answer the following questions to test your knowledge of the information in this chapter.

Q: If I'm not using any dimension filters, is there a difference between using a **Percent of Total** table calculation and using `FIXED`/`EXCLUDE` calculations?

A: While they will, in general, yield the same results, there a few exceptions that we have discussed in this chapter, and the main reason for the differences is the order of operations. FIXED calculations will remain unchanged by dimension and measure filters, EXCLUDE calculations will remain unchanged by measure filters (but not by dimension filters), and table calculations will be affected by both dimension and measure filters.

Q: Do LOD calculations have to use fields that are already included in the view? Can LOD calculations aggregate at a different level than the one determined by the fields chosen in the view?

A: As seen in the example of INCLUDE calculations, LOD calculations can be used to aggregate on fields that are not present in the view.

Q: Do LOD calculations always yield measures?

A: Not necessarily. In the example of cohorts in the second part of this chapter, we can use a FIXED LOD calculation to create a first purchase date, which will be treated as a dimension.

Further reading

You can check out the following links for more information about the topics that were covered in this chapter:

- *Top 15 Tableau LOD Expressions*: https://www.tableau.com/about/blog/LOD-expressions
- *Data Source Constraints for Level of Detail Expressions*: https://help.tableau.com/current/pro/desktop/en-us/calculations_calculatedfields_lod_constraints.htm
- *Which calculation is right for your analysis: simple, table, or LOD?* https://help.tableau.com/current/pro/desktop/en-us/calculations_calculatedfields_understand_which.htm

8
Leveraging Analytics Capabilities

In the previous three chapters, we learned how to create increasingly more complex calculations in Tableau. Now that we have the tools to develop powerful workbooks, let's see if we can leverage Tableau's analytics capabilities to bring some color to our data, either with graphical elements, such as reference lines or bands, or using forecasting to predict future data.

The following topics will be covered in this chapter:

- Basic tools in the Tableau Analytics pane
- Additional analytical options
- Using forecasting
- A practical example

Technical requirements

This chapter uses the Global Superstore dataset, which can be found at `http://www.tableau.com/sites/default/files/training/global_superstore.zip`.

Basic tools in the Tableau Analytics pane

Tableau holds a set of ready-made analytical tools that can be simply dragged and dropped onto a view. Those functions can be found in the **Analytics** pane, usually by clicking on the tab next to **Data**:

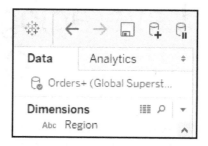

If you can't see this on the left-hand side of your screen, you can go to **Window** > **Show Side Bar** in the menu bar to display it. The pane holds tools that have been separated into three sections: **Summarize**, **Model**, and **Custom**.

Using the options

Each of the analytics tools in this toolbar functions in the same manner. You can either double-click the option or drag one of them onto the view, which will make a panel containing a few options appear:

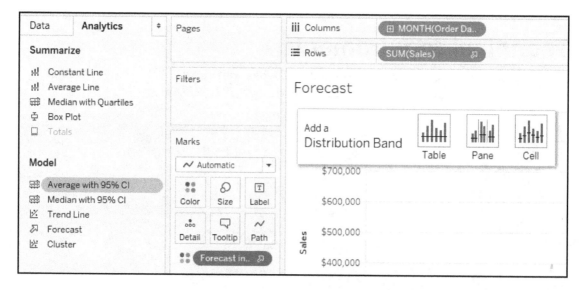

In general, it will display either three icons (**Table**, **Pane**, and **Cell**) or only one (when there is no choice to be made), with the exception of **Totals**. This will be an indication for Tableau as to which scope the calculation should consider, and you can drop your analytical tool on one of the icons. Taking the example of the **Average line** option, dropping it into each icon yields the following three possibilities:

If you select the **Table** icon, you will get the following output:

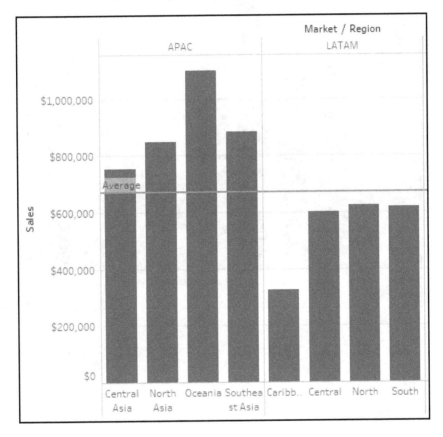

If you select the **Pane** icon, you will get the following output:

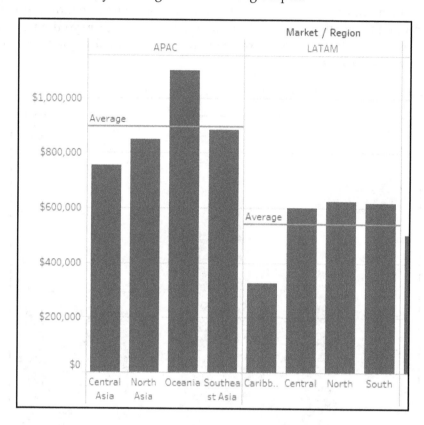

If you select the **Cell** option, you will get the following output:

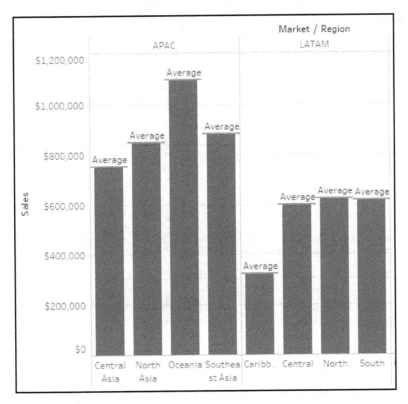

Whilst the **Table** represents the entire view, a **Pane** is the part of the view corresponding to an intersection of dimensions in rows and columns that are delimited by a *dividing line*. For instance, in the preceding examples, there are two panes, one under **APAC** and one under **LATAM**, as you can see a line between them. The **Cell** is the smallest intersection of dimensions and there are eight of them in the previous views.

 These are the same options we discussed in Chapter 6, *Tableau Table Calculations*.

We can also think about this by saying that the **Table** option is akin to a Grand Total and will hold only one value across the visualization; the **Pane** option akin to a subtotal across one dimension; and the **Cell** option akin to a subtotal at the lowest level possible and will make sense only when there are detail marks available (otherwise, it will just aggregate one value, as is the case here).

Once those analytical tools have been integrated into the view, it's possible to edit or remove them by clicking on their representation and using the relevant options in the tooltip:

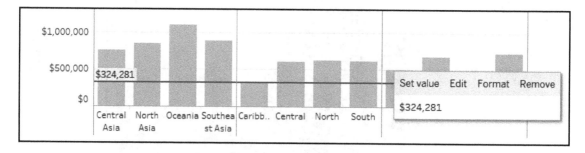

You can also perform the **Remove** action by simply dragging and dropping the reference lines off-view, just like you would with any other field.

Finally, you can use the **Format** option on the newly created lines or areas, including colors, fonts, and number formats.

Most of the tools are actually just shortcuts for the options that are available under **Custom**, so let's go through those first.

Creating reference lines

The different line options will create reference lines across your visualization at the scope you have chosen (either at the **Table**, **Pane**, or **Cell** level). Once you drop the **Reference Line** option onto your visualization, you can use the **Edit** window to switch between two main categories of values:

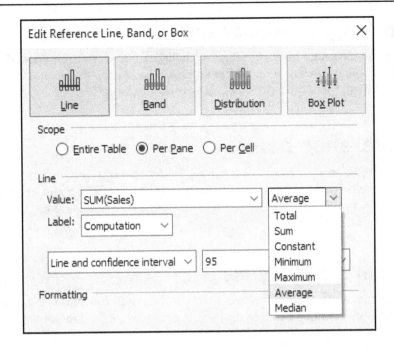

Here, you can choose the **Constant** option, which will display a single line across your representation, or one of several calculated options that will aggregate values at the scope you've chosen. The different possibilities for aggregation are displayed under the **Line** submenu, along with the **Constant** option.

Reference lines are the equivalent of a table calculation, which means the average that's displayed will be the average of marks present in the visualization, not of the underlying data.

Finally, it is also possible to choose a **confidence interval** and display it on the view under the same **Line** submenu and the label for the line can be customized (either to show the value, the name of the aggregation, or a calculated name, with the respective **Value**, **Computation**, and **Custom** options).

It is also possible to get back to this menu by clicking on an existing reference line and using the **Edit** option in the tooltip.

Shortcuts in the Analytics bar

The **Constant Line**, **Average Line**, **Average with 95% CI**, and **Median with 95% CI** options in the **Analytics** toolbar are shortcuts to the most common options for lines, but you can always drag and drop them onto the view and edit them later.

Using reference bands

A reference band will create two reference lines, as described in the previous section, and will color the space between those two lines with a light color. The **Band From** and **Band To** options in the **Edit** window are the same as for lines; you can use these to customize and format the upper and lower values of the band.

Shortcuts in the Analytics bar

There are no shortcuts for usual reference bands in the **Analytics** bar; you have to use the **Reference Band** option under **Custom** and select the relevant parameters.

Adding Distribution Bands

Distribution Bands allow users either to create bands as one or more multiples of a previous aggregate (for instance, 50%, 100%, or 150% of the median) or to create lines or bands based on statistical measures (for instance, percentiles, quantiles, and standard deviation). The resulting bands will be tinted in different shades of the main color that was chose to represent the intervals between two measures:

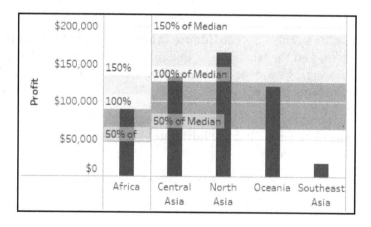

When using **Percentiles** in the **Edit** window, users have the option of using one of the selected values (**80, 90, 95, 99**) to show the respective percentile lines or using the **Enter One or More Values** option:

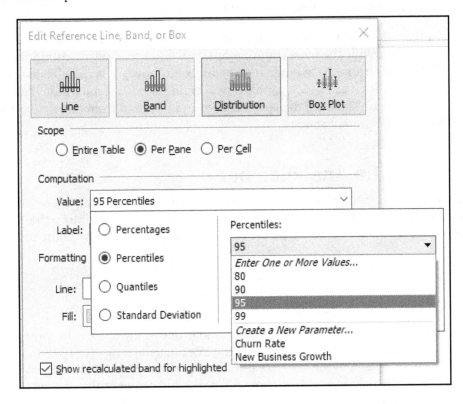

For example, to show the 20th, 60th, and 90th percentiles, select **Enter One or More Values** from the drop-down menu and enter the percentiles as comma-separated values; for example, 20, 60, 90.

If you want to create a reference line for a given percentile (for instance, the 90th percentile), you have to use the **Distribution** tab with the **Percentiles** option using one value, not the **Line** tab, as the **Percentiles** options are not available there.

For **Quantiles**, any value between 3 (terciles) and 10 (deciles) can be used, but all the quantiles will be shown in the view by default. If you wanted to show only a few selected quantiles, use the **Percentile** option with the selected calculated values instead (for instance, 10, 50, 90 to show the first, fifth, and ninth deciles only).

The **Standard Deviation** option creates bands that are multiples of the standard deviation away from the mean. While the most common option is -1, 1 to show distribution within one standard deviation from the average (one below, one above), it is possible to specify more complex bands, such as -0.5, 1, 2, to show a band from 0.5 standard deviations below the average to one standard deviation above, and a second from one to two standard deviations above in a different shade.

Shortcuts in the Analytics bar

The **Median with Quartiles** option in the **Analytics** toolbar is a shortcut to a common reference band (quartiles, **Quantiles** of degree 4), but you can drag and drop the **Distribution Band** option onto the visualization to create a custom view of the distribution of data.

Generating box plots

The box plot diagram (also called box and whiskers) is one of the most widespread statistical visualizations today. The box shows the interquartile range (or **IQR**, that is, the extent of the distribution between the first and third quartiles, also called **hinges**) with a line for the median, while the whiskers show either the full extent of the data or 1.5 times the interquartile range.

This is a very useful tool for depicting variations when you don't want to infer a normal distribution.

It is possible to create a box plot visualization by either dragging it from the **Analytical** pane or using the **Show me** button to create one:

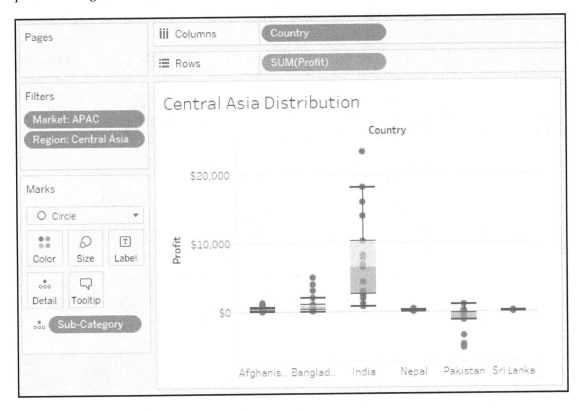

If the **Box Plot** option is grayed out in the toolbox, hovering over it will show what the issue is with the current view (for instance, **not enough marks in the view** or **can't be mixed with stacked marks such as bar charts**).

 Hovering over the box plot will show the values of the different limits of the box, starting from the bottom: **Lower Whisker**, **Lower Hinge** (first quartile), **Median**, **Upper Hinge** (third quartile), and **Upper Whisker**.

Using the **Edit** function in the tooltip will, as usual, take you to the **Edit** window, where you will be able to format the box and change the following two options:

- Whether the whiskers should extend to **data within 1.5 the IQR** or to the **maximum extent of the data**
- Whether to show or hide the marks that are not outside of the whiskers (outliers) with **Hide underlying marks (except outliers)**

Now that we've covered the basic analytical tools, you can see that they are actually the four types of visualizations that will be available at the top of the **Edit Reference Line, Band, or Box** window when editing any of them:

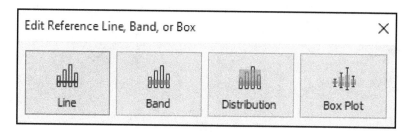

Adding one of them to the view will let you create any of them by just going to the **Edit** box. We'll continue our review of the different tools that remain in the next section.

Additional analytical options

There are four options remaining in the Analytics pane: **Totals**, **Trend Lines**, **Clustering**, and **Forecasting**. The last of these will be detailed in the next section, so let's focus on the first three.

Totals

The **Totals** option can be dragged onto the view to turn on totals either for all the rows, all the columns, or to add subtotals to all the rows or and columns:

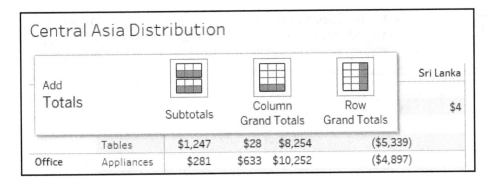

Central Asia Distribution

		Subtotals	Column Grand Totals	Row Grand Totals		Sri Lanka
Add Totals						$4
	Tables	$1,247	$28 $8,254	($5,339)		
Office	Appliances	$281	$633 $10,252	($4,897)		

It is not possible to turn on subtotals for selected dimensions; it has to be done for all or none.

Totals can also be turned on using the **Analysis > Totals** options, which can be found in the menu.

Trend lines

Tableau can create the usual **Trend Lines (Linear, Logarithmic, Exponential, Polynomial, Power)** using the option with the same name in the **Analytics** bar and dragging and dropping it onto the view:

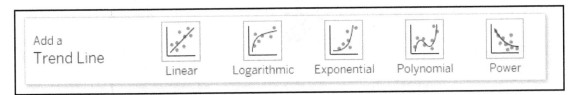

Add a Trend Line	Linear	Logarithmic	Exponential	Polynomial	Power

If the **Trend Line** option is not available for selection in the sidebar, this usually is because you need both axes to be measures, or a date and a measure. This will be indicated when hovering over the grayed-out option.

For instance, using the Global Superstore dataset, we can add `Profit` to rows, `Sales` to columns, `Order ID` to **Detail** marks, and filtering for orders where `Order Profitable?` is **Profitable**. Then, we can drop the **Trend Line** onto the **Linear** icon on the visualization. By doing this, we'll get the following output:

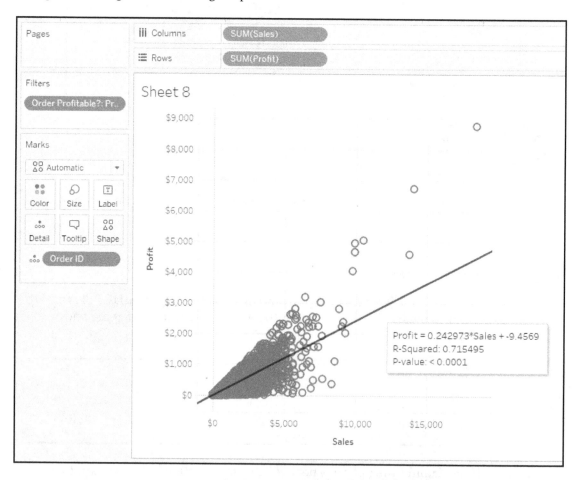

Hovering over the line will show the tooltip with the equation and the R^2 and **P** values, which will help you identify whether the trend is relevant or not.

If you need to edit the trend line or change the parameters, you can choose the **Edit** option in the tooltip to go to the **Trend Line Options** window.

Now, it's very easy to identify trends with a few clicks, thanks to the power of Tableau.

Clusters

While the **Clusters** option is not explicitly included in the exam syllabus, it is a valuable tool when we want to create a subdivision of our data. For instance, we can create a map view by including Country in rows, and SUM(Sales) as marks, and using the **Show me** option to create a quick map. Then, dragging **Clusters** onto the view will generate groups of countries based on their levels of sales value and will use them to color code the map. If we want to modify these parameters, we can click on the **Clusters** pill in **Marks** and select **Edit Clusters**:

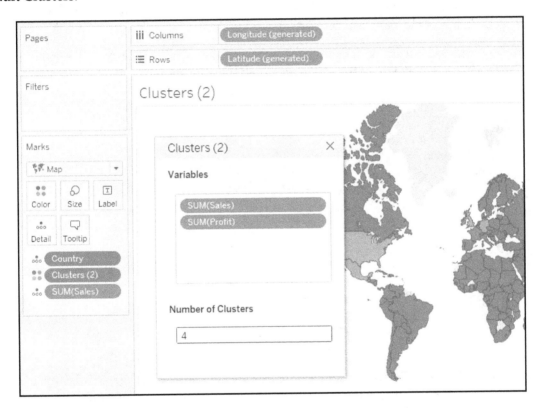

Then, we can add other variables to be included in the computation of the clusters and we can define a fixed number of clusters, rather than keep an automated number.

 For more information on how Tableau creates clusters, please refer to the *How Clustering Works* link in the *Further reading* section of this chapter.

When a cluster has been created, it is possible to drag its pill from the **Marks** section into **Dimensions** to transform it into a group. You will notice the icon is slightly different from the usual group icon (a combination of the cluster icon and a paperclip), and that is to signify that this group is not static and can be refitted using the **Refit** option. This means it can be updated with the latest data if the scope has changed.

The summary card

While the **Summary Card** is not part of the **Analytics** pane, it's a useful tool if you want to get a quick glance at the statistical properties of your dataset.

It can be turned on by using **Worksheet > Show Summary** in the menu. It will appear in the **Cards** section, below where the filters are when they are shown:

Summary	
Count:	18754
SUM(Profit)	
Sum:	$2,311,302
Average:	$123
Minimum:	$0
Maximum:	$8,762
Median:	$43
SUM(Sales)	
Sum:	$10,242,5...
Average:	$546
Minimum:	$2
Maximum:	$18,337
Median:	$229

By default, it will show the total number of marks and the **Sum, Average, Minimum, Maximum**, and **Median** for each measure. While using the drop-down menu in the card, you can select an additional set of calculations, including **Standard Deviation, First,** and **Third quartiles**.

It is important to remember that the results in this card are similar to table calculations: the median that's shown here is the median of the marks, not of the underlying data.

This wraps up our review of the basic analytical tools that are included with Tableau. There is one final tool to review, which we will do in the next section.

Using forecasting

While the previous tools were only performing analytics on existing data, the **Forecast** option allows us to extrapolate the data to get a glimpse into the future.

By default, Tableau includes a package that takes the best of a few options of models to create a simple forecast. Tableau uses an exponential smoothing model, which gives more weight to the recent data points over the older ones. Those forecasts can then be fine-tuned with the use of the options that can be found in the **Edit Forecast** toolbox.

To start using forecasts, simply drag and drop the **Forecast** option from the Analytics bar onto a chart or table that includes one and only one date field (otherwise, you will see a message indicating that no forecast can be created for views with multiple date fields). You can also use the **Analysis > Forecast > Show Forecast** menu to achieve the same result. Tableau will then create a best-guess forecast with automatic options, including a confidence range for a given period (based on how much past data is available).

For instance, using `Order Date` as columns (**Month**) and `Sales` as rows, we can drop the **Forecast** option onto the view:

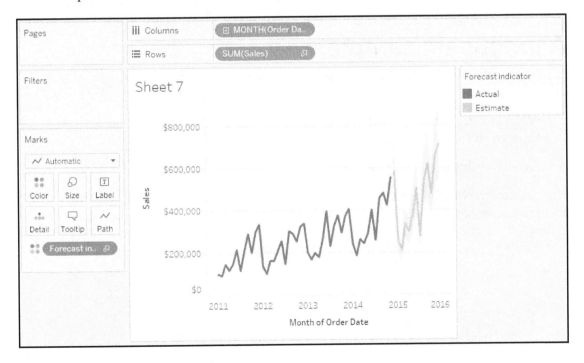

This will create a new color scheme so that we can differentiate between actual and estimated data, and a thick arrow will appear next to the **Sales** pill to confirm that the forecast is turned on. If you need to edit the forecast, you can use the **Edit** function in the tooltip when clicking on the forecast or use the **Analysis > Forecast > Forecast Options...** menu.

For basic users of this function and for the purpose of this exam, the only options that would be of interest are the **Forecast Length** (if you want to be able to manipulate it) and the **Ignore last** options, which are helpful when there are incomplete periods at the back of some data. Advanced users can use the **Learn more about forecast options** link to get a deeper understanding of what the different options can bring.

If you ever run into an issue where the forecast cannot be added (or where it doesn't appear), it is possible to hover over the **Forecast** option in the **Analytical** pane (or over the **No forecast** label on the view, respectively) to learn more about why a forecast cannot be generated.

This concludes our review of the different analytical tools that Tableau has to offer. Before we end this chapter, let's look at an example.

A practical example

Now that we know all about Tableau's analytical tools, let's see whether we can solve this sample exam question:

> *Which subcategories in the LATAM market are more than a standard deviation away from the mean for both sales and profit?*

We can answer this question in two ways.

First, we can go with the previous chapter and use INCLUDE statements to show the average and standard deviation of the sum of the two measures. Here, we will define {INCLUDE [Sub-Category]: SUM([Profit])} and {INCLUDE [Sub-Category]: SUM([Sales])} and look at the average and standard deviation of each, as follows:

By performing some simple additions, we can get the lower and upper bounds (for example, **$13,038 + $14,161 = $27,199** as the upper bound for profit and **$127,330-$111,886 = $15,444** as the lower bound for sales). Subsequently, we can plot Sales and Profit by Sub-category and get to the answer. But it's easy to overlook one of the subcategories when scanning down.

Instead, we can try to make the most of the **Analytics** pane. We can plot `Sales` and `Profit` along the rows and columns and use `Sub-Category` as **Detail** marks:

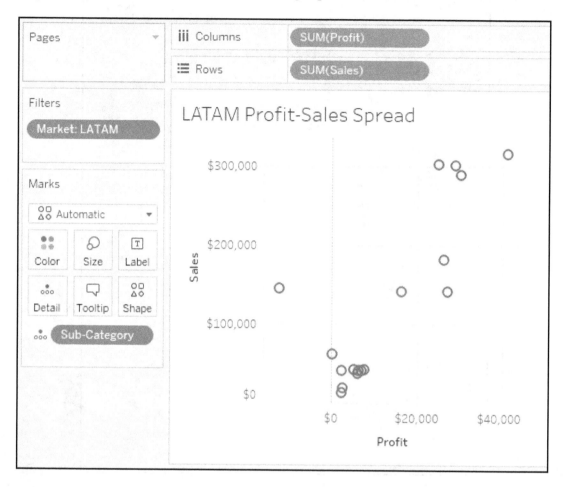

Now, we can drag and drop a **Distribution** band on the **Table** for both measures. Rather than the default **60, 80% of Average**, we can click **Standard Deviation** and keep the proposed **-1,1** factors, which means one standard deviation both below and above the mean:

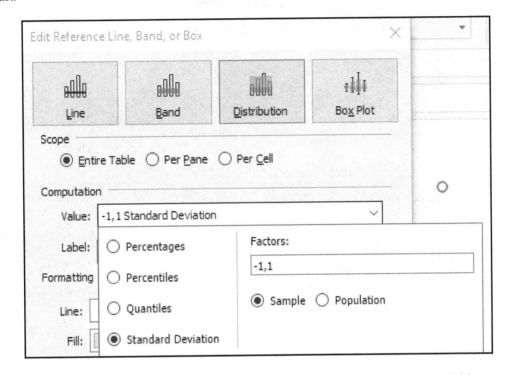

Note that you will probably need to adjust one of the bands as Tableau handles them one at a time and the second one will still show the default **60, 80% of Average**. To do so, click on one of the defining lines of the band and use **Edit** in the tooltip.

Now, we have a shaded area that represents the distribution within one standard deviation from the mean:

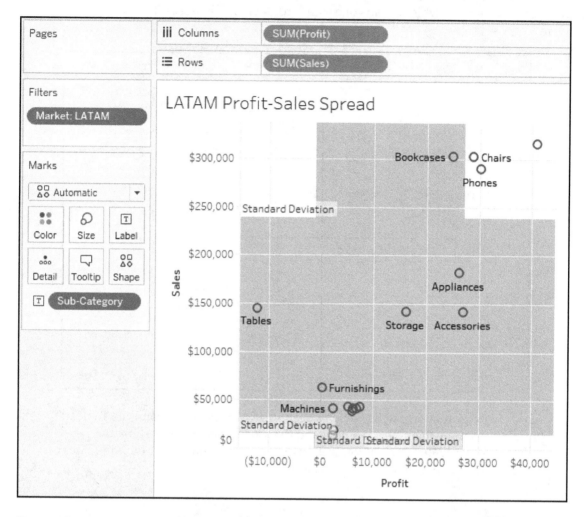

Due to this, it's easy to spot the three subcategories in the top-right corner that are outside both and get their names by hovering over the mark, if necessary on **Chairs**, **Phones**, and **Copiers**.

Summary

In this chapter, we covered some of Tableau's analytic tools, which allow us to create reference lines or bands, cluster data in similar buckets, identify trends, and forecast what our data will look like in the future. This allows us to highlight some of the useful information that might have been missing from the views (such as an average line or maybe a constant band to tell us when a project started and finished), and this helps bring meaningful insight to our data.

This chapter concludes our exploration of worksheets, for which we now have all the tools required for the exam. We will study how to link and present different worksheets in a single consolidated view using dashboards in the next and last chapter of this book.

Questions

Answer the following questions to test your knowledge of the information in this chapter.

Q: Using the Global Superstore dataset, if you create a forecast for `Sales` by `Year`, how many periods forward does Tableau forecast by default?

A: Two periods (with `Year(Order Date)` as columns and `SUM(Sales)` as rows, and dragging the **Forecast** option).

Q: How can you create a single line for the 90th percentile on a view?

A: By adding a **Distribution Band**, with **Percentile**, **90** as options, not by adding a **Reference Line**, as there are no options for percentiles.

Q: Using the Global Superstore dataset, which country in Central Asia has the widest distribution of profits, using interquartile ranges?

A: Creating a box plot, as described in this chapter, India is the country with the widest IQR (represented by the size of the box).

Further reading

You can check out the following links for more information about the topics that were covered in this chapter:

- Forecasting options: `https://help.tableau.com/current/pro/desktop/en-us/forecast_options.htm`.
- Forecast field results: `https://help.tableau.com/current/pro/desktop/en-us/forecast_field_results.htm`.
- How clustering works: `https://help.tableau.com/current/pro/desktop/en-us/clustering.htm#how-clustering-works`.

Building Your Dashboards

9

We have learned a lot about how to craft views of data thus far; now it is time to put everything together. The views you have created are often a means for a user to identify critical information. Dashboards allow us to combine multiple views onto a single page. By presenting multiple views of data on a single page, we are able to communicate information more efficiently.

However, presenting multiple views on a single page comes with a lot of challenges. You need to present the right combination of views without overwhelming the user. You also need to construct the dashboard in such a way that it is easy for users to use and understand. This chapter will walk you through features and best practices that will help you build actionable and informative dashboards. In this final chapter, we will discuss the following topics:

- Introduction to dashboards
- Effective design practices
- Exploring the Dashboard and Layout panes
- Telling stories
- Putting everything together

Introduction to dashboards

A dashboard is a visual display of important information on a single page. It usually consists of multiple related components that allows users to track changes or get information. Dashboards are embedded with controls that allow users to filter information. These filters often control multiple sheets on the dashboard. This allows users to view various related components without having to switch screens.

Filters are how users interact with the views in a dashboard – they allow users to answer questions. What distinguishes dashboards from reports is that dashboards are predominantly visual. While they can contain tabular summaries, they should emphasize visuals. There have been many studies that describe the importance of data visualization. The main findings are that data visualizations excel at revealing patterns, outliers, trends, and correlations that can't easily be found when looking at a table of numbers.

You can think of a dashboard as how you choose to present your sheets. A dashboard should be able to communicate key findings in the data. The visualizations that make up a dashboard are interactive via filters and controls. Effective information design is as much art as science. There is no one-size-fits-all method or technique to create robust and useful dashboards.

Dashboards can add a tremendous amount of value to an organization, but only if they are thought out. In the next section, we will discuss how to create dashboards that will help users make better sense of data.

Effective design practices

By the time you are ready to create a dashboard, you have already done a tremendous amount of work to create sheets. The sheets are the backbone of the dashboard; care must not only be taken in developing individual sheets but also how they are presented together in the dashboard. In this section, we will discuss best practices for effective dashboard design. While these tips are not exhaustive, they will provide you with a good starting point on your path to developing powerful dashboards.

Purpose

The most important item to consider before building any solution is to know the purpose. What questions will the dashboard answer? Having a list of specific questions to answer gives you a clear purpose. You should always have a have a clearly defined purpose when developing dashboards. Knowing the purpose forces you to address the needs of the viewers. In business, knowing the purpose of the dashboard usually involves understanding what **key performance indicators** (**KPIs**) users are interested in.

By knowing your audience and understanding their needs, you will be able to develop an actionable dashboard that users will want to use. At the end of the day, dashboards need to answer questions, keep people informed, and be easy to use. If these three components are not met, then everyone loses.

Good design principles

It can be easy to get caught up in building cool visualizations, with tons of slick features. Always remember the purpose of the dashboard. It should provide the information that users are looking for in a way that is easy to understand. When constructing a dashboard, there are many challenges you will face. Use the tips in the following section as you begin to face these challenges.

Limiting the number of sheets used

Limit the number of sheets used – you do not want to overwhelm users with sheets and clutter. A dashboard should not be hard to use (or understand). By limiting the number of sheets used in a dashboard, you limit the elements a user needs to pay attention to. One of the most common contributors to bad dashboard design is the inclusion of too many sheets. As a general rule, you should use no more than three visualizations in a dashboard.

Presenting multiple views allows you to include more information and finer details. More information also means that users can get lost in what is important and what is not. Thinking about the big picture when designing your dashboard can help mitigate this.

Being clear and concise

It is fun to create various chart types. Tableau makes it easy to include a large amount of extra information depending on the type of visual. Once again, it is important to know your audience. Try to make it easy for them to access the information they are looking for, even if it means simplifying your design. Design with your audience in mind. A good dashboard is one that people use. People are more likely to use simple dashboards as opposed to complex dashboards.

Constructing a cohesive story

Construct a cohesive story – dashboards should communicate information clearly and efficiently. One of the biggest obstacles you will face is how to present the various sheets in your workbook together in one dashboard in a manner that is seamless. Remember that you are trying to present a large amount of data in a limited space. You need to think about the relationship between sheets as you are working toward your end goal. The story you tell is dependent on what the audience wants and needs to see.

Now that we have described a few good design principles, let us discuss how to create dashboards using the **Dashboard** and **Layout** panes.

Exploring the Dashboard and Layout panes

There are two tabs in the menu on the left-hand side of the **Dashboard** pane. The two tabs are distinct panes – **Dashboard** and **Layout**. The **Dashboard** pane allows you to place sheets and objects in the dashboard. It is also where you set screen-sizing options. The **Layout** pane gives you finer control of how sheets and objects are formatted in the dashboard. The **Layout** pane allows you to precisely position and pad items in the dashboard. We will discuss both of these panes in the following section.

The Dashboard pane

In this section, we will begin building our dashboard. In order to create a dashboard, you must have created at least one sheet. A dashboard is a blank page where you can combine multiple sheets. Dashboards are interactive in a number of ways, primarily with the use of filters. To create a dashboard, click the **New Dashboard** button at the bottom of the workbook. The **Dashboard** tab is available at the bottom of the workbook:

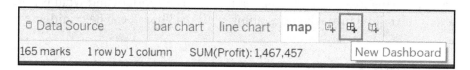

Once you have clicked on the **New Dashboard** button (bottom of the workbook), a blank dashboard page will open. Similar to the worksheets page, there are two tabs on the left pane – **Dashboard** and **Layout**. The **Dashboard** pane is the default view. The **Dashboard** pane contains four primary sections:

- **Device Preview**
- **Size**
- **Sheets**
- **Objects**

We will now discuss each of these sections in more detail. The following screenshot displays the four primary sections (**Device Preview**, **Size**, **Sheets**, and **Objects**) in the left pane:

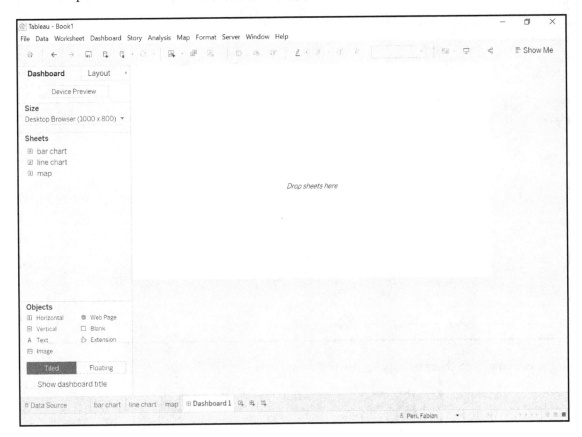

Sheets

To add a sheet to the view, either double-click the name under the **Sheets** portion of the pane, drag and drop the sheet to the canvas, or right-click the sheet name and select **Add to Dashboard**.

In the following example, the sheet titled **bar chart** was double-clicked. The sheet is now in the dashboard along with all the filters that were applied in the **bar chart** sheet:

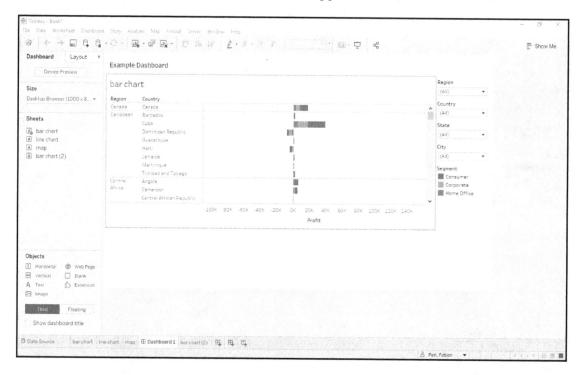

Right-clicking on a sheet brings up the following menu:

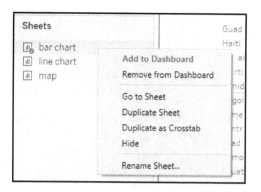

The following is a short description of each of the items:

- **Add to Dashboard**: Adds the selected sheet to the dashboard.
- **Remove from Dashboard**: Removes the selected sheet from the dashboard.

- **Go to Sheet**: Takes you to the selected sheet in the Tableau workbook.
- **Duplicate sheet**: Creates a copy of the selected sheet.
- **Duplicate as Crosstab**: The selected sheet is duplicated as a pivot table. This is an excellent way to see data used in a visualization as rows and columns. The following screenshot shows the crosstab version of the sheet (bar chart) that is in the dashboard:

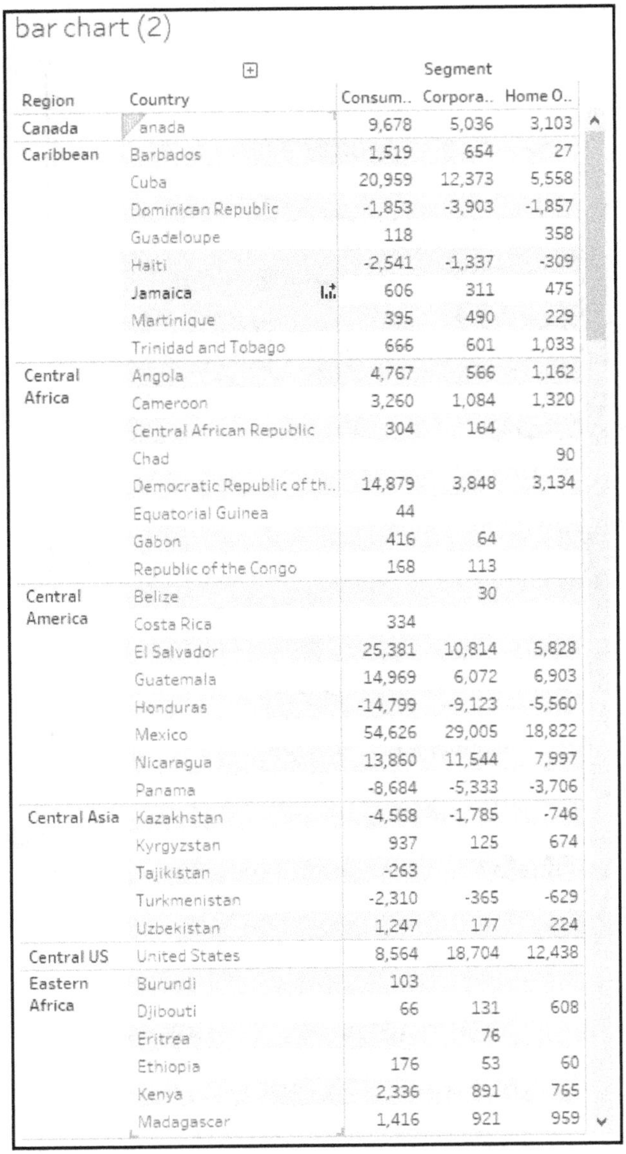

bar chart (2)

Region	Country	Segment		
		Consum..	Corpora..	Home O..
Canada	Canada	9,678	5,036	3,103
Caribbean	Barbados	1,519	654	27
	Cuba	20,959	12,373	5,558
	Dominican Republic	-1,853	-3,903	-1,857
	Guadeloupe	118		358
	Haiti	-2,541	-1,337	-309
	Jamaica	606	311	475
	Martinique	395	490	229
	Trinidad and Tobago	666	601	1,033
Central Africa	Angola	4,767	566	1,162
	Cameroon	3,260	1,084	1,320
	Central African Republic	304	164	
	Chad			90
	Democratic Republic of th..	14,879	3,848	3,134
	Equatorial Guinea	44		
	Gabon	416	64	
	Republic of the Congo	168	113	
Central America	Belize		30	
	Costa Rica	334		
	El Salvador	25,381	10,814	5,828
	Guatemala	14,969	6,072	6,903
	Honduras	-14,799	-9,123	-5,560
	Mexico	54,626	29,005	18,822
	Nicaragua	13,860	11,544	7,997
	Panama	-8,684	-5,333	-3,706
Central Asia	Kazakhstan	-4,568	-1,785	-746
	Kyrgyzstan	937	125	674
	Tajikistan	-263		
	Turkmenistan	-2,310	-365	-629
	Uzbekistan	1,247	177	224
Central US	United States	8,564	18,704	12,438
Eastern Africa	Burundi	103		
	Djibouti	66	131	608
	Eritrea		76	
	Ethiopia	176	53	60
	Kenya	2,336	891	765
	Madagascar	1,416	921	959

- **Hide**: Hides the selected sheet in the Tableau workbook.
- **Rename Sheet...**: Allows you to rename the selected sheet.

In addition to duplicating a sheet, you can duplicate a dashboard. To do this, go down to the **Sheets** menu, right-click the **Dashboard** tab, then select **Duplicate**:

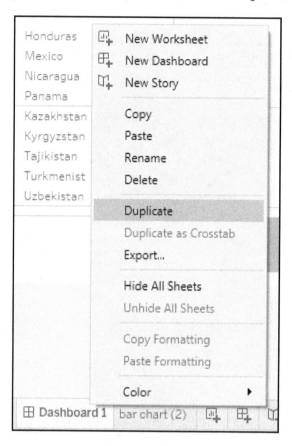

Duplicating a dashboard creates a new dashboard that looks exactly like the copied dashboard. The new dashboard still references all the same worksheets as the original dashboard. In the next section, we will discuss various objects that you can add to the dashboard other than sheets.

Objects

An object is an item that you can add to your dashboard. Objects allow you to customize the look of your dashboard as well as allowing for additional features. To add an object to the dashboard, either double-click the object name or drag and drop the object icon to the canvas. Depending on what object you choose, you will have a few options for customization. The following table gives a short description of each of the objects:

Icon	Sheet and description
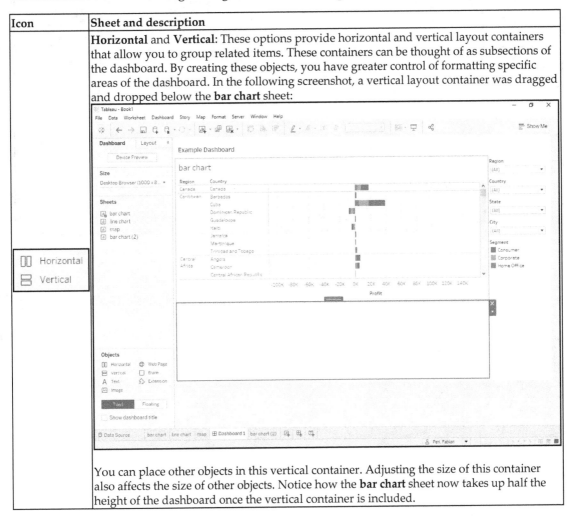	**Horizontal** and **Vertical**: These options provide horizontal and vertical layout containers that allow you to group related items. These containers can be thought of as subsections of the dashboard. By creating these objects, you have greater control of formatting specific areas of the dashboard. In the following screenshot, a vertical layout container was dragged and dropped below the **bar chart** sheet: You can place other objects in this vertical container. Adjusting the size of this container also affects the size of other objects. Notice how the **bar chart** sheet now takes up half the height of the dashboard once the vertical container is included.

Text: An object that allows you to enter in text for headers, descriptions, and other data. In the following screenshot, a text object was added to the top of the dashboard. The text says **Dashboard Title**. You can format the text however you like:

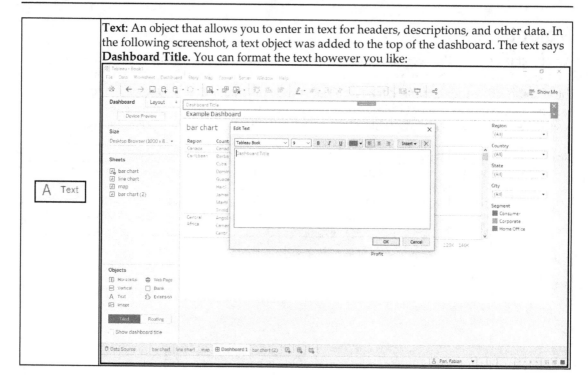

A   Text

Image: An object that allows you to enter an image. In the following screenshot, an image object was added below the bar chart:

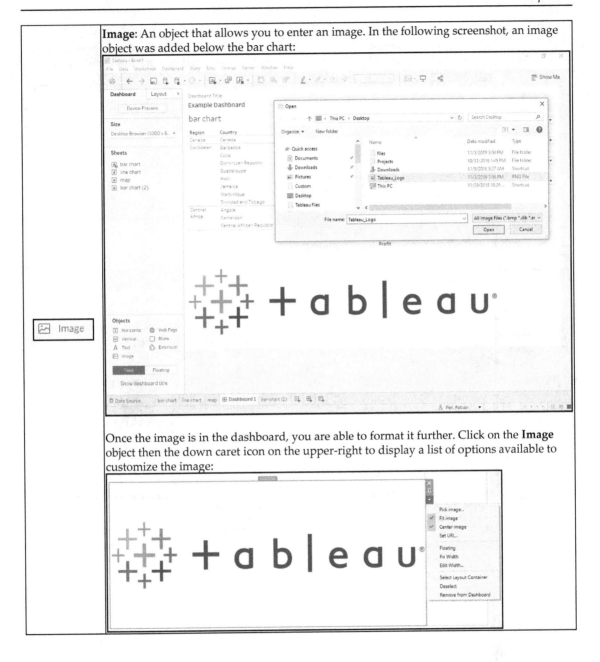

Image

Once the image is in the dashboard, you are able to format it further. Click on the **Image** object then the down caret icon on the upper-right to display a list of options available to customize the image:

Web Page: An object that allows you to embed a web page in the dashboard. In the following screenshot, the image object was replaced with a web page object. When the **Web Page** object icon is double-clicked or is dragged and dropped onto the dashboard, a URL window will appear. Enter the name of the web page URL here, then click **OK**:

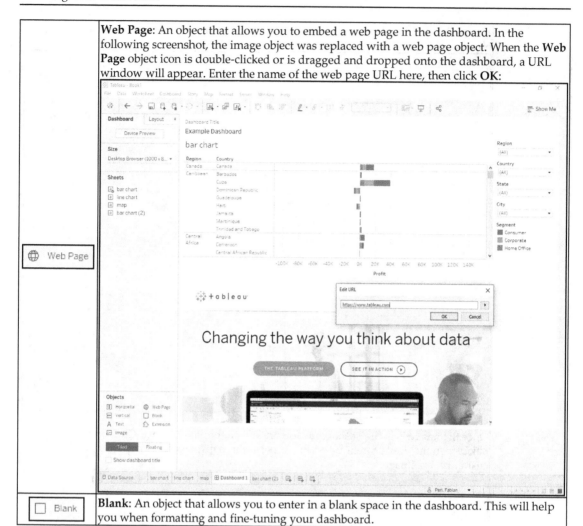

Blank: An object that allows you to enter in a blank space in the dashboard. This will help you when formatting and fine-tuning your dashboard.

Extension: Allows you to add extensions to your Tableau dashboard. In the following screenshot, an extension object was added to the dashboard where the web page object was. A **Choose an Extension** menu will appear:

 Extension

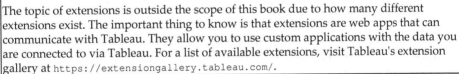

The topic of extensions is outside the scope of this book due to how many different extensions exist. The important thing to know is that extensions are web apps that can communicate with Tableau. They allow you to use custom applications with the data you are connected to via Tableau. For a list of available extensions, visit Tableau's extension gallery at `https://extensiongallery.tableau.com/`.

Not all web pages will appear when added to the web page object. This is mainly due to web security issues. If the page you are adding does not work, we suggest you google or check out the Tableau forms for a reason why.

Sheets and objects that are placed in dashboards are laid out in one of two ways: tiled or floating. In the next section, we will discuss the differences between them.

Tiled versus floating objects

The following screenshot shows the **Objects** menu. We have discussed each of the individual objects available in the preceding section. The toggle menu here allows you to choose between tiled objects and floating objects:

- **Tiled objects**: Each object in the dashboard is arranged using a grid mechanism. Tiled objects snap together with other tiled objects to form a view using grids that do not overlap. Tiled objects are much easier to work with. Tiled objects generally resize according to display settings much better than floating objects. Our suggestion is to use tiled objects whenever possible.
- **Floating objects**: Each object in the dashboard is free to be placed in any location. Floating objects can be placed on top of other objects – they are not constrained by grids. While floating objects give you the ability to make better use of space, this comes at a cost. That cost is how these objects are rendered when screen size changes. Tiled objects automatically resize based on the screen settings while tiled objects do not. One of the primary uses of floating objects is for legends.

When adding multiple sheets to a dashboard, you must think about how the user will be able to see the different visualizations. Best practices dictate that a user should not have to scroll to see different elements of a dashboard. We know that this is not always possible but selecting the right display settings can make a huge impact on how easy it is for a user to use the dashboard. We will discuss display sizing and the device preview option in the next section.

Display settings

To see the **Size** menu, click on the down caret to the right of the current size of the dashboard. A pop-up menu will appear, allowing you to select from commonly used resolutions for devices. The following screenshot shows the results:

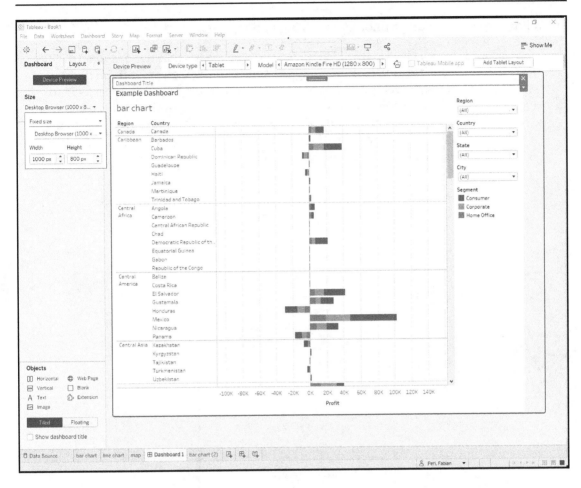

Clicking the down caret to the right of the current display size (**Fixed size**) brings up the sizing options. There are three sizing options, as seen in the following screenshot:

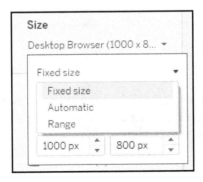

The following is a short description of the sizing options:

- **Fixed size**: This is the default size. A fixed size means that the dashboard stays the same size regardless of how big the screen of the viewer is. If the dashboard extends across or below the size of the screen then the user will be presented with scroll bars. There are pros and cons to each sizing option. With fixed-size dashboards, you can control the exact position of objects. If you choose to use floating elements, a fixed-size dashboard is the suggested option. When using a fixed-size dashboard, you can select from the following suggestions for specific devices:

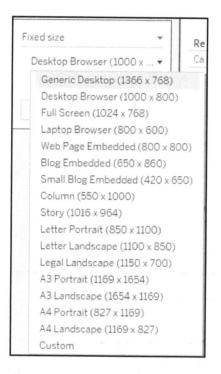

- **Automatic**: Select this option if you want Tableau to determine display settings. Tableau will attempt to resize the window based on the user's screen size.

- **Range**: With the **Range** setting, you select a minimum and maximum display size. The dashboard resizes to the minimum display if the user's display is smaller than the minimum selected. Similarly, the dashboard resizes to the maximum display if the user's display is larger than the maximum selected.

Device preview

After adding items to your dashboard, you can use the **Device Preview** option to see how the dashboard will render on different displays. The following screenshot highlights the **Device Preview** section that appears when the **Device Preview** button is clicked in the **Dashboard** pane:

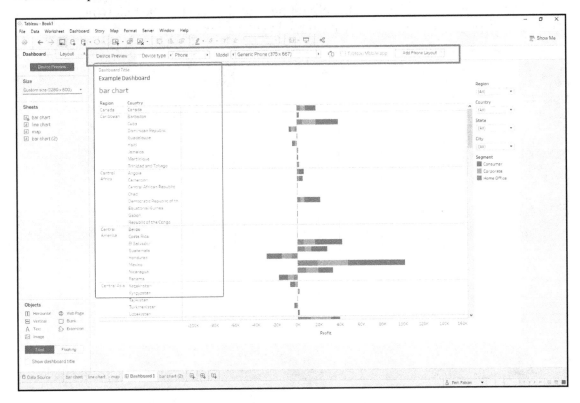

Use the device layout menu to see how the dashboard will look when viewed on different devices. This is a great way to see how your dashboard will be displayed on another user's device. Remember, just because a dashboard looks good on your device, it does not mean that it will look the same on another user's device.

Now that we have discussed the **Dashboard** pane, let us move on to the **Layout** pane.

The dashboard Layout pane

Proper sizing and arrangement make dashboards easier to use. Reorganizing sheet positions, shifting objects, and general formatting actions can help build a seamless user experience. In the preceding sections, we discussed display settings and arrangement options in the **Dashboard** pane. Now we will talk about additional formatting options that can be applied to sheets and objects to help refine your dashboard. The following screenshot displays the available options in the **Layout** pane:

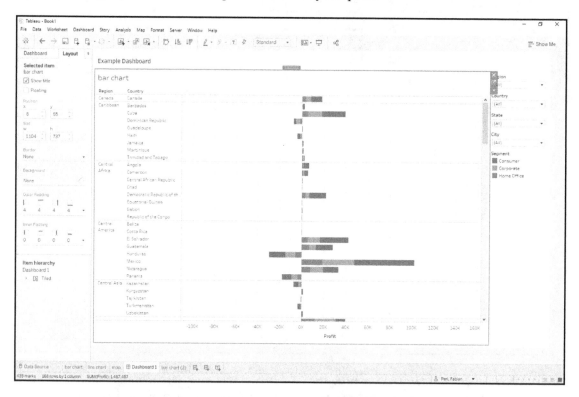

The following is a short description of the layout options:

- **Show title**: Select a sheet or object in the dashboard. Checking/unchecking the **Show title** checkbox displays this item's title. Use this to insert or remove a title.
- **Floating**: Select a sheet or object in the dashboard. Checking/unchecking the **Floating** checkbox changes the item from tiled to floating (or vice versa).

- **Position**: If you select a fixed size or range for the dashboard size, then you can fine-tune where sheets and objects are displayed on a dashboard. The **x** and **y** are offsets from the top-left corner signifying pixel length from this point.
- **Size**: If you change your sheets or objects to floating from tiled then you can manually set the width and height. The **w** is the width and **h** is the height in pixels.
- **Border**: Adds a border around a sheet or object.
- **Background**: Adds a background color to a sheet or object.
- **Outer Padding**: Adds outer padding to a sheet or object. Outer padding is space added to the outside of the element – it adds spacing for aesthetic purposes:

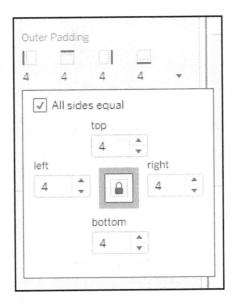

- **Inner Padding**: Similar to outer padding. This adds inner padding to a sheet or object. Inner padding is space added to the inside of the element – it adds spacing for aesthetic purposes.

- **Item hierarchy**: The item hierarchy shows you how objects are layered if you are using floating objects. Items are ordered from top to bottom, meaning objects that are higher up in the hierarchy are on top of the other items:

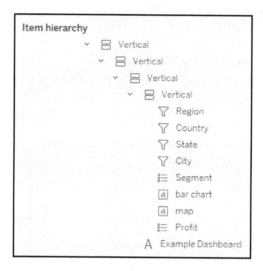

In the next section, we will go over another way to share your analysis with users – stories.

Telling stories

In this section, we will discuss stories. In order to create a story, you must have created at least one sheet. A story is a blank page where you can combine sheets with text and other objects. You create multiple story points and present them one after another to tell a story with the data. Stories are an excellent way to share the findings of your analysis. To create a story, click the **New Story** button at the bottom of the workbook. The **Story** tab is available at the bottom of the workbook:

Once you have clicked on the **New Story** button (bottom of the workbook), a blank story page will open. A story is a collection of visualizations presented in an ordered format. A story is similar to a PowerPoint presentation. The story comprises a series of story points. The following screenshot shows a blank story page:

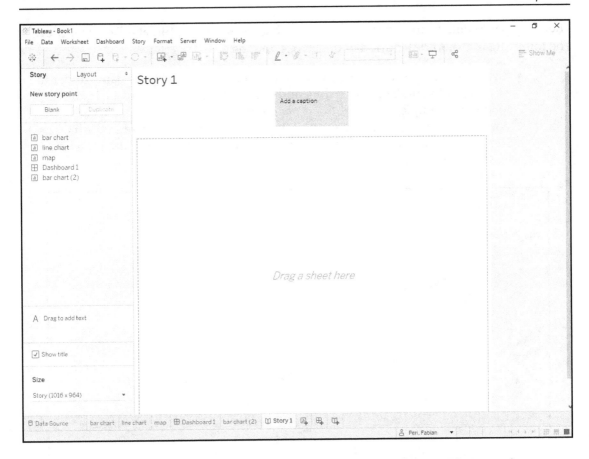

There are two tabs in the menu on the left-hand side of the story pane. The two tabs are distinct panes – **Story** and **Layout**. The layout of the Story page is similar to that of the dashboard page. The **Story** pane allows you to place sheets and objects in the story. It is also where you set screen-sizing options. The **Layout** pane gives you finer control of how to navigate through the story. We will discuss both of these panes in the following section.

The Story pane

Similar to dashboards, you should think about the purpose of your story. What data you present and how you present the data is a major component of storytelling. You are leading your viewers to a conclusion that should be supported with data. As with dashboards, we believe that you should have a plan or an outline before developing. Sitting down and crafting a narrative will help make your story better.

The **Story** pane contains four primary sections – **New story point**, **Sheets**, **Text**, and **Size**. The following is a short description of the layout options:

- **Sheets**: To add a sheet to the story point, either double-click the name under the **Sheets** portion of the pane or drag and drop the sheet to the canvas. In the following example, the sheet titled **bar chart** was double-clicked. The sheet is now in the Story pane along with all the filters that were applied in the **bar chart** sheet. The following screenshot displays the **Story** pane after adding the **bar chart** sheet:

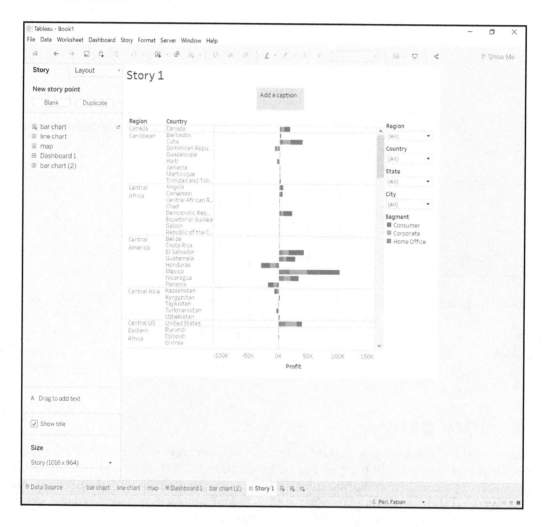

- **New story point**: If you think of your story as a presentation then a story point is a single slide. Stories are made of multiple story points in a sequence that conveys a point or message. The **New story point** section has two buttons – **Blank** and **Duplicate**. The **Blank** button creates a new story point for you to work on while the **Duplicate** button creates a copy of the current story point. In the preceding screenshot, there is only one story point – story points are represented by gray boxes in the middle of the pane under the story title. In the following screenshot, a blank story point was created – notice how there are now two gray boxes under the title of **Story 1** in the canvas:

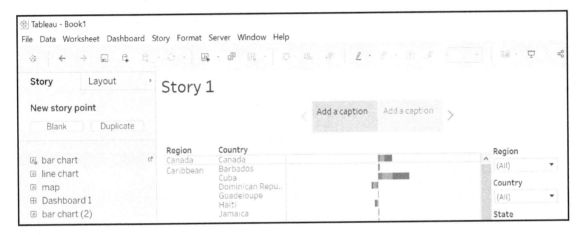

- **Text**: Click to add a text field to your story point. In the following screenshot, text was added to the story point. You can drag and drop the text field to anywhere on the story point as it is a floating object. The **Show title** checkbox controls whether or not to show the story point title (**Story 1** in the upper-left corner of the canvas in the following screenshot):

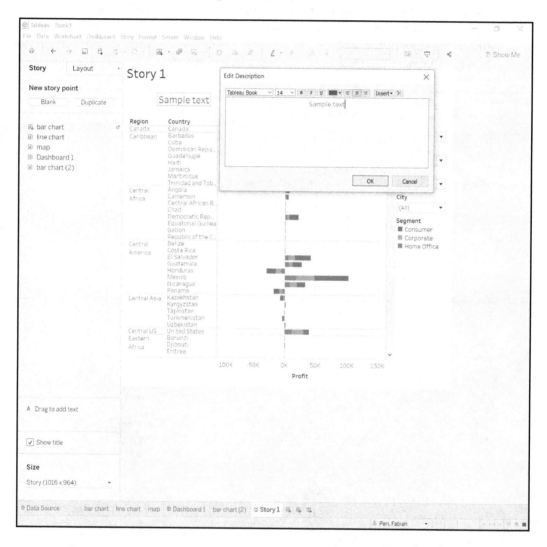

- **Size**: Select the display size of your story. This should be the size at which your users will view the story. There is a list of predefined screen sizes if you click the down caret in the **Size** options:

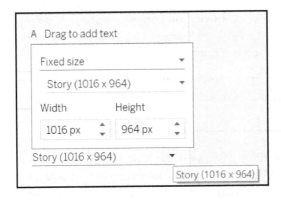

Now that we have had a quick walk-through of the **Story** pane, we will move onto the **Layout** pane.

The story Layout pane

The **Layout** pane contains options on how to present navigation options to users. You can select from caption boxes, numbers, dots, and arrows only. Play around with these settings to find what works best for your story:

Once you have completed your story, you can either share it using Tableau's presentation mode or publish the story to Tableau Server. The **Full screen** button is available in the upper-right corner of the menu ribbon:

So far in this chapter, we have discussed the features and options available to create dashboards and stories. You now have all the pieces necessary to create and share a professional view of the story you wish to tell. As we come to the end of our journey, we will close with our final thoughts on making compelling data visualizations.

Summary

Creating dashboards and stories is a combination of art and science. The visualizations you develop are only as good as the underlying data. If the data is not accurate then the solution is, at best, useless and, at worst, harmful. It is more beneficial for a user to have no information as opposed to incorrect information that they are led to believe is accurate. The message of the visualization needs to be true. Good visualizations enhance the message. They allow users to identify trends, spot patterns, and understand information more efficiently.

Throughout this book, you have learned how to work with Tableau. Some of the key concepts you should now feel comfortable with are the following:

- Connecting to and modeling your data
- Working with data in the worksheet
- Selecting the proper chart type depending on your data
- Plotting geographical data
- Creating custom calculations
- Understanding **Level of Detail** (**LOD**) expressions
- Using Tableau's embedded analytic features
- Sharing your analyses via dashboards and stories

We started our journey by explaining how Tableau can help you and your organization make better sense of your data. We hope that you have learned about the key features of Tableau and how to use them to take full advantage of your data. While the concepts presented in this book are not exhaustive, they are enough to help you pass the Tableau Desktop Certified exam. The best way to get better at Tableau is to start using it. You now have a solid foundation on which to build. Our final advice to you is to find questions that you wish to answer, get the data to do so, and use the methods you have learned in this book to help you create accurate, intuitive, and visually stunning reporting solutions.

Mock Test A + B (Assessment)

Mock tests A and B

For the mock tests A and B, you will require the following data:

- **Sample Superstore dataset:** `http://www.tableau.com/sites/default/files/training/global_Superstore.zip`
- **FIFA match results:** `https://public.tableau.com/s/sites/default/files/media/world_cup_results.xlsx`
- **2018 FIFA rosters:** `https://public.tableau.com/s/sites/default/files/media/world_cup_2018_squads.xlsx`
- **Titanic passenger list:** `https://public.tableau.com/s/sites/default/files/media/titanic%20passenger%20list.csv`
- **Star Wars character details:** `https://public.tableau.com/s/sites/default/files/media/starwarscharacterdata.json`
- **Apples data:** `https://www.ers.usda.gov/webdocs/DataFiles/51035/apples.xlsx?v=0`
- **NFL stats:** `https://public.tableau.com/s/sites/default/files/media/Resources/NFL%20Offensive%20Player%20stats%2C%201999-2013.xlsx`
- **Brewing production size:** `https://docs.google.com/spreadsheets/d/1fjA0jSVPecI7rCeSx5MUzIw3Z0pOJeYbT1q80bW1SsM/edit?usp=sharing`
- **Tableau job market dashboard:** `https://public.tableau.com/workbooks/Practiceworkbook-TableauJobMarket.twb`

The exam comprises the following sections:

Calculations 1-7

Data Connections 8 - 13

Analytics 14 - 19

Organizing Data 20 - 23

Bins 24 - 26

Dashboards 27 - 28

Mapping 29 - 30

Test A

Question 1: Answer the following question using the Superstore dataset. What was the percentage change in the profitability between 2013 and 2014 for segments other than the consumer segment?

1. 23.89%
2. 40.17%
3. 24.17%
4. 32.74%

Question 2: Answer the following question using the Star Wars dataset. What is the most common first letter for male characters with orange eyes?

1. S
2. A
3. T
4. C

Question 3: Answer the following question using the Superstore dataset. What is the total sales value for all products in 2014 by customers who also ordered in 2012?

1. 2,677,439
2. 4,139,150
3. 587,457
4. 4,299,866

Question 4: Answer the following question using the Titanic passenger list data. How many people with the last name Davies were on the passenger list?

1. 1
2. 7
3. 18
4. 2

Question 5: The COUNTD function returns the number of distinct items in the group. Is it true or false that *null* items are counted as a separate item?

1. True
2. False

Question 6: Answer the following question using the FIFA 2018 rosters. What is the percentage of players born before 1990 that scored more than 10 goals.

1. 19.29%
2. 80.71%
3. 11.96%
4. 88.04%

Question 7: For any aggregate calculation, is it true or false that you cannot combine an aggregated value and a disaggregated value?

1. True
2. False

Question 8: Using the Superstore dataset, answer the following question: What was the total sales value for Southeast Asia in 2014 for items that were never returned?

1. 23,161
2. 212,726
3. 306,769
4. 323,068

Question 9: Using the Apples dataset, answer the following question: What is the average price for fresh and frozen apples?

1. 2.126
2. 0.51
3. 1.616
4. 1.063

Question 10: Answer the following question using the FIFA match results and 2018 FIFA rosters data. How many players who were born before 1990 played on the team in 2018 that ranked number 1 winner by the number of times they won in all previous years?

    1. 12

    2. 4

    3. 0

    4. 23

Question 11: Answer the following question using the brewing production size dataset. What is the difference in percentage of exported products between 2017 and 2018 for breweries that have a production size of less than one barrel?

    1. -45.51%

    2. -16.35%

    3. 45.5%

    4. 7.24%

Question 12: Answer the following question using the Superstore dataset. What was the name of the manager that gave the fewest discounts in the consumer segment?

    1. Anna Andreadi

    2. Alejandro Ballentine

    3. Shirley Daniels

    4. Nicole Hansen

Question 13: When would be the best time to use data blending rather than join?

    1. When you are unable to combine data sources through JOIN

    2. When data blending is the only option available

    3. When JOIN doesn't give the flexibility required

    4. When you need to avoid data duplication without losing unrelated data

Question 14: Answer the following question using the FIFA match results dataset. Create a bar graph for the year and goals scored. Add a distribution band for 65 to 80 percent. What is the value of the 65% average?

    1. 77.3175

    2. 65

    3. 95.16

    4. 73.65

Question 15: Answer the following question using the NFL stats dataset. Create a scatter plot using College Wins and Age detailed by Player. What is the standard error for the linear trend line?

1. <0.001
2. 0.800443
3. 86.3054
4. 148.27

Question 16: Answer the following question using the NFL stats dataset. Using a box plot, find out what is the value for the lower quartile for players' height?

1. 66
2. 71
3. 73
4. 76

Question 17: When can the linear trend lines be considered significant?

1. When t-value >= 0.5
2. When the standard error <= 5.0
3. When R-squared >= 0.05
4. When p-value <= 0.05

Question 18: What are the two methods Tableau uses to determine seasonality in forecasting?

1. Temporal and non-temporal
2. Granular and non-granular
3. Linear and non-linear
4. Seasonal and non-seasonal

Question 19: Which Tableau option would you use to distinguish marks (single data point) and call out their position on the X/Y axis in the view?

1. Tool tip
2. Axis Lines
3. Drop Lines
4. Reference Lines

Question 20: Answer the following question using the 2018 FIFA roster dataset. Create a hierarchy Group - Position. How many goals were scored by Position whose players appeared the most on the National Team (Cap count) in Group B?

1. 268
2. 340
3. 414
4. 0

Question 21: Answer the following question using the 2018 FIFA roster dataset. Looking at the FW position, what percentage of goals were scored by the top three players?

1. 88.86%
2. 6.03%
3. 48.14%
4. 11.14%

Question 22: Is it true or false that you can manually sort data using a legend?

1. True
2. False

Question 23: Is it true or false that fixed **Level Of Detail (LOD)** filters are executed before context filters?

1. True
2. False

Question 24: Answer the following question using the NFL stats dataset. What is the moving average of the age of the players by draft year in the five years prior to 2013?

1. 24.50
2. 23.89
3. 24.15
4. 24.32

Question 25: Answer the following question using the NFL Stats dataset. Using a histogram, create a visualization for the players' weight using a bin size of 10. What is an average broad jump for players that weigh 230-240 lb?

1. 88.27
2. 91.94

3. 73.89

4. 109.46

Question 26: Knowledge Based. Is it true or false that, in Tableau, bins can be used for continuous measure?

1. True
2. False

Question 27: Answer the following question using the Tableau Job Market workbook. What title holds the largest average salary for Architect position?

1. Business intelligence architect
2. Data warehouse architect
3. Tableau server administrator
4. Security administrator

Question 28: Knowledge Based. Is it true or false that, while building dashboards, strings and dates slow the performance down more than numbers and Booleans?

1. True
2. False

Question 29: Answer the following question using the sample Superstore dataset. What is the sum of profits of the cities that fall within a 30 km range of Seattle?

1. 29,156
2. 27,391
3. 56,024
4. 31,887

Question 30: Answer the following question using the sample Superstore dataset. Using Maps answer the following: which groups of states raised the most profit?

1. Idaho, Montana, North Dakota
2. Wyoming, South Dakota, Nebraska
3. Minnesota, Wisconsin, Iowa
4. Utah, Colorado, New Mexico

Answer Key Test A

Answer 1: 3. 24,17%

Add both **Order Date** and **Profit** to the view:

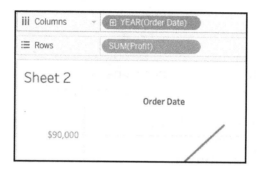

Create a **Quick Table Calculation** to see the percentage difference:

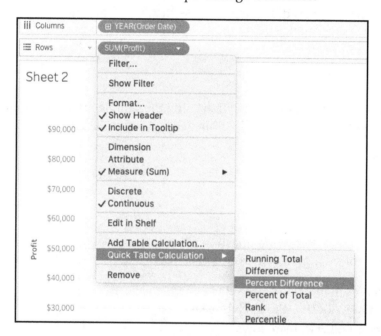

Create a filter to exclude **Consumer**:

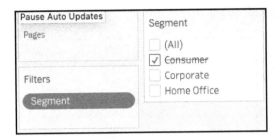

Select text tables to view the data:

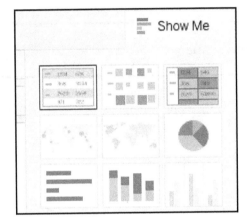

Your answer should look similar to this. The correct answer is 4.01%:

	Order Date		
2011	2012	2013	2014
7.61%	40.17%		24.17%

Answer 2: 1. S

First create a calculated field:

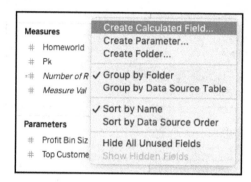

Then, create the following calculation:

Add it to the view:

Create filters for the gender:

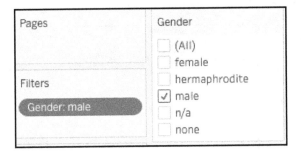

Create filters for the eye color:

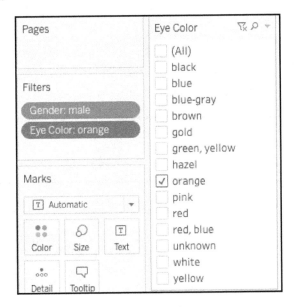

Now double-click on the **Number of Records**:

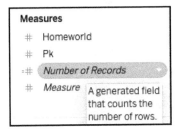

Your answer should look like this. There are two records for R and S. S is the only option available for the correct answer:

Answer 3: 2. 4,139,150

First create the LOD calculated field on [customer name]:

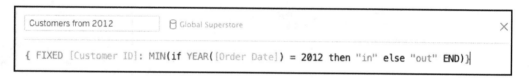

Then, add the year, category, and sales to the view:

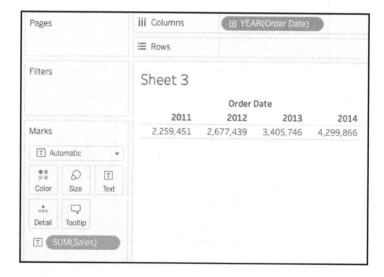

Create a filter with the `Customers from 2012` calculated field we created, and filter out the results that match the criteria. Note that the filter had no effect on the column for 2012, but did adjust the rest to match the customers that also ordered in 2012:

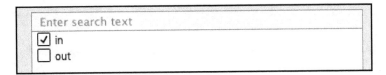

Your answer should look like this:

	Order Date		
2011	2012	2013	2014
2,168,573	2,677,439	3,265,753	4,139,150

Answer 4: 2. 7

While adding the data source, split the `name` field in order to divide the column:

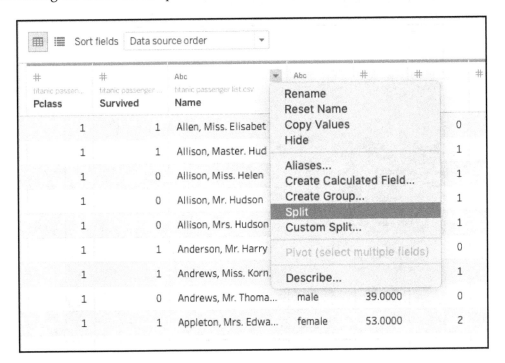

Rename the `split 1` column to `Last name`:

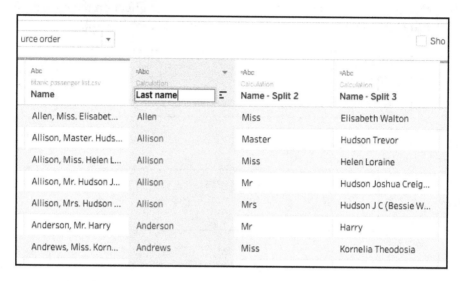

Add `Last name` and `number of records` to the view:

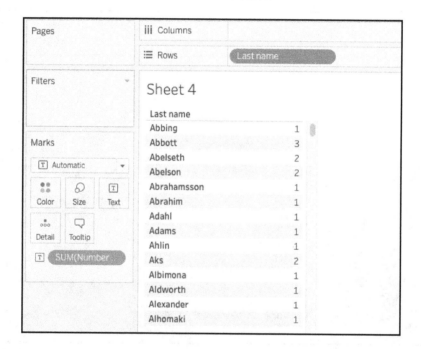

Scroll down to the last name **Davies**. The correct answer is 7:

Answer 5: 2. False

NULL values are not counted:

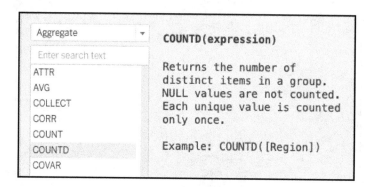

Answer 6: 1. 19.29%

Add the data source, making sure all the fields, especially DOB, are identified as such:

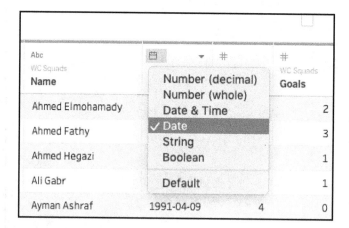

Create the calculated field in order to separate players into two groups: `more than 10` and `less than 10`:

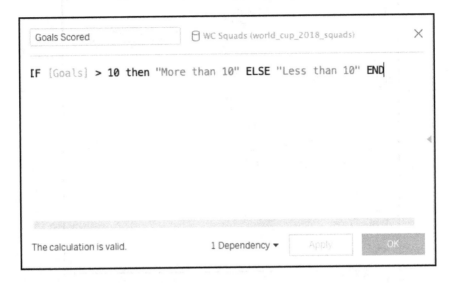

Create a filter for players who were born before 1990:

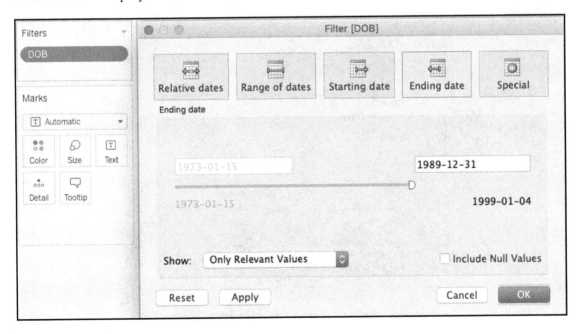

Now, add the `Goals Scored` and `Number of records` fields to the view:

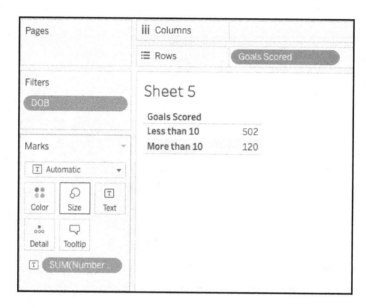

Now, create a quick table calculation to find out the percentage of the total for the number of records:

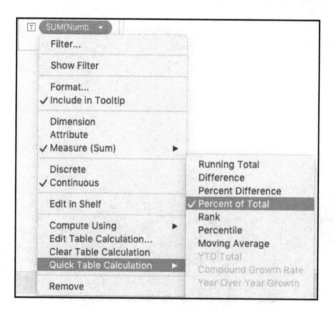

Your answer should look like this, with the answer showing the percentage of players scoring more than 10 goals being 19.29%:

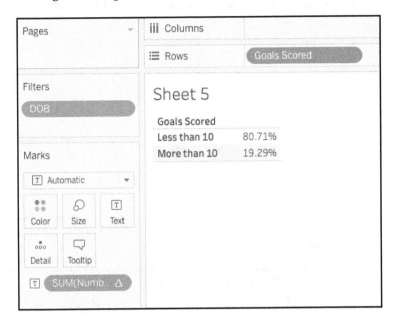

Answer 7: 1. True

For any aggregate calculation, you cannot combine an aggregated value and a disaggregated value. For example, *SUM(Price)*[Items]* is not a valid expression because *SUM(Price)* is aggregated and Items is not. However, *SUM(Price*Items)* and *SUM(Price)*SUM(Items)* are both valid. For further information, refer to `https://help.tableau.com/current/pro/desktop/en-us/calculations_calculatedfields_aggregate_create.htm`.

Answer 8: 3. 306,769

First we need to join the **Orders** and **Returns** tables using **Left** JOIN on **Order ID**:

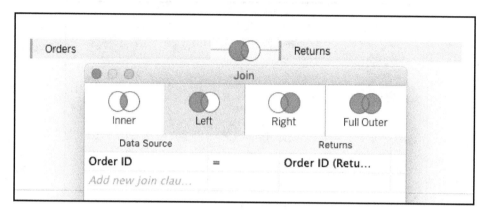

Then, add **Order Date**, **Region**, and **Sale** to the view:

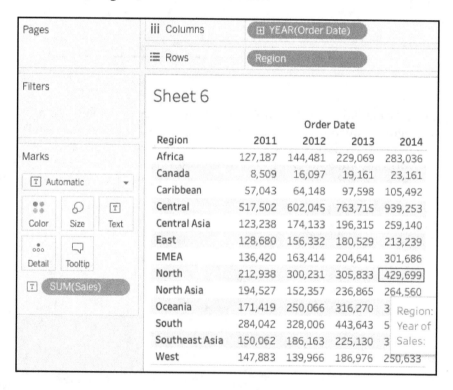

Exclude Returned Items via a filter:

Enter search text
☐ Null
☑ ~~Yes~~

Your answer should look like this:

	Order Date			
Region	2011	2012	2013	2014
Africa	127,187	144,481	229,069	233,036
Canada	3,509	16,097	19,161	23,161
Caribbean	53,908	57,993	93,721	108,090
Central	480,114	565,481	719,057	893,043
Central Asia	118,534	170,701	194,862	245,046
East	118,293	145,223	175,696	197,587
EMEA	136,420	163,414	204,641	301,026
North	186,053	262,887	271,114	384,021
North Asia	147,913	131,796	202,308	212,728
Oceania	186,372	240,629	306,220	352,358
South	278,263	306,585	419,463	500,627
Southeast Asia	148,159	173,005	217,812	306,769
West	136,223	118,869	204,485	193,458

Answer 9: 4. 1.063

First use the data interpreter while adding the data source to clean the data:

☑ Cleaned with Data Interpreter
Review the results. (To undo changes, clear the check box.)

As a result, you should see the following columns:

Abc	#	Abc	#	#	Abc	#
Apples	Apples	Apples	Apples	Apples	Apples	Apples
Form	Average retail price	Average retail pric...	Preparation yield f...	Size of a cup equiv...	Size of a cup equiv...	Average price per ...
Fresh1	1.61553	per pound	0.900000	0.24251	pounds	0.435312

Filter out the form of apple we are looking for:

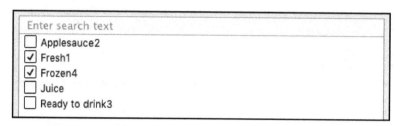

Add the average retail price measure to the view:

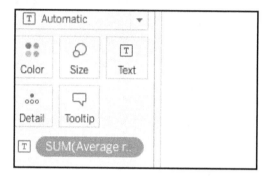

Note that measures are added as a SUM by default. We need an average, so switch it to **AVG**:

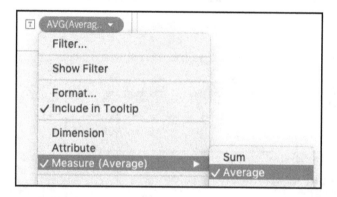

Your answer should look like this:

1.063

Answer 10: 1. 12

For this question we would have to use data blending. This will allow us to use two data sources without JOIN, thus eliminating any possibility of extra rows added to the dataset.

First add the relationship between the data sources:

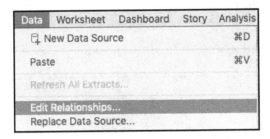

Select the WorldCups in the list

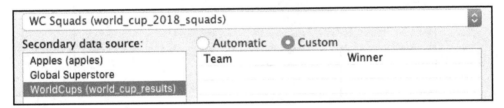

Next, using the WC squads data, filter players by their DOB:

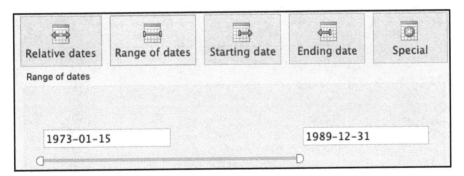

In the WorldCups datasource, create a calculation field that ranks the winners by the number of wins they have:

Add the Rank Winners and Winners fields to the view:

Keep only Brazil:

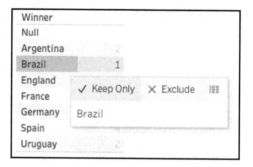

Add the Name field to the view:

Look at the bottom left of the screen. You have 12 rows of data. This is the answer:

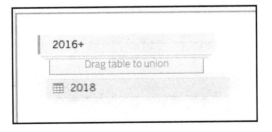

Answer 11: 1. -45.51%

First, we need to UNION all three tables:

Next, use **Data Interpreter** to clean up the table:

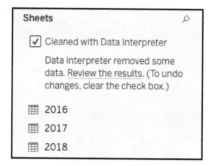

Rename the table column to **Year** and change the data format to date:

Bring **Year**, **Barrels**, and **Total Shipped** into the view:

Keep only the breweries with production under 1 Barrel:

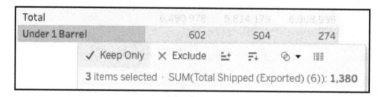

Using **Quick Table Calculation,** calculate the percentage difference between the years:

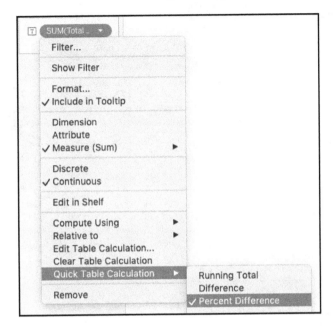

Your answer should look like this:

	Year		
	2016	2017	2018
Barrels (31 gall..			
Under 1 Barrel		-16.35%	-45.51%

Answer 12: 4. Nicole Hansen

First LEFT JOIN two tables, **People** and **Orders** using **Region** as key:

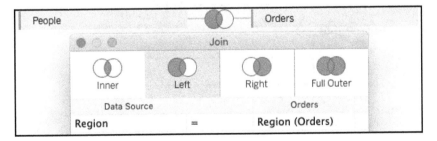

Then bring the **Segment**, **People**, and **Discount** fields into the view:

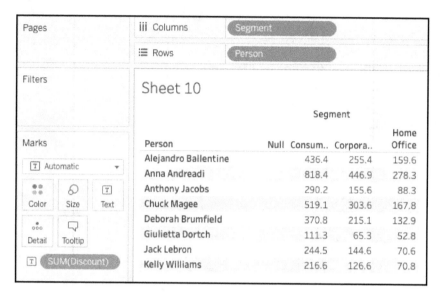

Keep only **Consumer**:

Sort the data in descending order:

Your answer should look like this:

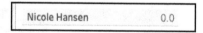

Answer 13: 4. When you need to avoid data duplication.

In some instances, changing JOIN conditions is not enough to avoid data duplication, as well as certain unlinked data may not be included in the JOIN. Data blending would then be the best option, creating the combined data source with combined data from all sources, without duplication.

Answer 14: 1. 77.3175

First add **Year** and **Goals Scored** to the view:

Change **Year** from **Continuous** to **Discrete**:

Add Table Distribution Band using the Analytics tab on the left. Change the lower percent brakes in the distribution to reflect the range 65 to 80 percent:

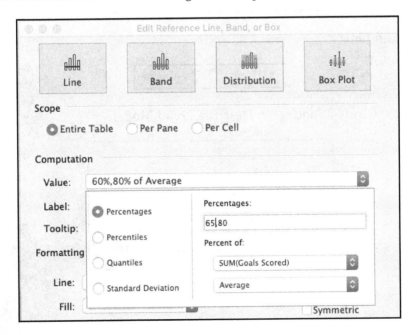

Hover over `65% of Average`. Your answer should look like this:

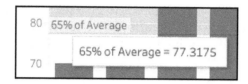

Answer 15: 4. 148.27

Add **College Wins** and **Age** to the view:

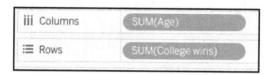

Drop **Player** on detail in Marks:

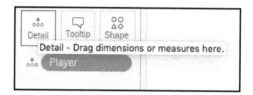

Add Linear **Trend Line**:

Right click on the trend line and select **Describe Trend Model**:

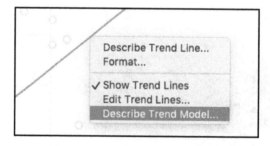

Your answer should look like this:

MSE (mean squared error):	21984.1
R–Squared:	0.800443
Standard error:	148.27
p–value (significance):	< 0.0001

Answer 16: 2. 71

First let's add **Height** and **Player** to the view. You will right away see that for some players such as Alex Smith the height is 1,300 inches. Clearly, we have some data duplication. So let's create a simple LOD calculation that would give us only one value per player. Create a calculated field with the following formula:

Add this new measure along with **Player** into the view:

Select Whisker Plot in in Show Me:

Hover over the visualization. The lower quartile is another name for **Lower Hinge**. Your answer should look like this:

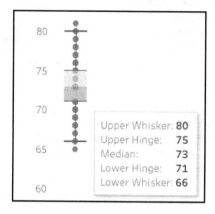

Answer 17: 4. When p-value <= 0.05

`https://help.tableau.com/current/pro/desktop/en-us/trendlines_add.htm.`

Answer 18: 1. Temporal and non-temporal

`https://help.tableau.com/current/pro/desktop/en-us/forecast_how_it_works.htm.`

Answer 19: 3. Drop Lines

`https://help.tableau.com/current/pro/desktop/en-us/inspectdata_droplines.htm.`

Answer 20: 1. 268

First make the hierarchy, dragging dimension **Position** onto dimension **Group**:

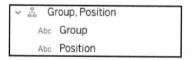

Then, add the newly created position to the view, as well as **Caps** and **Goals** by double-clicking them:

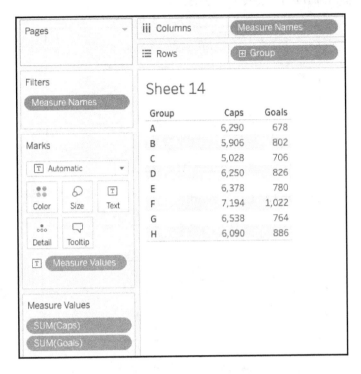

Expand the hierarchy, and sort the data in the descending order:

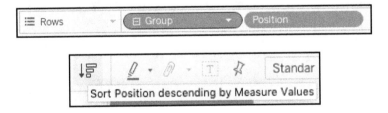

Your answer should look like this:

Answer 21: 4. 11.14%

First let's create a set for the top three players:

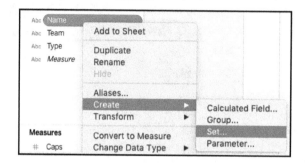

You want to create a set using the Goals field:

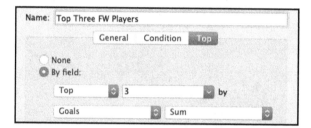

Next add the new set along with **Position** and **Goals** to the view:

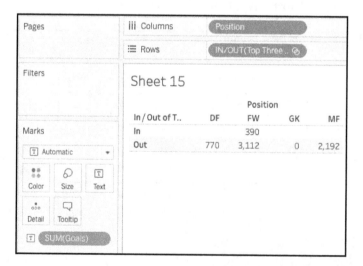

Now we need to create a table calculation using **Percent of Total** calculated through Table down:

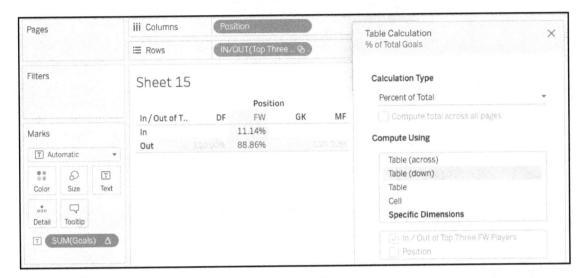

Your answer should look like this:

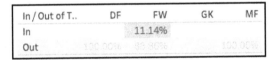

Answer 22: 1. True

`https://help.tableau.com/current/reader/desktop/en-us/reader_sort.htm.`

Answer 23: 2. False

`https://help.tableau.com/current/pro/desktop/en-us/order_of_operations.htm.`

Answer 24: 3. 24.15 Years

Fist change the data type for **Draft Year** to **Date**:

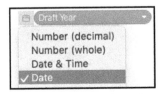

Convert it to Discrete:

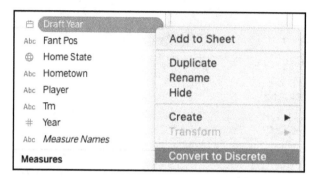

Add **Draft Year** and **Age** to the view:

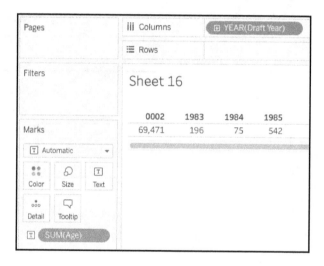

Change Age **SUM** to **AVG**:

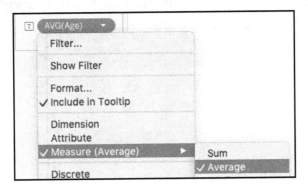

Add the **Moving Average** table calculation:

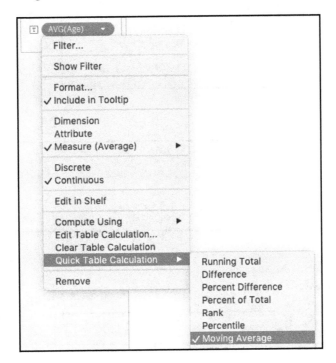

Edit **Table Calculation**. Select the average for five last data points, and deselect the current value, as we don't want data for 2013 to be included in the calculation:

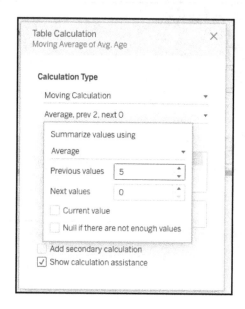

Your answer should look like this:

Answer 25: 1. 88.27

Add **Weight** to the view:

Select **Histogram** from **Show Me**:

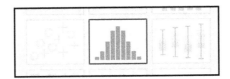

You will notice that `Weight (bin)` appeared in **Dimensions**. Click **Edit** and select bin size `10`:

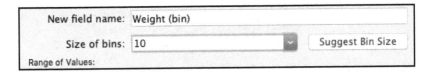

Drag Broad Jump to the **Tooltip** card in **Marks**, and switch from SUM to **AVG**:

Hover over the bin "230-240". Your answer should look like this:

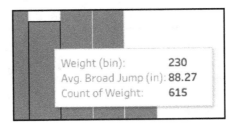

Answer 26: 1. True.

`https://help.tableau.com/current/pro/desktop/en-us/calculations_bins.htm`.

Answer 27: 1. Business intelligence architect

First expand the **Position** hierarchy:

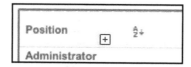

Now sort the **Average Estimated Salary** in the descending order:

Your answer should look like this:

Architect	Business Intelligence Ar..	$207,500	3
	Teradata Architect/Deve..	$172,800	1
	Enterprise BI Architect	$165,000	1

Answer 28: 1. True

https://help.tableau.com/current/pro/desktop/en-us/performance_tips.htm.

Answer 29: 4. 31,887

First, add **City** and **Profit** to the view:

Select the map symbol from the **Show Me** menu.

Find Seattle:

Go to the map, then **Map Options**, and select units to be **Metric**:

Use the **Radial Selection** tool to measure the distance:

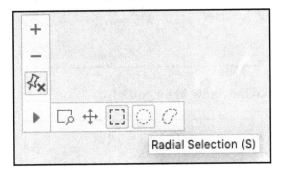

Stretch the measuring tool to reflect 30 km:

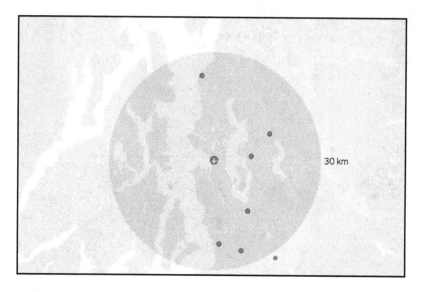

Look at the bottom left. Your answer should look like this:

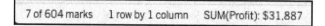

7 of 604 marks   1 row by 1 column   SUM(Profit): $31,887

Answer 30: 1. Idaho, Montana, North Dakota

Add **State** and **Profit** to the view:

Select the map symbol from the **Show Me** menu:

Group the states together:

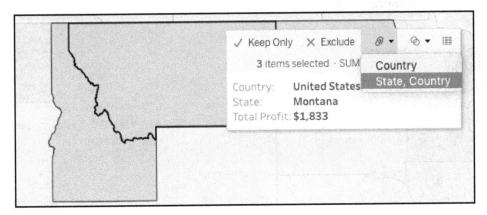

Collapse the state pill to only show the country:

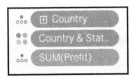

Mouse over the states to see which one is the most profitable. Your answer should look like this:

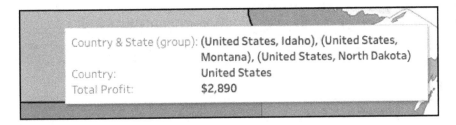

Test B

Question 1: Answer the following question using the Superstore dataset. What was the percentage change in the sales between 2012 and 2013 for all segments?

1. 23.48%
2. 32.37%
3. 25.16%
4. 23.92%

Question 2: Answer the following question using the Star Wars dataset. What is the most common first letter for female characters with blue eyes?

1. A
2. J
3. B
4. N

Question 3: Answer the following question using the Superstore dataset. What is the total sales value for all segments in 2014 by customers who ordered items from the consumer segment?

1. 1,194,052
2. 1,503,262
3. 1,463,760
4. 1,766,155

Question 4: Answer the following question using the Titanic passenger list data. What was the most common last name on the passenger list?

1. Sage
2. Johnston
3. West
4. Smith

Question 5: Is it true or false that the median function returns a value in an ordered set of values, below and above which there is an equal number of values?

1. True
2. False

Question 6: Answer the following question using FIFA 2018 Rosters. What is the percentage of players that were born after January 01, 1992 who scored more than 15 goals?

1. 97.29%
2. 17.24%
3. 9.92%
4. 2.03%

Question 7: Is it true or false that, if you don't have all the data values you need on the visualization, it is a perfect time to use quick table calculation?

1. True
2. False

Question 8: Using the Superstore dataset answer the following question: What was the total sales value for Central Asia in 2013 for items that were returned?

1. 14,094
2. 44,658
3. 4,833
4. 1,453

Question 9: Using the Apples dataset, answer the following question: What is the average price per cup equivalent for fresh and ready to drink apples?

1. 0.4353
2. 0.3754
3. 0.3156
4. 0.2973

Question 10: Answer the following question using the FIFA Match results and 2018 FIFA rosters data. How many players who were born before 1988 play on the teams in 2018 that ranked number 4 by the number of times they won in all previous years?

1. 3
2. 5
3. 7
4. 18

Question 11: Answer the following question using the brewing production size dataset. Which production size (by barrel) saw the biggest increase in the number of breweries in 2018?

1. Under 1 barrel
2. 1 to 1k barrels
3. 1k to 7,5k barrels
4. 7,5k to 15k barrels

Question 12: Answer the following question using the Superstore dataset. What was the name of the manager who is in charge of the least profitable region in the corporate segment?

1. Anthony Jacobs
2. Shirley Daniels
3. Kelly Williams
4. Alejandro Ballentine Corporate

Question 13: Is it true or false that, if your file type is not listed under **Connect**, the only option is to cover the file to supported format?

1. True
2. False

Question 14: Answer the following question using the FIFA match results dataset. Create a bar graph using year and matches played. Add the distribution band for the standard deviation -0.5,0.5. What is the value of the standard deviation above the mean?

1. 50.409
2. 33.190
3. 47.753
4. 12.874

Question 15: Answer the following question using the NFL Stats dataset. Create a scatter plot using College Wins and College Losses detailed by Player. May a linear trend line for this data be considered significant?

1. Yes
2. No

Question 16: Answer the following question using the NFL Stats dataset. Using a box plot, find out what is the value for upper whisker for players wins?

1. 546
2. 349
3. 721
4. 1168

Question 17: Is it true or false that, with Tableau, you can create forecasts and that all you need is a dimension and a measure?

1. True
2. False

Question 18: What is the number of parameters needed to completely specify the model called?

1. Model observations
2. Model data point
3. Model degrees of freedom
4. Model Parameters

Question 19: Is it true or false that you can use clustering for any dimension in the view?

1. True
2. False

Question 20: Answer the following question using the 2018 FIFA Roster dataset. Create a hierarchy Group - Position. Which group had the most goals scored by the FW position?

1. F
2. H
3. A
4. D

Question 21: Answer the following question using the 2018 FIFA Roster dataset. Looking at the FW position, out of all the players what, percentage of appearances on national teams (Caps) were done by top ten players based on their goals?

1. 7.86%
2. 6.03%
3. 20%
4. 12.59%

Question 22: Is it true or false that you cannot manually sort data in the view within a hierarchy?

1. True
2. False

Question 23: Is it true or false that measure filters are always executed before dimension filters?

1. True
2. False

Question 24: Answer the following question using the NFL Stats dataset. What is the moving average of the wins of the youngest players (last three years) based on their date of birth?

1. 50,998
2. 28,476
3. 72,427
4. 63,596

Question 25: Answer the following question using the NFL Stats dataset. Using a histogram, create a visualization for a broad jump by the players using the bin size of two inches. What is an average height of the players that conducted the longest jumps?

1. 73.21
2. 71.45
3. 73.89
4. 72.57

Question 26: Knowledge Based. What are custom fields that define a subset of data based on some conditions called?

1. Groups
2. Parameters
3. Sets
4. Fields

Question 27: Answer the following question using the Tableau Job Market workbook. How many job postings are there for a Tableau developer?

1. 52
2. 109
3. 33
4. 2

Question 28: Knowledge Based. Can web pages be included in the Tableau dashboard?

1. True
2. False

Question 29: Answer the following question using the sample Superstore dataset. What is the sum of the sales of the cities that fall within 10 mile range of Lehi?

1. 1,517
2. 4,511
3. 17,366
4. 9,821

Question 30: Answer the following question using the sample Superstore dataset. Using Maps answer the following: which state around Indiana sold the largest quantity of items?

1. Illinois
2. Michigan
3. Kentucky
4. Ohio

Answer Key Test B

For the procedures on how to answer each question, refer to Answer Key for Test A, as they follow the same structure.

Answer 1: 2. 32.37%

Answer 2: 3. B

Answer 3: 2. 1,503,262

The formula for the LOD calculation you are looking for is: { FIXED [Order ID]: MIN(IF [Segment] = "Consumer" then "in" else "out" END)}

Answer 4: 1. Sage

Answer 5: 1. True

Question 6: 4. 2.03%

Answer 7: 2. False (https://help.tableau.com/current/pro/desktop/en-us/calculations_calculatedfields_understand.htm)

Answer 8: 4. 1,453

Answer 9: 2. 0.3754

Answer 10: 4. 18

Answer 11: 1. Under 1 barrel

Answer 12: 4. Alejandro Ballentine Corporate

Answer 13: 2. False (https://help.tableau.com/current/pro/desktop/en-us/basicconnectoverview.htm)

Answer 14: 1. 50.409

Answer 15: 1. Yes, based on the p-value <= 0.05

Answer 16: 4. 1168

Answer 17: 2. False (https://help.tableau.com/current/pro/desktop/en-us/forecasting.htm)

Answer 18: 3. Model degrees of freedom

Answer 19: 2. False (https://help.tableau.com/current/pro/desktop/en-us/clustering.htm)

Answer 20: 1. F

Answer 21: 3. 20

Answer 22: False

Answer 23: False (https://help.tableau.com/current/pro/desktop/en-us/order_of_operations.htm)

Answer 24: 2. 28,476

Answer 25: 1. 73.21

Answer 26: 3. Sets (https://help.tableau.com/current/pro/desktop/en-us/sortgroup_sets_create.htm)

Answer 27: 3. 33

Answer 28: 1. True (`https://help.tableau.com/current/pro/desktop/en-us/dashboards_best_practices.htm`)

Answer 29: 2. 4511

Answer 30: 1. Illinois

This is it. Well done!

Other Books You May Enjoy

If you enjoyed this book, you may be interested in these other books by Packt:

Tableau 2019.x Cookbook
Dmitry Anoshin, Teodora Matic, Et al

ISBN: 9781789533385

- Understand the basic and advanced skills of Tableau Desktop
- Implement best practices of visualization, dashboard, and storytelling
- Learn advanced analytics with the use of build in statistics
- Deploy the multi-node server on Linux and Windows
- Use Tableau with big data sources such as Hadoop, Athena, and Spectrum
- Cover Tableau built-in functions for forecasting using R packages
- Combine, shape, and clean data for analysis using Tableau Prep
- Extend Tableau's functionalities with REST API and R/Python

Mastering Tableau 2019.1 - Second Edition

David Baldwin, Marleen Meier

ISBN: 9781789533880

- Get up to speed with various Tableau components
- Master data preparation techniques using Tableau Prep
- Discover how to use Tableau to create a PowerPoint-like presentation
- Understand different Tableau visualization techniques and dashboard designs
- Interact with the Tableau server to understand its architecture and functionalities
- Study advanced visualizations and dashboard creation techniques
- Brush up on powerful Self-Service Analytics, Time Series Analytics, and Geo-Spatial Analytics

Leave a review - let other readers know what you think

Please share your thoughts on this book with others by leaving a review on the site that you bought it from. If you purchased the book from Amazon, please leave us an honest review on this book's Amazon page. This is vital so that other potential readers can see and use your unbiased opinion to make purchasing decisions, we can understand what our customers think about our products, and our authors can see your feedback on the title that they have worked with Packt to create. It will only take a few minutes of your time, but is valuable to other potential customers, our authors, and Packt. Thank you!

Index